Cambridge English Lexicon

A graded word list for materials writers and course designers

Roland Hindmarsh

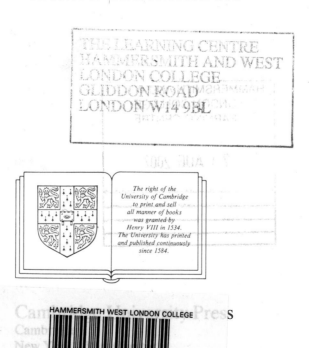

*The right of the
University of Cambridge
to print and sell
all manner of books
was granted by
Henry VIII in 1534.
The University has printed
and published continuously
since 1584.*

Cambridge University Press

Cambridge
New York
Melbourne   Sydney

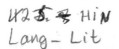

Published by the Press Syndicate of the University of Cambridge
The Pitt Building, Trumpington Street, Cambridge CB2 1RP
40 West 20th Street, New York, NY 10011–4211, USA
10 Stamford Road, Oakleigh, Melbourne 3166, Australia

© Cambridge University Press 1980

First published 1980
Fifth printing 1991

Printed in Great Britain at the University Press, Cambridge

British Library cataloguing in publication data

Hindmarsh, Roland

Cambridge English lexicon.
1. English language – Glossaries, vocabularies, etc.
I. Title
428′.1   PE1680   79–41656

ISBN 0 521 21623 0

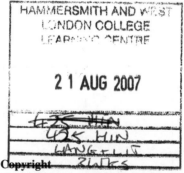
The law allows a reader to make a single copy of part of a book
for purposes of private study. It does not allow the copying of
entire books or the making of multiple copies of extracts. Written
permission for any such copying must always be obtained from the
publisher in advance.

Contents

Acknowledgements

I wish here to thank some of those who helped me in a variety of ways to get the work completed. At the outset John Trim, then Head of the Department of Linguistics in Cambridge, and Professor John Sinclair of Birmingham; in the same period and on later occasions Harold Otter and Bill Shephard of the Local Examinations Syndicate. My thanks are also due to Andree Blakemore for collating frequency values in 1974; Michael O'Shea for exploring gradings at pre-FCE levels of language learning in 1975; Vivienne Mosback for assigning gradings to the main list items in 1976; Ann Brumfit, David Sweetman and Susan Morris for help in the selection and expression of semantic values in 1977; and Kay McKechnie for editorial work in the final stages. In addition I am grateful to several British Council and other ELT colleagues for shorter or longer discussions, but especially to Adrian du Plessis of Cambridge University Press; without his steady interest, his readiness to assist with arrangements and discussions at all stages of development, and his professional understanding of the issues involved, this work would never have been accomplished.

Roland Hindmarsh
Brussels 1980

Future development of the *Cambridge English Lexicon*

The *Lexicon* is now in use in many countries, where it is being used by materials writers and others (including examining authorities such as the University of Cambridge Local Examinations Syndicate) as a guide to vocabulary selection.

A second edition of the Lexicon will be prepared and all users are invited to contribute suggestions for new inclusions, changes of grading and other comments that may serve to improve what has become a basic reference work for the English Language Teaching profession.

Write to Roland Hindmarsh, ELT Department, Publishing Division, Cambridge University Press, Shaftesbury Road, Cambridge CB2 2RU, England. All suggestions will be carefully considered.

Introduction

My interest in word lists was aroused in the mid 1950s when I was working in a secondary school in Uganda. Many of the comprehension texts we used in class contained items of vocabulary that were of no conceivable use to my students. The texts were often literary, sometimes archaic, and in content and style intended vaguely to edify. Worse, the examination texts were in the same genre. Something needed doing to make the texts fit the context of learning and use better.

What that might be I first learnt from John Bright, who came to Makerere in Kampala in early 1956. Through him I started to understand what a professional approach to ESL means, and I acknowledge his inspiration with gratitude. One method he advocated for dealing with the problem of textual accessibility was vocabulary selection and control: not out of any antagonism to literature, but rather out of respect for its merits. When the task was one of training in reading comprehension, he held it essential to ensure that the text was within the capacity of the students to grasp its meaning; yet in the process they should feel stretched, and so derive from the experience a sense of achievement.

This approach to reading comprehension I took as one of my basic operating principles. It followed that I did not want to have rigid vocabulary ceilings, since that makes progression from one level of vocabulary to the level above it seem to proceed in a series of unnatural leaps. I wanted a system of flexible control: the content and purpose of a given text would require vocabulary items varying in their degree of frequency or accessibility; yet this variation should average out at a level the student could handle.

Vocabulary grading was, at that time, nothing new in ESL. Michael West and Laurence Fawcett had used it already in the 1930s. But in the 1950s it gained momentum and in the early 1960s it swept all before it in the ESL field. That decade also saw the first series of structurally graded readers. ESL syllabuses too, whether for curricula or for examinations, expressed themselves mainly in blocks of vocabulary and structure for each identified level of study. The principal focus in preparing pedagogical materials passed gradually from vocabulary to structure; this movement was much assisted by Chomsky's work on syntax and the development of transformational-generative grammar. The focus of debate shifted then to TG itself, and led later to criticisms of its

Introduction

theoretical position, and to the dominant influence of sociolinguistics in the 1970s. The sociolinguistic approach to language implies diversity: language is essentially related to context and purpose, and to the participants engaged in the relevant communicative functions. We seem now to have come a long way from the grading of vocabulary. But the teaching and learning of languages has to be systematic in some sense, not merely haphazard. Purposive communication calls for the deployment of language skills and these are used to manipulate the content to specified ends. Purpose, context, tone, mode and medium can be orchestrated to produce a language specification: but that specification can – and I maintain must – be graded in some measure to make it right for where the learner is now.

At this stage of development or production, certain instruments of language selection are required. These instruments cannot be allowed to dominate syllabus ever again; they are however needed to ensure good husbandry in learning to use language in specified situations. The less easy it is to specify the context, purpose and tone, the more weight will tend to be given to language grading instruments. Among these instruments, those for vocabulary grading form a part; those for syntactic grading another part; and the as yet unwritten instruments of discourse grading the third part. All such instruments must be used flexibly in the generation of language learning programmes; but that they are an essential part of this process there can be no doubt.

It is my hope therefore that this book will be used not to produce artificially rigid barriers to learning, but to enable the language appropriate to various contexts, purposes and messages to be wisely controlled. For some users this may mean no more than an occasional check on vocabulary items; for others a filter at a particular stage in the production of language learning materials; for yet others, a careful scrutiny to establish that a reading comprehension passage for an examination does not contain vocabulary items that exceed a given learning level by more than the agreed degree of variation.

The particular orientation of the lexicon in this book is towards the First Certificate in English (FCE) examination of the University of Cambridge Local Examinations Syndicate. In fact it was during a one-year attachment jointly to the Syndicate and to the Department of Linguistics of the University of Cambridge (1970-1) that the lexicon originated, as is described more fully below. But its application reaches much more widely, I believe, into the production of materials at all levels as far as upper-intermediate and even beyond, as well as into their assessment and selection.

Introduction

The list is based on a large number of lexicographical and pedagogical sources worked and reworked in a sequence of often laborious procedures. But the outcome is unique: it is the only word list to upper-intermediate level with graded meanings. What the gradings represent is explained below in the 'Note to users'.

At first sight it may appear that making a lexicon ought to be easy enough; all one should need is a set of clear working principles, and the will to apply them. But language is too subtle a matter to submit to such regimentation; exceptions begin to occur almost at once, and the principles lose their clarity of contour. The aim of such a list as this is to assist the professional user to make sensible decisions on lexical accessibility for the student; the handling of each item tries to serve this aim, and does so in a variety of ways, as appears to suit the context best. But the learning of languages takes place in a variety of cultural contexts too; in a lexicon, it is not possible to grade items flexibly to indicate how accessible they are in every cultural context of learning. That is why, for example, the four-letter words now (correctly) included in the *Oxford Advanced Learner's Dictionary of Current English* and the *Longman Dictionary of Contemporary English* are not taken up in this list, since their use is highly subject to variations deriving from the cultural context of learning.

Development of the *Cambridge English Lexicon*

1 Background

For the academic year 1970-1 I was attached by the British Council to the Local Examinations Syndicate and to the Department of Linguistics of the University of Cambridge. The task assigned to me was to look into the feasibility of making a specification of the language syllabus appropriate to what is now the First Certificate in English (FCE; then LCE), and to the Certificate of Proficiency in English (CPE). These two examinations, together with the Diploma in English Studies, form the Examinations in English as a Foreign Language, administered jointly by the University of Cambridge Local Examinations Syndicate and the British Council.

The Syndicate stated in information literature then available that it considered Michael West's *General Service List of English Words* (GSLEW; Longman, 1953) to represent approximately the comprehension vocabulary needed by a candidate to pass the LCE. I therefore decided first to study GSLEW in order to see how far

Introduction

the words listed there did in fact match the comprehension vocabulary required for the various types of passage given to candidates in the FCE examination.

2   Research findings

My investigations showed up a number of lexicographical anomalies in GSLEW, and led me to make a revised version of it, consisting of a total of 3300 entries. This list was made by cutting certain items (and types of item) out from GSLEW; nothing new was added.

It became clear to me from comparative studies that I carried out that neither GSLEW nor its revised form GSLEW 3300 could be held to state the vocabulary comprehension level appropriate to FCE, and I reported accordingly.

3   Development of an interim FCE lexicon

After being posted to Iran in 1971, I complemented GSLEW 3300 with items from a number of sources in order to see whether a more rounded lexicon could not be produced which would serve the original purpose, i.e. to give a guide as to the approximate comprehension vocabulary level appropriate to FCE. The sources used were:
i)   Three commonly used series of readers in simplified English, spanning the vocabulary ranges 2000-2340.
ii) A number of basic English vocabulary lists, spanning the vocabulary ranges 850-1490.
iii) Three frequency counts, including in each case the most common 2000 items.
The revision produced the *Intermediate English Word List* (IEWL), containing 4200 lexical items. Comparisons with examination texts suggested that this total represented more closely the vocabulary that an FCE candidate would need to understand moderately well to make reasonably sure of managing the lexical comprehension tasks demanded of him.

4   A new initiative

Instead of working onwards from IEWL, and thus ultimately still basing myself on GSLEW, I began afresh by seeing what sort of lexicon would be produced by taking the words entirely from the frequency list compiled by E.W. Thorndike and I. Lorge (1944). My intention was to produce a word list of about 5000 items, the

Introduction

total which is generated by a Thorndike–Lorge frequency of 13 or
14 occurrences per million words. I therefore took frequency 13 as
my main focal point, but broadened the focus up and down the
frequency scale so that I ranged in fact from 19 down to 8, using a
teacher's discretion in so doing.

To the words generated in this way I added a limited number
drawn from the then *New Oxford English Readers for East Africa*
(OUP) Books 1-5, which provided the lexicon for my *Understand
and Write* (CUP); and also all the words from the list in *Longman
Structural Readers Handbook* not already included. These
compilations produced a list of about 4700 words.

I then added to this lexicon by putting in items not already listed
drawn from two other frequency counts.

i) The word count made by Henry Kučera and W. Nelson Francis
of Brown University (1967): I again drew items from the 19 to 8
frequency range; for this it was necessary to compound the
frequencies in order to group syntactic items as had been done
by Thorndike–Lorge.

ii) The word list drawn up by C. W. Wright (1965): most of the
items in his first 5000.

This gave me a lexicon of approximately 5400 items. I now cut
away some 200 items whose frequency did not meet certain criteria
of statistical constancy through the three frequency lists, giving
5200 items.

I then added to the 5200 list all the words from IEWL that had
not already been included; these amounted to some 800, giving a
lexicon of about 6000 items. This lexicon could however only be
regarded as an intermediate stage in the production of further word
lists, since the 6000 word list did not appear to correspond to any
existing examination level of wide recognition.

5 A fuller lexicon for FCE

Studies had shown that the comprehension lexicon for passing FCE
lay approximately in the 4000-5000 word range. The 6000 word list
was therefore pared down to reach a level of about 4000. In doing
this many of the slightly archaic terms from Thorndike–Lorge were
cut, as well as some academic and specialised terminology from
C.W. Wright. The computer-based anomalies in Kučera–Francis
had already been disqualified in an earlier process.

The aim was to produce a lexicon worth teaching and learning at
the intermediate level of FCE. At this stage the cutting out process
was therefore radical and based principally on intuitions of teachers
of EFL. At the same time lexical items reflecting the world today

Introduction

were drawn together from a number of sources and added to the list.

As work progressed, the need for appendices became more and more apparent, especially for phrasal verbs (which no frequency list hitherto has tackled fairly). These came to form an integral part of the list, and many items listed in their various categories in the appendices were also included in the main list.

Work then proceeded on grading the items up to FCE level; these were organised first in 10 levels for the main list, then simplified to 5 levels. Items in the appendices were also graded from 1 to 5 where it was felt this served the overall aim of the lexicon.

Semantic values were supplied for all items in the main list where there could be differences either in values or word functions for these items; and gradings were given to each of these values or functions. Four people were involved in this pioneering task; in draft form, the list with the semantic values was used by text editors of Cambridge *English Language Learning* readers to obtain feedback.

In its final form, the main list now totals a little over 4500 items, with over 8000 semantic values.

Main source materials used

NO	AUTHOR/EDITOR	TITLE OF SOURCE MATERIAL	PUBLISHER	DATE	ITEMS	REMARKS
1	Michael West	*A General Service List of English Words*	Longman	1953	3500	Starting material for research.
2	—	*Longman Structural Readers Handbook*	Longman	1968	2340	Headwords and derivatives (see source 14).
3	Leslie Hill	*Advanced Stories for Reproduction*	OUP	1965	2075	Builds on L. A. Hill's 1500 word list, in *Intermediate Stories for Reproduction.*
4	C. K. Ogden & I. A. Richards	*Basic English*	Kegan Paul	1930	850	An early essential word book.
5	Council for Cultural Co-operation	*Systems Development for Adult Language Learning*	Council of Europe	1973	922	Initial list, superseded in 1975 (see source 12 below).
6	Michael West	*An International Reader's Dictionary*	Longman	1965	1490	The defining vocabulary. For grading semantic values.
7	—	*Ladder Series Dictionary*	Ladder Books	(n.d)	5000	The first 2000 words fully; the remainder selectively.

Introduction

NO	AUTHOR/EDITOR	TITLE OF SOURCE MATERIAL	PUBLISHER	DATE	ITEMS	REMARKS
8	Henry Kučera & W. Nelson Francis	*Computational Analysis of Present-Day American English*	Brown University Press, RI	1967		The commonest 2000 initially; the commonest 5000 later.
9	C. W. Wright	*An English Word Count*	National Bureau of Educational & Social Research, Pretoria	1965	10000	The commonest 2000 initially; the commonest 5000 later.
10	E. W. Thorndike & I. Lorge	*The Teacher's Wordbook of 30,000 Words*	Teachers' College Columbia, NY	1944	30000	The commonest 5000.
11	J. B. Carroll	*The American Heritage of English Wordlist*				The commonest 5000.
12	J. A. Van Ek	*The Threshold Level*	Council of Europe	1975	1600	This list superseded source 5 above.
13	Paul Proctor & A. W. Frisby	*Longman Dictionary of Contemporary English (Specimen)*	Longman	1974	2100	The defining vocabulary.
14	—	*Longman Structural Readers Handbook*	Longman	1976	2850	In conjunction with source 15.
15	L. G. Alexander and others	*English Grammatical Structure*	Longman	1975	—	Levels I to V parallel with CEL 1 to 5, for broad working purposes.
16	Ann Baker	*English to Get on With*	Heinemann Educational Books	1975	—	Grading phrasal verbs.
17	A. S. Hornby	*Oxford Advanced Learner's Dictionary of Current English*	OUP	1974	61000	For stating and grading semantic values.

Note to users

1   The *Cambridge English Lexicon* (CEL) is a word list prepared for use by text editors, curriculum planners, examination setters and course writers at or below the level of reading comprehension required for the First Certificate in English (FCE) examination of the University of Cambridge Local Examinations Syndicate.

2   The word list includes about 4500 lexical items, and is supported by 22 appendices as listed on the contents page. The items in the main list have been compiled from several sources including four major frequency counts and a number of other vocabulary lists found in widely-used EFL textbooks of various kinds (see explicit list on pages x-xi above). The appendices collate, exemplify or amplify the items found in the main list.

3   The lexical items in the main list, and virtually all items in the appendices too, are graded on a five-point scale. Level 5 corresponds to the comprehension vocabulary necessary for the FCE examination; levels 4 to 1 represent progressively earlier stages. Semantic values are given where necessary (without being closely defined) to show which meaning of a word is intended.

4   The lexical grading in CEL can appropriately be associated with the syntactic grading in *English Grammatical Structure* (EGS) by L.G. Alexander and others (Longman, 1975). For working purposes it can be assumed that there is a one-to-one correspondence between levels 1 to 5 of CEL and levels I to V of EGS. In addition a good deal of level VI in EGS can be considered as corresponding to level 5 in CEL.

5   It is emphasised that the gradings given in CEL are not intended as a straitjacket on the materials producer or other user, but as a guide to help him control levels consistently. It is fully appreciated that the demands of context may frequently override the level assignment given by lexical grading.

6   Each margin entry is printed in bold type and constitutes a lexical item, irrespective of whether or not:

Note to users

    i)   it is a derivative of another listed or unlisted word (act; action)

   ii) it consists of more than one word (owing to; carry out)

  iii) it has more than one semantic value (bank; come up)

  iv) it has more than one grammatical function (about; acid)

   v) it is a compound of other self-standing words listed or unlisted (car-park; chairman; bus stop)

  vi) it is an abbreviation of another listed or unlisted word (can't, cannot; ad, advertisement).

This clarification is provided in order to avoid the confusion that has tended to arise owing to the various ways in which 'word', 'headword' and 'lexical item' are used.

7   The items are listed in generally the same order as in the *Oxford Advanced Learner's Dictionary of Current English* (OALDCE).

8   Each item carries a grading on its left from 1 to 5. Level 5 means that the item is approaching or at FCE level. Level 1 means that the item is at beginner or post-beginner level. The totals for the five levels are as follows for items in the main list.

Level	Total	Cumulative total
1	598	598
2	617	1215
3	992	2207
4	1034	3241
5	1229	4470

9   Many items within the comprehension of students at levels 1-5 have more than one meaning. Such items are provided with semantic values, each with its own grading. Over 8000 semantic values are expressed by means of a definition, a context of use, or an example; or some combination of these. The OALDCE was often consulted over definitions etc. and the indebtedness is gratefully acknowledged.

    The gradings go beyond 1-5 to include levels 6 and 7 because the user may find it helpful to know some of the meanings that are somewhat beyond level 5, and thus decide whether to exclude or include them in a passage, depending on his purpose. Level 7 relates to a reading comprehension level estimated provisionally, on the basis of some initial research, as appropriate for the Certificate of Proficiency in English:

Note to users

about 8500 lexical items appear to be involved. Level 6
represents a reading comprehension level halfway between
FCE and CPE, at about 6500 items.

Some items have more than one grammatical function (noun,
verb, etc). These functions are also given separate gradings.

10 Proper names are subsumed for reference and amplified in
    appendices A-H. Appendices K-S subsume grammatical items
    from the list, and sometimes amplify them. Appendices T-X
    deal with various other features of language; few of the items
    in these appendices are in the main list.

11 The appendices complement the main list in various ways:
    i)   They subsume certain items listed and graded in the main
         list and present them in collated form under categories of
         reference.
    ii) They extend beyond the listed items in some categories of
         reference to give guidance on how to handle items whether
         complex or simple in grading terms.
    iii) They present reference tables for certain features of
         language such as modals, strong verb forms, prefixes and
         suffixes.
    iv) They present gradings for new sets of material integral to
         CEL, such as abbreviations, symbols and layout.

12 A particular difficulty occurs with proper names in some of the
    appendices A-H. This is that the cultural context strongly
    affects the knowledge that a student has of items of this kind.
    It is therefore extremely difficult to make a selection, and even
    more difficult to grade. For this reason, where it has been
    unavoidable, the assumption has been made that the student is
    living in a West European context.

Abbreviations used in the text

abbr.	abbreviation	*int.*	interjection
adj.	adjective	lang.	language
adv.	adverb	*n.*	noun
aux.	auxiliary	nat.	national
colloq.	colloquial	opp.	opposite
conj.	conjunction	*pl.*	plural
det.	determiner	*prep.*	preposition
fig.	figurative	*pron.*	pronoun
gen.	generally	*v.*	verb

xiv

A

1 **a/an**
  1 *det.* one of a set: *it's a camera/an aeroplane*
  1 *det.* profession: *he's a doctor*
  1 *det.* genus: *a mouse is a small animal*
  2 *prep.* per: *three times a week*
  4 *det.*: *a friend of mine*
  5 *det.*: kind of: *a fish you can eat*
  5 *det.*: sort of: *a love of skiing*
5 **ability**
  5 *n.* potential capacity: *to the best of my ability*
  6 *n.* cleverness: *a man of great ability*
2 **able**
  2 *adj.* having ability/capacity: *am/was able to*
  5 *adj.* skilful
1 **about**
  1 *adv.* around: *walking about*
  2 *prep.* approximately: *about 3 o'clock*
  3 *prep.* on the subject of: *it's about flowers*
  4 *prep.* here and there: *books lying about the room*
  5 *adv.* on the point of: *about to go*
2 **above**
  2 *prep.* at a higher level: *above the clouds*
  4 *adj.* mentioned earlier: *the above example*
  7 *prep.* more than: *honour above life*
3 **abroad**
  3 *adv.* in a foreign country
  7 *adv.* far and wide: *he's travelled abroad for years*
4 **absence**
  4 *n.* state of being away from
  4 *n.* period of being away
  5 *n.* lack of, non-existence
4 **absent**
  4 *adj.* not present at
  6 *adj.* abstracted, lost in thought

  7 *v.* stay away from: *she absented herself from all meetings*
4 **absolute** *adj.* complete, unconditional
5 **absolutely**
  5 *adv.* completely
  6 *int.* definitely
5 **academic**
  5 *adj.* of teaching
  7 *n.* scholar
  7 *adj.* theoretical, not practical
5 **accelerate** *v.*
4 **accent**
  4 *n.* way of speaking: *a Cockney accent*
  6 *n.* emphasis: *the accent in this project lies on . . .*
  7 *n.* symbol in writing or printing
2 **accept**
  2 *v.* receive
  5 *v.* agree
3 **accident**
  3 *n.* crash in traffic
  3 *n.* happening without immediately perceived cause
4 **accommodation** *n.* dwelling
5 **accompany**
  5 *v.* go with: *I accompanied her to the station*
  7 *v.* play music together with: *he accompanied the singer at the piano*
5 **accord** *v./n.*
5 **according to** *prep.*: *according to the Bible, it is wrong to steal*
3 **account**
  3 *n.* as in financial affairs
  4 *n.* report
  4 *prep.* because of: *on account of*
  6 *v.* give reason for
5 **accountant** *n.*
4 **accurate** *adj.*
4 **accuse** *v.*
5 **accustom** *v.*

3 **ache**
  3 *v.* hurt
  3 *n.* dull continuous pain
4 **achieve** *v.*
5 **achievement** *n.*
4 **acid**
  4 *n.* liquid used in chemistry
  6 *adj.* bitter: *an acid comment*
1 **across** *prep./adv.*
3 **act**
  3 *n.* thing done: *a cruel act*
  3 *v.* carry out action
  4 *n.* part of a play
  7 *n.* law: *act of parliament*
4 **action**
  4 *n.* process of doing something
  5 *n.* opposite of reflection
  7 *n.* legal action, process in law
  7 *n.* military activity: *killed in action*
4 **active**
  4 *adj.* energetic
  6 *adj.* functioning: *active volcano; active service*
5 **actively** *adv.*
4 **activity**
  4 *n.* forms of work or play: *classroom activities*
  6 *n.* state of using energy: *the activity of the machine can be regulated*
3 **actor** *n.*
3 **actress** *n.*
3 **actual**
  3 *adj.* real: *our actual needs*
  4 *adj.* true: *the actual place of his birth*
3 **actually**
  3 *adv.* in fact: *money actually paid*
  6 *adv.* as much as: *he actually dared return*
4 **ad** *n.* advertisement (abbr.)
3 **add**
  3 *v.* count together
  4 *v.* go on, say further
  5 *v.* increase: this adds to the total
4 **addition**
  4 *n.* process of adding
  4 *prep./adv.* as well (as): *in addition (to)*

5 *n.* something added: *an addition to the family*
5 **additional** *adj.*
1 **address**
  1 *n.* postal details of place
  6 *v.* indicate destination: *address a letter*
  7 *v.* give speech or talk
5 **adequate** *adj.*
5 **adjective** *n.*
4 **adjust**
  4 *v.* put right: *adjust the TV*
  7 *v.* adapt to: *adjust to society*
5 **administration**
  5 *n.* management of affairs
  7 *n.* the government
  7 *n.* the giving of an examination/punishment
5 **admiration** *n.*
3 **admire** *v.*
4 **admission**
  4 *n.* reception into/acceptance by an institution
  7 *n.* statement admitting something
3 **admit**
  3 *v.* permit to enter
  6 *v.* grant a thing to be true
  7 *v.* allow: *the words admit of no other meaning*
4 **adopt**
  4 *v.* take a child into one's family
  5 *v.* accept other customs
  7 *v.* accept a proposal: *the motion was adopted*
4 **adult** *n./adj.*
3 **advance**
  3 *v.* come or go forward
  6 *v.* put forward, put earlier
  7 *n.* pre-payment
5 **advanced** *adj.* superior: *at an advanced age*
3 **advantage** *n.* something useful or helpful
2 **adventure** *n.*
5 **advertise** *v.*
3 **advertisement** *n.*
3 **advice**
  3 *n.* informed opinion
  7 *n.* information: *letter of advice*

3 **advise**
   3 *v.* give advice to
   7 *v.* inform
1 **aeroplane** *n.*
3 **affair**
   3 *n.* concern: *personal affairs;*
   business affairs
   4 *n.* sexual relationship
4 **affect**
   4 *v.* have effect on: *this music affects*
   me deeply
   7 *v.* pretend to feel something
5 **affection** *n.*
3 **afford** *v.* able to find the time or
   money
2 **afraid**
   2 *adj.* frightened of
   3 *adj.* regretful: *I'm afraid we're going*
   to be late
   4 *adj.* apprehensive, doubtful: *I was*
   afraid to hurt his feelings
2 **Africa** *n.*
4 **African** *n./adj.*
1 **after**
   1 *prep.* subsequent: *after dark; run*
   after him
   2 *adv.* later in time, behind in place
1 **afternoon** *n.*
3 **afterwards** *adv.*
1 **again**
   1 *adv.* once more, one more time: *do*
   it again
   3 *adv.* as earlier: *you'll soon be well*
   again
2 **against** *prep.*
1 **age**
   1 *n.* length of life
   4 *n.* period of time: *the Middle Ages*
   6 *v.* become older
5 **agency** *n.* business, place of business
   of an agent
4 **agent** *n.* one who acts for others
5 **aggressive**
   5 *adj.* quarrelsome
   6 *adj.* go-ahead, not afraid of
   resistance
   7 *adj.* for offensive purposes:
   aggressive policies
2 **ago** *prep.*

2 **agree**
   2 *v.* share view
   5 *v.* concord
4 **agreement** *n.*
4 **agriculture** *n.*
4 **agricultural** *adj.*
3 **ah** *int.*
3 **ahead** *adv.*
3 **ahead of** *prep.:* *please go ahead of me*
4 **aid**
   4 *v.* assist
   4 *n.* help: *aid programme*
   5 *n.* support: *visual aids*
3 **aim**
   3 *v.* intend to do
   4 *v.* point towards
   5 *n.* objective
5 **aimless** *adj.*
1 **air**
   1 *n.* atmosphere
   5 *v.* ventilate: *to air a room*
2 **aircraft** *n.*
2 **airline** *n.*
4 **airmail** *n.*
5 **airman** *n.*
2 **airport** *n.*
5 **airtight** *adj.*
5 **alarm**
   5 *n.* a warning sound
   7 *v.* create the feeling of anxiety
4 **album**
   4 *n.* blank book for collection of
   photographs etc.
   5 *n.* protective covering for a record
   5 *n.* a longplaying record
3 **alcohol** *n.*
5 **algebra** *n.*
5 **alien**
   5 *n.* foreigner
   7 *adj.* differing in nature or character
4 **alike** *adj.*
2 **alive**
   2 *adj.* living
   4 *adj.* alert: *alive to change*
   7 *adj.* swarming with: *alive with grubs*
1 **all**
   1 *det.* (idea of wholeness): *all day;*
   with all my heart
   1 *det.* (idea of number): *all men*

3 *pron.* everything: *that's all*
4 *adv.* completely: *all alone*
5 *pron.* everything (with relatives): *all that I own; all of which*
3 **allow**
  3 *v.* permit: *dogs are not allowed here*
  5 *v.* pay regularly: *how much money does your father allow you?*
  5 *v.* include in planning: *we must allow for delay*
  7 *v.* accept: *the judge allowed the claim*
5 **allowance**
  5 *n.* money for regular or special purpose: *dress allowance*
  6 *n.* inclusion in calculation: *make allowance for the future*
  7 *n.* regular provision: *an allowance of food for the prisoners*
2 **almost** *adv.* nearly
2 **alone**
  2 *adv.* unaccompanied: *he lives alone*
  4 *adv.* only: *he alone knows*
  5 *adj.* isolated: *he is alone in that opinion*
2 **along**
  2 *prep./adv.* in a given direction: *run along the road*
  3 *prep.* alongside: *trees along the road*
  5 *adv.* over: *I'll go along to his house; move along!*
3 **aloud**
  3 *adv.* audibly: *read the story aloud*
  4 *adv.* loudly: *he called aloud for help*
5 **alphabet** *n.*
2 **already**
  2 *adv.* before a certain time: *I've completed it already*
  2 *adv.* so quickly: *have you done it already?*
  4 *adv.* previously: *I've been there already*
2 **also** *adv.*
5 **alter** *v.*
3 **although** *conj.* (see **though**)
1 **always**
  1 *adv.* at all times: *the earth always rotates on its own axis*

2 *adv.* repeatedly: *he's always asking for money*
5 **amateur** *n.*
5 **amaze** *v.*
4 **ambition** *n.*
5 **ambitious** *adj.*
4 **ambulance** *n.*
1 **American**
  1 *adj.*
  2 *n.* (nat.)
2 **among**
  2 *prep.* within group: *one among many*
  3 *prep.* surrounded by: *villages among the hills*
  4 *prep.* one of (+superlative): *Cambridge is among the most beautiful cities in England*
  5 *prep.* between: *he divided his money among his sons*
5 **amongst** *prep.* within/one of/between: (as for **among**)
2 **amount**
  2 *n.* quantity: *a small amount of sugar*
  3 *v.* add up to a total: *the cost amounts to*
  7 *v.* be equivalent to : *this amounts to a threat*
3 **amuse**
  3 *v.* cause to laugh: *the story amused me*
  5 *v.* pass the time: *TV amuses the children*
5 **amusement**
  5 *n.* relaxation: *he does it for his own amusement*
  7 *n.* sources of entertainment: *an amusement arcade*
5 **analyse**
  5 *v.* split into components for examination
  7 *v.* carry out psychological process
5 **analysis**
  5 *n.* process or product of analysing
  7 *n.* process of psychological treatment
5 **anchor**
  5 *n.* metal weight
  7 *v.* attach firmly to stable object

4 **ancient** *adj.* belonging to times long past: *ancient Rome*

1 **and**
  1 *conj.* connecting: *a table and four chairs*
  2 *conj.* replacing an if-clause: *work hard and you will pass*
  2 *conj.* intensive repetition: *for hours and hours*
  4 *conj.* to: *try and come early*

4 **anger** *n.*

5 **angle**
  5 *n.* corner: *the three angles of a triangle*
  7 *n.* an approach: *a new angle on the problem*

1 **angry**
  1 *adj.* greatly irritated: *I am angry with him for lying to you*
  5 *adj.* disturbed: *angry weather/sea*

1 **animal**
  1 *n.* all living things (except man)
  3 *n.* all living things (including man)
  7 *adj.* opp. of the spiritual side of man's nature

4 **ankle** *n.*

3 **announce**
  3 *v.* declare beforehand
  5 *v.* introduce programmes on radio/TV
  7 *v.* make known someone's arrival

5 **announcer** *n.*

3 **annoy**
  3 *v.* be irritated: *I was annoyed by the delay*
  4 *v.* irritate: *he annoyed the bull with a red flag*

5 **annoyance** *n.*

4 **annual**
  4 *adj.* every year: *the annual parade*
  4 *adj.* for one year: *his annual income*
  6 *n.* book
  7 *n.* plant

1 **another**
  1 *det.* a second: *have another cup of tea*
  2 *det.* similar: *he's another Edison*
  3 *det.* different: *at another time and in another place*

1 **answer**
  1 *v.* reply
  2 *n.* reply
  6 *v.* be responsible: *answer for*
  7 *v.* correspond: *he answers the description given*

5 **ant** *n.*

4 **Antarctic** *n.*

5 **antique**
  5 *n.* an old object
  7 *adj.* belonging to the distant past

5 **anxiety**
  5 *n.* unease: *anxiety about the future*
  7 *n.* eagerness: *in her anxiety to please*

3 **anxious**
  3 *adj.* uneasy
  5 *adj.* eager

1 **any**
  1 *det.* some: *have you any money? No, I haven't any*
  3 *det.* no matter what: *any food is better than none*
  5 *det.* whatever: *at any rate; in any case*
  5 *adv.* somewhat: *is he any better?*

2 **anybody**
  3 *pron.* no matter who: *anybody can do it*
  2 *pron.* someone: *is anybody there?*
  7 *pron.* person of importance: *was she anybody before she married?*

3 **anyhow**
  3 *adv.* whatever happens: *I shall go, anyhow, whether it rains or not*
  5 *adv.* in any possible way: *get there anyhow you like*
  6 *adv.* moreover: *it's too late now, anyhow*
  7 *adv.* carelessly: *don't do it anyhow, take care over it*

2 **anyone** *pron.*

2 **anything**
  2 *pron.* something: *has anything happened?*
  3 *pron.* no matter what: *I'll eat anything*

3 **anyway** (see **anyhow**)

2 **anywhere**
  2 *adv.* somewhere: *has she gone anywhere special?*
  3 *adv.* no matter where: *put the box down anywhere*
3 **apart**
  3 *prep.* not counting: *apart from that; joking apart . . .*
  4 *adj.* separated: *I can't get these two things apart*
  5 *adv.* distant: *those two pubs are a mile apart*
  7 *adj.* withdrawn: *she holds herself apart*
3 **apart from** *prep.: apart from anything else, she is too ill to travel*
4 **apartment** *n.*
4 **apologise** *v.*
5 **apology** *n.*
5 **apparatus** *n.*
5 **apparently** *adv.*
4 **appeal**
  4 *v.* request earnestly
  4 *n.* an earnest request
  5 *n.* power of attraction: *sex appeal*
  7 *v.* try to reverse a court decision
2 **appear**
  2 *v.* come into view, arrive
  6 *v.* seem to be
4 **appearance**
  4 *n.* act of appearing: *it was his first public appearance*
  6 *n.* something which seems to be: *the appearance of being half starved*
  7 *n.(pl.)* outward show: *keep up appearances*
5 **appetite** *n.*
5 **applause** *n.*
1 **apple** *n.*
5 **applicant** *n.*
4 **application**
  4 *n.* request: *to make an application to join*
  6 *n.* use on skin surface: *for external application only*
  7 *n.* assiduity: *if you show application in your work. . .*
3 **apply**
  3 *v.* request

  5 *v.* use
  7 *v.* show diligence
4 **appoint** *v.*
4 **appointment**
  4 *n.* rendezvous
  5 *n.* selection for office
4 **appreciate**
  4 *v.* value: *I appreciate your efforts*
  6 *v.* evaluate: *to appreciate poetry*
  7 *v.* rise in money value: *the land has greatly appreciated*
3 **approach**
  3 *v.* get closer to: *they approached the castle*
  7 *v.* take up a matter: *make an approach to the boss*
5 **approval** *n.* acceptance: *it meets with my approval*
3 **approve**
  3 *v.* accept, agree with: *I approve of this*
  7 *v.* ratify: *the minutes are approved*
4 **approximately** *adv.*
1 **April** *n.*
5 **Arab** *n.*
5 **arch**
  5 *n.* architectual feature
  6 *v.* shape into arch
5 **architect** *n.* one who designs buildings
4 **Arctic** *n./adj.*
3 **area**
  3 *n.* surface measure: *the area of this room is. . .*
  3 *n.* region of earth's surface: *tropical areas*
  6 *n.* sphere: *an area of agreement*
3 **argue**
  3 *v.* disagree, quarrel: *they are always arguing*
  4 *v.* maintain a case: *argue for or against*
  5 *v.* persuade: *they tried to argue him out of it*
  5 *v.* debate: *the lawyers argued for hours*
3 **argument**
  3 *n.* quarrel
  5 *n.* piece of reasoning
5 **arise** *v.* come into existence: *a new difficulty has arisen*

5 **arithmetic** *n.*
1 **arm**
  1 *n.* limb: *the human arm*
  3 *n.* arm-like part: *arm of a chair; arm of a coat*
  7 *n.* armed Forces: *the infantry arm*
5 **arms** *n.(pl.)* weapons
3 **army**
  3 *n.* military forces of a country
  5 *n.* organised body: *the Salvation Army*
5 **around**
  5 *adv.* on every side
  6 *adv.* near: *I'll be around if you want me*
  7 *adv.* travelling round about: *he's been around a lot*
3 **arrange**
  3 *v.* put in order: *she's good at arranging flowers*
  4 *v.* make plans in advance: *I have arranged to get there by 10 o'clock*
  4 *v.* agree on a plan with somebody: *I've arranged with John about the car*
3 **arrangement**
  3 *n.* order
  4 *n.* plan
  4 *n.* agreement
4 **arrest**
  4 *v.* seize: *the police arrested four persons*
  4 *n.* seizure by police
  7 *v.* stop movement: *the dam arrested the flow of water*
3 **arrival**
  3 *n.* act of arriving
  6 *n.* persons who arrive: *there are several new arrivals*
2 **arrive**
  2 *v.* reach a place: *arrive home*
  5 *v.* come to be: *yesterday her baby arrived*
  6 *v.* reach a stage/point: *arrive at a decision*
5 **arrow**
  5 *n.* sign to show direction
  6 *n.* weapon

3 **art**
  3 *n.* painting, sculpture etc: *the fine arts*
  6 *n.* skill/craftsmanship: *made not by nature but by art*
  7 *n.* as opposed to science: *he took a degree in Arts*
3 **article**
  3 *n.* piece of writing
  5 *n.* thing: *an article of furniture*
  7 *n.* point in a written legal agreement
5 **artificial** *adj.*
3 **artist**
  3 *n.* one who practises a fine art
  4 *n.* person who does something with skill and good taste: *an artist in words*
5 **artistic**
  5 *adj.* done with skill and good taste especially in the arts
  6 *adj.* of art and artists generally
1 **as**
  1 *adj.* like: *it can be used as a knife*
  1 *conj.* showing relationship: *as heavy as gold*
  3 *conj.* because: *as you aren't ready, I shall go alone*
  4 *conj.* in addition to: *John came as well as Jane*
  5 *conj.* while: *as I stood there, the King passed by*
  5 *conj.* showing purpose: *so as to . . .*
2 **as far as** *conj.: as far as I know, they are still coming*
5 **as for** *prep.: as for him, the proposal is out of the question*
4 **as if** *conj.: behave as if you don't understand the language*
4 **as long as** *conj.: as long as you're satisfied, we can go ahead*
5 **as regards** *prep.: as regards your application, we shall let you know*
3 **as soon as** *conj.: I'll call you as soon as possible*
3 **ash** *n.*
3 **ashamed** *adj.*
5 **ashore** *adv.*
4 **Asian** *n./adj.*

5 **aside**
    5 *adv.* on or to one side: *he laid the book aside*
    6 *adv.* apart: *joking aside*
    7 *n.* utterance in theatre: *an aside*
1 **ask**
    1 *v.* enquire: *ask a question; ask about the matter*
    2 *v.* make a request: *ask him a favour; ask for the manager*
    4 *v.* invite: *ask him to dinner; I wasn't asked*
5 **ask after** *v.* enquire about someone's welfare
2 **ask for** *v.* request
2 **asleep**
    2 *adj.* sleeping
    6 *adj.* numb: *my left arm's asleep*
4 **aspirin** *n.*
5 **assemble**
    5 *v.* gather together: *the students assembled*
    6 *v.* fit or put together: *assemble a watch*
5 **assignment** *n.*
4 **assist** *v.*
3 **assistant**
    3 *n.* shop assistant
    4 *adj.* helper, deputy: *assistant warden*
4 **associate**
    4 *v.* join or connect with: *associate one thing with another*
    5 *n.* colleague: *a business associate*
    6 *v.* be often in the company of: *don't associate with drug-peddlers*
    6 *adj.* assistant: *associate professor*
5 **association**
    5 *n.* society with specific aim: *the Automobile Association*
    6 *n.* collaboration, acquaintance: *I benefited from my association with him*
    7 *n.* connection of ideas
3 **astonish** *v.*
5 **astonishment** *n.*
5 **astrology** *n.*
1 **at**
    1 *prep.* of time: *at 9 o'clock*

2 *prep.* showing position: *the lines meet at a point*
2 *prep.* showing direction of activity: *rush at; look at*
3 *prep.* special use in regard to towns (but *not* the capital city): *at Leeds*
4 *prep.* with adj.: *good at; clever at*
4 *prep.* showing level on a scale: *at 35°C.; at £3 a bottle*
1 **at breakfast**
2 **at church**
5 **at all costs**
5 **at ease**
5 **at all events**
1 **at first**
5 **at first sight**
5 **at hand**
1 **at home**
2 **at last**
3 **at least**
5 **at a loss**
2 **at once**
3 **at peace**
3 **at present**
5 **at a profit**
4 **at any rate**
1 **at school**
2 **at sea**
2 **at a time**
3 **at the same time**
4 **at times**
3 **at war**
1 **at work**
5 **athletics** *n.*
2 **Atlantic** *n./adj.*
3 **atmosphere**
    3 *n.* air in any place
    5 *n.* mixture of gases surrounding the earth
    6 *n.* feeling, sense: *an atmosphere of peace and calm*
3 **atom**
    3 *n.* smallest unit of an element
    6 *n.* very small bit: *there's not an atom of truth in it*
3 **atomic** *adj.*
4 **attach**
    4 *v.* fasten or join: *attach labels to the luggage*

5 *v.* join oneself to: *attach oneself to a political party*
6 *v.* be bound to by love or affection: *she's deeply attached to her younger brother*
7 *v.* attribute: *attach importance to what he says*

3 **attack**
3 *n.* assault: *an attack on the government*
3 *v.* go and fight against

5 **attain**
5 *v.* succeed in doing or getting: *attain one's hopes*
7 *v.* reach, arrive at: *attain perfection*

3 **attend**
3 *v.* be present: *attend a meeting*
5 *v.* give service to: *are you being attended to?*
6 *v.* give ear/mind to: *attend to the teacher/one's business*

5 **attendance**
5 *n.* being present: *regular attendance by the students*
7 *n.* number of people attending: *a large attendance at the lecture last night*

5 **attendant**
5 *n.* a servant, doorman
6 *n.* a medical assistant

3 **attention**
3 *n.* act of directing one's thoughts: *pay attention*
6 *n.* drill position: *at attention*

3 **attitude**
3 *n.* way of feeling/thinking or behaving: *what is your attitude towards this question?*
6 *n.* manner of placing or holding the body

3 **attract**
3 *v.* draw interest: *the side shows attracted many people*
6 *v.* draw closer: *a magnet attracts iron*

5 **attraction**
5 *n.* power of pulling towards: *the attraction she felt for him*
6 *n.* that which attracts: *the attractions of a big city*

3 **attractive** *adj.*

3 **audience**
3 *n.* gathering of persons to listen
7 *n. the Pope granted him an audience*

1 **August** *n.*

3 **aunt** *n.*

3 **Australia** *n.*

3 **Australian** *n./adj.*

4 **author**
4 *n.* writer
7 *n.* creator or initiator: *God, the author of our being*

4 **authority**
4 *n.* power or right to give orders
6 *n.* person or group having authority: *the municipal authority*
7 *n.* right given to execute: *only the treasurer has the authority to make payments*
7 *n.* person or object with special knowledge: *this book is the main authority on Byzantine coins*

5 **automatic**
5 *n.* weapon
5 *adj.* self-acting, self-moving, of a machine
6 *adj.* of actions done without thought: *breathing is automatic*

1 **autumn** *n.* season

4 **available** *adj.*

4 **avenue**
4 *n.* a wide road
6 *n.* line of objects: *an avenue of trees*
7 *n.* way of proceeding: *explore every avenue*

3 **average**
3 *n./adj.* the arithmetical mean: *the average price*
4 *adj.* ordinary: *the average man*
6 *v.: our takings average £100 a day*

3 **avoid** *v.*

2 **awake**
2 *v.* wake: *he awoke at 4 o'clock this morning*
6 *v./adj.* become aware: *awake to his opportunities*

5 **award**

  5 *n.* decision made by a judge or arbiter

  6 *n.* something given as the result of such decision

  7 *n.* money granted to a university student

4 **aware** *adj.*

2 **away**

  2 *adv.* movement from a place: *run away*

  2 *adv.* separation from a position: *the manager is away*

  3 *adv.* aside: *put your work away*

  5 *adv.* idea of decline/diminution: *fade away*

  6 *adv.* idea of continuing: *work away without stopping*

  7 *adv.* intensive: *right away! fire away!*

2 **away from** *prep.: the village lies a few miles away from the coast*

4 **awful** *adj.*

4 **awfully** *adv.*

5 **awkward**

  5 *adj.* clumsy, having little skill: *he's awkward with his hands*

  6 *adj.* badly designed, difficult to use: *an awkward staircase*

  6 *adj.* difficult to handle: *he was an awkward man to deal with over money*

  7 *adj.* (colloq.): *an awkward customer*

5 **axe** *n.*

5 **axle** *n.*

B

1 **baby**

  1 *n.* a young child

  6 *n.* youngest: *which of you is the baby?*

  7 *adj.* not fully developed: *baby marrows*

4 **baby-sitter** *n.*

1 **back**

  1 *adv.* towards the rear: *head winds drove them back*

  1 *n.* part of the body or of an object, opposite of front: *the back of his head*

  2 *adv.* to a former state: *back to life*

  2 *adv.* in return: *to have the money back*

  3 *adv.* of time: *back in the Middle Ages*

  4 *adv.* in retaliation: *answer back; hit back*

  4 *v.* reverse: *he backed the car away*

  6 *v.* gamble on: *back a cause*

5 **back out of** *v.* withdraw

5 **back up** *v.* support

5 **backbone**

  5 *n.* spine

  7 *n.* main strength: *backbone of the crew*

4 **background**

  4 *n.* part of a view

  7 *n.* setting: *the background to the report*

5 **backwards**

  5 *adv.* away from front: *go backwards*

  5 *adv.* reverse order: *say the letters backwards*

5 **backyard** *n.*

1 **bad**

  1 *adj.* useless: *a bad worker*

  1 *adj.* unpleasant, incorrect: *bad manners*

  1 *adj.* immoral: *a bad man, bad behaviour*

  2 *adj.* painful: *I've got a bad head*

  4 *adj.* rotten: *go bad*

1 **badly**
  1 *adv.* roughly, untidily: *badly made*
  2 *adv.* much: *badly in need of repair*
  5 *adv.* very much: *she wants it badly*
  6 *adv.* poor: *badly off*
5 **badge** *n.* sign of occupation, office, membership
1 **bag**
  1 *n.* container for carrying solid things
  7 *n.* lots of: *bags of money*
  7 *v.* get by hunting: *bag some duck*
3 **baggage** *n.* luggage
2 **bake**
  2 *v.* cook
  3 *v.* harden: *these pots were baked in our kiln*
  7 *v.* warm one's body: *baking in the sun at the resort*
2 **baker** *n.*
3 **balance**
  3 *v.* cause to be steady: *balance a ruler on one finger*
  5 *n.* instrument for weighing
  6 *v.* equate: *balance the accounts*
  6 *n.* state of equilibrium: *balance of power*
  7 *n.* outstanding amount: *hand in the balance*
5 **balcony**
  5 *n.* platform on exterior of building
  7 *n.* raised level of seating in theatre
4 **bald** *adj.* without hair on head
1 **ball**
  1 *n.* round object: *cricket ball; meatball; a ball of wool*
  6 *n.* dance: *May Ball*
5 **ballet** *n.*
2 **balloon** *n.* bag or envelope filled with air
4 **ballpoint** *n.*
1 **banana** *n.*
3 **band**
  3 *n.* group of persons, generally musicians
  4 *n.* connecting piece: *rubber bands*
  6 *v.* join together
  6 *n.* strip: *a band of colour*
5 **bandage** *n.*

5 **bang**
  5 *n.* sudden loud noise
  6 *n.* a violent blow
  6 *v.* strike: *bang in that nail with a hammer*
2 **bank**
  2 *n.* establishment for handling money
  5 *n.* a ridge: *bank of earth*
  6 *v.* place securely: *to bank one's money*
3 **Bank Holiday** *n.*
5 **banker** *n.*
5 **bankrupt** *adj.*
2 **bar**
  2 *n.* a drinking place
  4 *n.* a rod of wood or metal: *a bar of gold*
  5 *v.* obstruct: *to bar the door*
  5 *n.* obstacle: *a bar across the road*
  7 *n.* place in court: *prisoner at the bar*
4 **barber** *n.*
3 **bare**
  3 *adj.* naked: *bare skin; bare head*
  6 *adj.* mere: *kill with your bare hands*
  6 *adj.* very slight: *a bare majority*
  7 *v.* make naked: *bare one's head*
3 **bargain**
  3 *v.* negotiate by argument: *you have to bargain in a Persian bazaar*
  5 *n.* thing bought cheaply
  5 *n.* agreement: *strike a bargain*
3 **bark**
  3 *v.* cry (dogs, foxes)
  3 *n.* cry so made
  6 *v.* shout sharply: *he barked his orders*
5 **barman** *n.*
4 **barrel**
  4 *n.* round container: *a barrel of beer*
  7 *n.* tube: *barrel of a rifle*
4 **base**
  4 *n.* foundation: *base of a pillar*
  5 *v.* establish on foundation: *base the argument*
  6 *n.* headquarters, main office: *go back to base for supplies*
  7 *adj.* dishonourable: *acting from base motives*
4 **basement** *n.*

4 **basic** *adj.*
3 **basin**
   3 *n.* bowl for washing, etc
   4 *n.* dish for cooking/storing food
   5 *n.* hollow place where water collects
   7 *n.* deep part of harbour
5 **basis** *n.* foundation: *the basis of morality*
2 **basket** *n.*
2 **bath**
   2 *v.* wash: *bath the baby*
   3 *n.* act of washing: *take a cold bath*
   3 *n.* container: *a porcelain bath*
2 **bathroom** *n.*
2 **bathe**
   2 *v.* apply liquid to, soak: *the nurse bathed the wound*
   4 *v.* go into the sea: *we bathed every morning*
3 **battle**
   3 *n.* military engagement
   5 *n.* struggle: *a battle of wills*
   7 *v.* fight
4 **bay**
   4 *n.* curved edge of sea or lake
   7 *n.* architectural feature: *bay window*
   7 *n.* area outside main stream of activity: *loading bay; sick bay*
1 **be**
   1 *v.* be present in space: *Mary is upstairs*
   1 *v.* exist: *there are two ways of doing it*
   1 *aux.* present continuous: *she is cooking*
   2 *aux.* past simple forms: *they were ill that week*
   3 *aux.* past continuous: *I was reading when you rang*
   3 *aux.* passive uses: *it was broken yesterday*
   3 *v.* visit: *he's been to Rangoon*
   4 *v.* plan: *I'm to make the first draft*
   5 *v.* be obliged: *you're to report every Monday*
   6 *v.* take place: *but the meeting she hoped for was never to be*
2 **beach** *n.* the sea shore
5 **beak** *n.* horny part of bird's mouth

5 **beam** *n.*
5 **bean** *n.*
3 **bear**
   3 *n.* animal
   5 *v.* carry: *bearing a burden*
   6 *v.* stand: *bear pain*
   6 *v.* tolerate: *I can't bear him*
   7 *v.* yield: *bear fruit*
5 **bear up** *v.* remain firm
3 **beard** *n.*
5 **beast**
   5 *n.* four-footed animal
   6 *n.* cruel or disgusting person
2 **beat**
   2 *v.* conquer
   3 *v.* strike rhythmically: *beat a drum*
   4 *n.* rhythmic stroke: *heart beats*
   5 *v.* punish: *beat him*
   6 *v.* mix: *beat an egg*
1 **beautiful** *adj.*
3 **beauty**
   3 *n.* quality
   4 *n.* beautiful person or thing: *she was a famous beauty*
   7 *n.* beautiful feature: *her eyes are her chief beauty*
1 **because** *conj.* as: *I do it because I like it*
2 **because of** *prep.* owing to: *we didn't go out because of the storm*
2 **become**
   2 *v.* come to be: *he became a doctor*
   5 *v.* happen to: *what will become of the children*
   7 *v.* suit well: *her new hat becomes her*
1 **bed**
   1 *n.* piece of furniture
   5 *n.* patch of ground: *flower bed*
   6 *n.* the bottom level: *bed of a lake*
5 **bedclothes** *n.(pl.)*
5 **bedding** *n.*
2 **bedroom** *n.*
5 **bedside** *n.*
5 **bedsitter** *n.*
5 **bee** *n.* insect
5 **beef** *n.* meat
3 **beer** *n.*

1 **before**
1 *prep.* anterior in time: *before 1937*
2 *conj.: tell me before he comes*
5 *prep.* in front of: *the options before us*
5 *adv.* earlier: *you should have told me before*
5 **beg**
5 *v.* ask for charity
6 *v.* request humbly
5 **beggar** *n.* person who begs (for a living)
2 **begin** *v.* start: *we begin at 7*
2 **beginner** *n.*
2 **beginning** *n.*
3 **behave**
3 *v.* conduct oneself
5 *v.* (of machines) function: *how is your new car behaving?*
4 **behaviour**
4 *n.* human actions and conduct
5 *n.* functioning of machines/systems: *the behaviour of the ship*
1 **behind**
1 *prep./adv.* at the rear, to the rear: *walking just behind (me)*
3 *prep.* on the further side of: *behind the trees there is a lake*
7 *adj.* late: *behind in payments*
4 **belief**
4 *n.* religious faith, tenets
5 *n.* trust, credence: *unworthy of belief*
3 **believe**
3 *v.* think: *I believe that he came*
5 *v.* give credence to: *I don't believe you*
5 *v.* have faith in: *believe in God*
1 **bell** *n.*
2 **belong**
2 *v.* be part of, connected with: *where does this button belong*
3 *v.* be owned by: *that land belongs to me*
2 **below**
2 *prep.* under: *below the surface*
5 *adv.* underneath: *try it from below*
3 **belt**
3 *n.* item of clothing put around waist

4 *n.* endless strap used to connect wheels
5 *n.* wide strip or band, a surrounding area: *commuter belt*
5 **bench** *n.* seat
3 **bend**
3 *v.* force into a curve or angle
4 *n.* turning in the road
5 *v.* stoop: *bend down/over*
7 *v.* direct: *all eyes were bent on me*
3 **beneath** *prep.* below or under: *beneath the same roof*
4 **benefit**
4 *n.* advantage, profit, help: *benefit from your holiday; benefit of the doubt*
6 *v.* do good to
5 **berry** *n.*
1 **beside**
1 *prep.* at the side of, close to: *come and sit beside me*
3 *prep.* compared with: *you're quite tall beside your sister*
5 *prep.* as well as: *and all the supporters were there, besides the players*
6 *adv.* moreover: *and besides, he's stupid too*
1 **best**
1 *adj.* superlatively good: *the best dinner I ever had*
2 *adv.* in the most excellent way: *he works best in the mornings*
5 *adj.* the outstanding person/thing: *we're the best of friends*
6 *adv.* should (with had): *you had best see him soon*
7 *adv.* most: *he's the best hated man in the village*
4 **bet**
4 *v.* risk money
4 *n.* a wager
7 *v.* be (almost) sure: *I bet you they've gone*
1 **better**
1 *adj.* superior: *better wine*
2 *adv.: get better; do it better*
5 *adv.* should (with had): *you'd better do as he asked*

5 *adv.: the sooner, the better*
6 *adj.* greater: *for the better part of three hours*
6 *adj.* richer, wiser: *better off*

1 **between**
  1 *prep.* showing division: *a choice between two alternatives*
  2 *prep.* of position or time: *standing between A and B*
  3 *prep.* joining: *a railway between two cities; a marriage between Mr A and Miss B*
  5 *prep.* amongst: *between ourselves*

2 **beyond**
  2 *prep.* at, on, to the farther side of: *the house is beyond the bridge*
  3 *prep.* past (of time): *don't stay beyond 10 o'clock*
  5 *prep.* exceeding, out of reach of: *beyond his powers*
  7 *prep.* apart from: *he has nothing beyond his pension*

4 **bible** *n.*

1 **bicycle** *n.*

1 **big**
  1 *adj.* large in measurement/volume: *a big building*
  3 *adj.* important: *a big man*
  7 *adv.* boastfully: *to talk big*

1 **bike** *n.*

3 **bill**
  3 *n.* statement of financial charges
  4 *n.* notice, poster
  6 *v.* send a statement of financial charges
  7 *n.* list of foods/performers: *top of the bill*

2 **billion** *n.*

3 **bind**
  3 *v.* tie up a person or a thing
  4 *v.* tie up a wound, tie onto: *she bound a cloth round his head*
  7 *v.* constrain by oath or law: *bind by a promise*

1 **bird**
  1 *n.* creature
  7 *n.* (colloq.) girl

3 **birth**
  3 *n.* act of being born
  6 *n.* family: *of noble birth*

3 **birth control** *n.*

2 **birthday** *n.*

2 **biscuit** *n.* flat crisp cake

1 **bit**
  1 *n.* small part of anything: *a few bits of wood; a bit of advice*
  3 *adv.* little: *wait a bit; not a bit*

1 **bite**
  1 *v.* seize/sever with teeth
  3 *n.* act of biting
  5 *n.* sting: *a mosquito bite*
  6 *n.* a small amount of food: *a bite to eat*

3 **bitter**
  3 *adj.* of taste: *bitter beer*
  4 *adj.* of pain: *bitter disappointment*
  5 *adj.* virulent, angry: *a bitter attack*

5 **bitterness** *n.*

1 **black**
  1 *adj.* opposite of white, dark: *black clouds; black skin*
  3 *n.* a black person: *blacks in America*
  5 *adj.* illegal: *black market*
  7 *adj.* malignant, sad: *black looks*

1 **blackboard** *n.*

5 **blade**
  5 *n.* cutting part of knife or sword
  6 *n.* flat part of piece of grass
  7 *n.* flat thing: *blade of an oar; shoulder blade*

3 **blame**
  3 *v.* attribute guilt: *blame him for doing it*
  4 *n.* responsibility for error: *lay the blame on*

4 **blank**
  4 *adj.* unwritten on: *blank sheet of paper*
  5 *adj.* empty, without interest or expression: *a blank look*
  6 *adj.* unrhymed: *blank verse*
  6 *n.* spaces in a document: *fill in the blanks*

3 **blanket**
  3 *n.* a woollen covering
  7 *adj.* covering all cases or classes: *blanket insurance*

7 *v.* cover entirely: *the valley was blanketed with fog*

3 **bleed**
  3 *v.* lose blood: *if you cut your finger it will bleed*
  6 *v.* feel great distress: *our hearts bleed for you*

5 **bless**
  5 *v.* wish happiness or favour to: *bless you my boy*
  6 *v.* ask God's favour for: *the priest blessed the people*
  6 *v.* consecrate: *the buildings were blessed by the Bishop*

5 **blessing**
  5 *n.* something one is glad of: *what a blessing it is that we didn't get wet*
  6 *n.* the favour of God: *ask a blessing*

3 **blind**
  3 *adj.* not able to see: *blind from birth*
  5 *v.* dazzle
  6 *adj.* insensitive: *blind to the beauties of nature*
  6 *v.* deprive of sight
  7 *adj.* hidden, having no opening: *a blind alley*

3 **block**
  3 *n.* mass: *a block of stone, wood etc.*
  4 *n.* set of buildings: *a block of houses*
  5 *v.* obstruct: *the road is blocked*
  6 *n.* blockage: *a traffic block*
  7 *n.* rectangle limited by streets: *she lives two blocks away*

5 **blond(e)** *adj.*

3 **blood**
  3 *n.* liquid
  4 *n.* idea of emotion: *hot blood; in cold blood*
  6 *n.* idea of family, breeding: *royal blood*
  7 *n.* idea of life: *to shed blood*

5 **bloody**
  5 *adv.* very (vulgar): *it's bloody awful*
  5 *adj.* nasty, unpleasant: *the interview was bloody*
  7 *adj.* covered with blood

4 **blouse** *n.*

2 **blow**
  2 *v.* move (of wind): *the wind is blowing from the north*
  3 *n.* hit: *strike a blow*
  4 *v.* exhale, puff or inflate: *to blow up a balloon etc.*
  5 *v.* play (of wind instruments): *to blow a trumpet*
  4 *v.* explode: *to blow up a bridge; the gun blew up*
  7 *n.* disaster: *what a blow!*

1 **blue**
  1 *n./adj.* colour
  5 *adj.* sad: *he's feeling blue*
  6 *adj.* pornographic: *blue films*

4 **blunt**
  4 *adj.* without a sharp point or edge
  7 *adj.* forthright: *a blunt speaker*
  7 *v.* impair sharpness

1 **board**
  1 *n.* piece of wood: *floorboard; noticeboard*
  4 *n.* meeting: *there's to be a selection board soon*
  5 *n.* committee: *he's on the board of directors*
  5 *n.* food: *board and lodging*
  6 *n.* ship: *on board*
  6 *v.* get on or into: *board a boat or train*
  7 *v.* interview for selection: *we'll board them next week*

5 **boast**
  5 *v.* praise oneself: *he boasts about his money*
  6 *n.* self-praise: *his loud boasts*

1 **boat** *n.* water-borne vessel

1 **body**
  1 *n.* physical organism: *my body feels hot*
  2 *n.* corpse: *bury the body*
  5 *n.* a group: *a body of men*
  6 *n.* trunk: *draw the body then add the arms and legs*
  7 *n.* distinct from chassis: *the body of a car*
  7 *n.* object in science: *heavenly body*

15

3 **boil**
  3 *v.* bubble with heat: *the water is boiling*
  3 *v.* heat: *boil the water*
  7 *n.* swelling on skin: *a boil on his back*
5 **boiler** *n.* metal container in which water is heated
3 **bold**
  3 *adj.* brave: *a bold leader*
  6 *adj.* striking: *a bold design*
  7 *adj.* heavy (printing): *bold type*
  7 *adj.* immodest: *a bold dress*
5 **boldness** *n.*
3 **bomb** *n./v.*
5 **bomber** *n.*
5 **bombing** *n.*
3 **bone**
  3 *n.* part of the body: *she's broken her hip-bone*
  5 *n.* substance: *this brooch is made of whalebone*
  7 *v.* remove bones: *bone a chicken*
1 **book**
  1 *n.* a number of sheets of paper, printed or blank, fastened together in a cover
  3 *n.* set of similar items: *a book of stamps*
  4 *v.* reserve: *to book a place (theatre)*
4 **bookshelf** *n.*
4 **bookshop** *n.*
4 **boot** *n.* covering for the foot and ankle/leg
4 **border**
  4 *n.* frontier: *within our borders*
  5 *n.* edge: *at the border of the garden*
  5 *n.* of cloth: *coloured border on a dress*
  6 *v.* form edge: *fields bordered by woods*
4 **bore**
  4 *v.* make a hole
  5 *v.* weary by tediousness
  6 *n.* someone or something tiresome
4 **boss**
  4 *n.* person in charge
  5 *v.* give orders (gen. fussily)

1 **both**
  1 *pron.* the two together: *both are dead*
  2 *adj.* one and the other: *both my friends; on both days*
  4 *adj./adv.* at the same time, conjointly: *both men and women*
4 **bother** *v./n.* trouble
1 **bottle**
  1 *n.* receptacle
  5 *v.* place in receptacle: *bottle fruit*
5 **bottom**
  5 *n.* foundation: *the bottom of this tower*
  5 *n.* the lowest part: *bottom of a valley*
  5 *n.* buttocks: *a baby's bottom*
  6 *n.* deepest region: *from the bottom of my heart*
  7 *n.* bed of the sea/lake: *to touch bottom*
  7 *n.* the basis or first cause: *I'll get to the bottom of this*
5 **bound**
  5 *adj.* connected: *their prospects are bound up with tourism*
  6 *adj.* forced: *I'm bound to say*
  7 *adj.* travelling: *homeward bound*
4 **boundary** *n.* line that marks a limit
5 **bow**
  5 *v.* incline body
  6 *n.* weapon: *bows and arrows*
  6 *n.* kind of knot: *tie a bow*
  7 *n.* the front of a ship
5 **bowl**
  4 *n.* deep round hollow dish
  5 *n.* anything bowl-shaped: *the bowl of a pipe*
  6 *v.* hurl a ball
  7 *n.(pl.)* game with wooden balls
1 **box**
  1 *n.* container
  3 *v.* fight with gloves
  6 *n.* compartment in a theatre
  7 *v.* enclose: *box up/in*
5 **boxing** *n.* sport
5 **Boxing Day** *n.*
1 **boy** *n.* a male child, a son: *he has two boys and one girl*

3 **bra** *n.*
5 **bracelet** *n.*
3 **brain**
   3 *n.* the organ: *the brain is contained in the skull*
   7 *n.* cleverness: *he has a fine brain*
5 **brains** *n.(pl.)*
4 **brake**
   4 *v.* reduce speed of vehicle
   4 *n.* device for reducing speed
2 **branch**
   2 *n.* limb of a tree
   4 *n.* subsidiary office of a business: *branch of a bank*
   5 *n.* section of subject: *a branch of mathematics*
   5 *n.* subsidiary line/course: *of a river/railway*
   6 *v.* take a side turning: *branch off to the left*
5 **brand**
   5 *n.* trademark: *a brand of soap*
   6 *adj.* completely: *brand new*
   7 *v.* mark with owner's symbol: *brand cattle*
5 **brass**
   5 *n.* bright yellow metal
   7 *n.* section of a band
2 **brave**
   2 *adj.* courageous: *as brave as a lion*
   4 *adj.* splendid: *brave new world*
5 **bravery** *n.*
5 **Brazil** *n.*
5 **Brazilian** *n./adj.*
1 **bread**
   1 *n.* foodstuff: *a loaf of bread*
   2 *n.* nourishment: *I earn my bread*
5 **breadth**
   5 *n.* distance or measure from side to side: *10 ft in breadth*
   7 *n.* tolerance: *breadth of mind*
1 **break**
   1 *v.* smash: *break the window*
   4 *n.* pause for relaxation: *they went on all day without a break*
   5 *v.* interrupt: *to break one's journey*
   6 *v.* overcome constraints: *break a contract*

3 **break down**
   3 *v.* fail to go on working (system, car)
   5 *v.* collapse (in tears)
5 **break in**
   4 *v.* enter a building by force
   5 *v.* interrupt (a conversation)
4 **break off** *v.* end suddenly
4 **break out**
   4 *v.* escape
   5 *v.* burst into speech
5 **break through** *v.* overcome an obstacle
3 **break up**
   3 *v.* separate (partners in marriage)
   4 *v.* smash into many pieces
5 **breakdown**
   5 *n.* collapse of will or mental state: *a nervous breakdown*
   6 *n.* mechanical failure
1 **breakfast**
   1 *n.* meal
   6 *v.* have this meal
5 **breast**
   5 *n.* part of woman's body
   6 *n.* chest or upper front part of human body
3 **breath**
   3 *n.* air into or from the lungs: *to draw breath*
   7 *n.* air in movement: *there wasn't a breath of air*
3 **breathe**
   3 *v.* exhale/inhale: *breathe again*
   7 *v.* reveal: *don't breathe a word*
5 **bribe** *n./v.*
3 **brick** *n.*
4 **bride** *n.*
4 **bridegroom** *n.*
2 **bridge**
   2 *n.* construction for crossing a divide
   5 *n.* control deck of a ship
   7 *n.* upper/boney part of nose
   7 *v.* put bridge over gap: *bridge (a river)*
   7 *n.* game of cards
4 **brief**
   4 *adj.* concise: *please be brief*
   6 *n.(pl.)* close fitting underpants
   7 *n.* set of instructions: *a legal brief*

2 **bright**
  2 *adj.* giving out or reflecting much light
  4 *adj.* cheerful and happy: *a bright smile*
  5 *adj.* quick witted: *he's a bright boy*
5 **brighten** *v.*
1 **bring**
  1 *v.* carry, convey: *bring your book*
  2 *v.* cause to reach a certain state: *bring to an end*
4 **bring about** *v.* cause to happen
2 **bring back** *v.* return something to someone
4 **bring in** *v.* introduce an element
5 **bring off** *v.* succeed against expectations
5 **bring out** *v.* make clear
5 **bring round** *v.* help back to consciousness
3 **bring up** *v.* raise (child)
1 **Britain** *n.*
1 **British** *adj.*
5 **Briton** *n.*
2 **broad**
  2 *adj.* opposite of narrow: *a broad river*
  3 *adj.* extensive: *broad horizons*
  7 *adj.* comprehensive: *a broad view of the matter*
4 **broadcast**
  4 *v.* send out by radio/TV: *the BBC broadcasts in many languages*
  4 *n.* a radio/TV programme
5 **broaden** *v.*
1 **brother**
  1 *n.* son of same parents
  7 *n.* member of a religious brotherhood
5 **brow** *n.* arch of hair above the eye
1 **brown**
  1 *n./adj.* colour
  4 *v.* turn brown: *the toast is nicely browned*
5 **bruise** *v./n.*
2 **brush**
  2 *n.* instrument used for cleaning/painting

3 *v.* clean with a brush: *brush the crumbs from the table*
  5 *v.* polish, smarten: *brush your shoes*
  7 *v.* touch lightly: *brush against*
4 **bubble**
  4 *n.* spherical shape
  5 *v.* give off bubbles
2 **bucket** *n.* vessel for holding/carrying water
5 **Buddhist** *n./adj.*
5 **budget**
  5 *n.* estimate of probable future income and expenditure
  7 *v.* allow or arrange for future expenditure
5 **bug**
  5 *n.* insect
  6 *n.* (colloq.) virus: *the flu bug*
  7 *v.* (colloq.) use small hidden microphone: *bug an embassy*
2 **build**
  2 *v.* erect structure, construct: *build a house/ship*
  5 *v.* accumulate: *traffic is building up*
  6 *v.* strengthen: *he is building up his reserves*
  7 *n.* shape, structure: *he's the same build as me*
3 **builder** *n.*
2 **building**
  2 *n.* structure for living or working in
  4 *n.* art of constructing houses
5 **bulb**
  5 *n.* rooted stem of plant such as onion
  6 *n.* anything with bulb shape: *electric light bulb*
3 **bullet** *n.*
5 **bunch**
  5 *n.* group of similar things together: *bunch of keys*
  7 *v.* form into a bunch: *bunch up*
4 **bundle** *n.* articles fastened together
2 **burn**
  2 *v.* consume with fire: *burn down the house*
  4 *n.* mark of burning: *burn on my hand*

3 burst
    3 *v.* break from internal pressure: *the bottle burst*
    4 *v.* break out: *burst into tears*
    4 *v.* break through or into: *burst open the door*
    5 *n.* explosion: *a burst of flame*
    6 *n.* sudden output of energy: *a burst of speed*
4 burst in *v.* enter suddenly
5 burst out *v.* explode from a confined space
3 bury
    3 *v.* put in the ground: *bury a body*
    4 *v.* hide away: *buried in the country / buried treasure*
    7 *v.* sink deep or hide: *he buried his hands in his pockets*
1 bus
    1 *n.* means of transport
    7 *v.* transport by bus
2 bush
    2 *n.* shrub
    7 *n.* outback, jungle
2 business
    2 *n.* work, occupation: *the grocery business*
    3 *n.* duty: *here on business*
    4 *n.* commerce: *go into business*
    5 *n.* going concern: *sell the business*
    6 *n.* affairs: *mind your own business*
    7 *n.* affair, event: *that business of last Friday*
    7 *n.* agenda: *the business before the meeting is. . .*
4 businessman *n.*
2 busy
    2 *adj.* working: *he's busy now and cannot see you*
    3 *adj.* full of work or activity: *a busy day, a busy town*
    7 *v.* work at: *busy oneself with*
1 but
    1 *conj.* contrast: *it's not cheap but it's very good*
    6 *prep.* except: *last but one; none but the brave*
    7 *adv.* only: *had but a single rival*

1 butcher
    1 *n.* person who sells meat
    7 *n.* person who causes unnecessary death
1 butter
    1 *n.* substance
    4 *v.* spread the substance
2 button
    2 *n.* fastening: *there's a button missing on the sleeve*
    4 *v.* fasten with buttons: *button up your coat*
5 buttonhole
    5 *n.* hole for a button in jacket, coat or dress
    7 *n.* flower to put into buttonhole
1 buy
    1 *v.* get in return for money: *buy a new hat*
    4 *n.* purchase: *a very good buy*
    7 *v.* obtain at a sacrifice: *he bought fame at the expense of his health*
2 by
    2 *prep.* position, near: *stand by his side*
    3 *prep.* agent: *written by Shakespeare; proved by time*
    4 *prep.* motion, near: *pass by your window*
    4 *prep.* before: *do it by Wednesday*
    4 *adv.*: *stand by; a house near by; I saw him pass by*
    5 *prep.* according to: *paid by the hour; moved by inches*
    6 *prep.* beside: *I always keep some by me*
4 by accident
1 by air
1 by bus
1 by car
4 by chance
3 by day
5 by far
5 by hand
4 by heart
1 by land
4 by all means
4 by means of *prep.*: *thoughts are expressed by means of words*

3 **by mistake**
3 **by name**
3 **by night**
2 **by oneself**
1 **by plane**
2 **by post**
1 **by sea**

2 **by ship**
3 **by sight**
4 **by surprise**
1 **by train**
2 **by yourself**
1 **bye-bye** *int.*
4 **bypass** *n.*

C

5 **cabbage** *n.*
4 **cabin** *n.*
5 **cable**
    5 *v.* send message by telegraph
    5 *n.* message sent by telegraph
    6 *n.* form of rope or wire
2 **café** *n.*
3 **cage**
    3 *n.* a framework of wires or bars for keeping birds or animals in
    6 *v.* put/keep in a cage
1 **cake** *n.*
4 **calculate**
    4 *v.* work out mathematically: *we need to calculate the costs*
    6 *v.* plan: *this advertisement is calculated to attract attention*
4 **calendar** *n.*
1 **call**
    1 *v.* give/have as name: *their daughter is called Prunella*
    3 *v.* summon: *call the police*
    4 *v.* wake: *call me at seven*
    4 *n.* (with telephone): *a telephone call*
    4 *v.* phone: *call her up on this number*
    4 *v.* shout: *did you hear me call?*
    6 *n.* signal: *bugle call*
    7 *n.* cry (animal): *the call of a bird*
3 **call away** *v.* summon to carry out another activity
4 **call by** *v.* visit briefly while on a journey
3 **call for**
    3 *v.* collect someone

    5 *v.* require
3 **call in**
    3 *v.* visit (place or person)
    5 *v.* ask to visit
4 **call off** *v.* abandon, cancel
4 **call on** *v.* visit (person)
5 **call up** *v.* mobilise (troops)
3 **calm**
    3 *adj.* peaceful (weather): *a calm day; calm sea*
    4 *adj.* untroubled, not excited: *keep calm*
    5 *v.* regain composure: *calm down*
5 **calmness** *n.*
4 **camel** *n.*
5 **camera** *n.* apparatus for taking photographs
3 **camp**
    3 *n.* place where people live in tents
    3 *v.* establish sleeping quarters
    7 *n.* body of opinion: *we belong to different political camps*
1 **can/cannot**
    1 *v. modal* ideas of capacity: *can you see me?; he can speak French*
    2 *n.* container
    2 *v. modal* being permitted = may: *can I have one of these?*
    3 *v. modal* idea of possibility: *it can't be true*
3 **Canada** *n.*
3 **Canadian** *n./adj.*
4 **canal**
    4 *n.* channel for water cut through land

20

5 *n.* connecting passage (in general)
4 **cancel**
    4 *v.* annul an arrangement already made: *cancel a meeting*
    6 *v.* cross out, prevent re-use
    7 *v.* balance, equate: *cancel out*
5 **cancer**
    5 *n.* the illness
    7 *n.* the sign of the Zodiac
3 **candle** *n.*
5 **canteen** *n.* a place for eating
5 **canvas** *n.*
3 **cap**
    3 *n.* covering on head: *boy's cap; soldier's cap*
    4 *n.* cap-like cover, e.g. on a milk bottle
    5 *v.* cover a container (usually liquid)
    7 *v.* go one better: *cap a story/remark*
4 **capable**
    4 *adj.* gifted, able: *a very capable doctor*
    5 *adj.* able to perform: *show your teacher what you are capable of*
3 **capital**
    3 *n.* city with centre of national government: *Paris is the capital of France*
    4 *n./adj.* shape (printing): *a capital letter*
    4 *n.* funds: *the company has a capital of £1m*
    7 *adj.* involving killing criminals: *capital punishment*
2 **captain**
    2 *n.* leader
    6 *v.* lead
1 **car**
    1 *n.* vehicle
    5 *n.* wagon (on railway)
3 **car park** *n.*
4 **caravan**
    4 *n.* trailer behind motor vehicle
    6 *n.* gypsy wagon
5 **carbon**
    5 *n.* non-metallic element
    7 *n.* carbon copy
1 **card**
    1 *n.* a playing card

2 *n.* small piece of cardboard: *a visiting card*
4 **cardboard** *n.*
3 **care**
    3 *n.* responsibility: *take care of the baby*
    4 *v.* feel concern for: *he cares only for himself*
    4 *n.* caution: *take care or you'll fall*
    6 *v.* love: *does she really care for him?*
    7 *n.(pl.)* anxieties: *put your cares aside*
    7 *v.* wish: *would you care to read this?*
3 **care about** *v.* be concerned
4 **care for**
    4 *v.* like
    5 *v.* look after: *the baby was well cared for*
4 **career** *n.* way of making a living
1 **careful**
    1 *adj.* attentive: *be careful not to break the eggs*
    4 *adj.* done with care: *a careful piece of work*
2 **careless**
    2 *adj.* inattentive: *he is careless with money*
    3 *adj.* done without care: *a careless mistake*
5 **cargo** *n.*
5 **Caribbean** *n./adj.*
5 **carpenter** *n.*
2 **carpet** *n.* soft thick covering for floors
4 **carriage**
    4 *n.* a wheeled vehicle: *a railway carriage*
    7 *n.* act of carrying: *the carriage of goods*
5 **carrot** *n.*
1 **carry**
    1 *v.* move while supporting: *he carried the boxes on his head*
    2 *v.* bring, take: *the pipe carrying water to the house*
    4 *v.* support: *pillars carry the arch*
    5 *v.* transfer: *carry the case to a higher court*

6 *v.* win: *carry the motion by a small majority*

7 *v.* reach: *the guns won't carry so far*

4 **carry off** *v.* seize and take away

3 **carry on** *v.* continue

3 **carry out** *v.* complete a task

3 **cart** *n.* means of transport

2 **case**
 2 *n.* a piece of luggage/a container
 2 *n.* an example/combination of circumstances: *in my case*
 3 *conj.* lest: *carry an umbrella in case it rains*
 5 *n.* occurrence in medicine: *a case of measles*
 6 *n.* dispute in law: *bring a case against*

4 **cash**
 4 *n.* money in coin or notes: *I have no cash with me*
 5 *n.* money in any form: *I'm short of cash*
 5 *v.* convert into notes/coins: *cash a cheque*

4 **cassette** *n.*

3 **castle** *n.*

1 **cat** *n.*

5 **catalogue**
 5 *n.* list
 6 *v.* make a catalogue

2 **catch**
 2 *v.* run after, seize and hold: *the cat caught the mouse*
 3 *v.* take: *catch the train*
 4 *v.* overtake: *you'll catch him if you hurry*
 5 *v.* succumb to: *catch a disease*
 7 *n.* device: *the catch on a door*
 7 *n.* snag: *there's a catch in it somewhere*

5 **catch on**
 5 *v.* become popular
 5 *v.* understand

4 **catch up with** *v.* draw level with

5 **Catholic** *n./adj.*

2 **cause**
 2 *v.* bring about: *the moon causes the tides*

3 *n.* the thing which produces an effect: *the cause of the tide*

4 *n.* reason for action: *she had good cause to leave*

7 *n.* common interest or purpose: *traitors to the cause*

5 **caution**
 5 *n.* prudence: *cars approached the crossing with caution*
 5 *n.* warning: *said a word of caution*
 7 *v.* warn: *the judge cautioned the prisoner*

4 **cautious** *adj.*

3 **cave** *n.* hollow place in a cliff

1 **ceiling**
 1 *n.* overhead surface of a room
 7 *n.* maximum height of aircraft/prices/wages etc.

5 **celebrate** *v.* honour a day or event: *we celebrate Christmas*

5 **cellar** *n.*

3 **cement**
 3 *n.* material used in building for floors, jointing etc.
 4 *n.* any similar substance in dentistry
 7 *v.* strengthen/unite firmly: *to cement a friendship*

2 **cent** *n.*

5 **centigrade** *n.*

2 **centimetre** *n.*

4 **central**
 4 *adj.* of/at/from/near the centre: *my house is very central*
 5 *adj.* chief/most important: *the central idea of an argument*

1 **centre**
 1 *n.* middle: *the centre of a circle; the town centre*
 4 *v.* focus: *their hopes are centred round the young king*
 6 *n.* gathering point: *Hampstead has long been a centre for artists*

3 **century**
 3 *n.* period of a hundred years
 7 *n.* score of 100 in some sports

4 **ceremony**
 4 *n.* solemn ritual: *church ceremony*
 7 *n.* formal way of behaving: *we were received with much ceremony*

2 **certain**
  2 *adj.* particular: *a certain person*
  3 *adj.* sure: *be certain of your facts*
2 **certainly** *adv.* definitely
4 **certainty**
  4 *n.* state of being certain: *we have no certainty of success*
  5 *n.* something that is certain: *prices have to go up, that's a certainty*
5 **certificate** *n.*
3 **chain**
  3 *n.* metal cord made of links
  5 *v.* fasten by a chain
  5 *n.* sequence in time or space: *a chain of events/lakes*
  7 *n.* the idea of bondage: *man is everywhere in chains*
1 **chair**
  1 *n.* seat
  7 *n.* position of professor: *the Chair of English*
  7 *v.* preside over meeting: *he chaired the meeting*
5 **chairman** *n.*
1 **chalk**
  1 *n.* substance
  6 *v.* mark with chalk
4 **champion**
  4 *n.* a winner
  7 *v.* support a person or cause
2 **chance**
  2 *n.* opportunity: *give me a second chance*
  3 *n.* possibility, probability: *there is a chance that . . .*
  4 *n.* idea of hazard/risk: *by chance; take a chance*
  7 *v.* happen: *I chanced to meet him*
2 **change**
  2 *n.* alteration: *a change for the better*
  3 *v.* substitute one thing for another: *I'll change my clothes*
  3 *v.* alter: *this has changed my ideas*
  4 *v.* become altered: *the weather changed*
  4 *n.* money: *count your change*
4 **channel**
  4 *n.* a stretch of water
  6 *n.* band of frequencies on radio/TV

7 *n.* route: *secret channels of information*
  7 *v.* route
5 **chap**
  5 *n.* (colloq.) man, boy, fellow
  7 *v.* become rough or cracked (skin)
2 **chapter**
  2 *n.* division of a book
  6 *n.* period: *a dismal chapter in British rule in Ireland*
  7 *n.* series, group: *a chapter of accidents*
4 **character**
  4 *n.* moral nature: *he has a weak character*
  5 *n.* special nature: *the character of this enterprise*
  6 *n.* person: *a public character; characters in a book*
  7 *n.* a letter in printing
3 **charge**
  3 *v.* require to pay: *I was charged £50*
  4 *v.* attack: *the cavalry charged*
  5 *n.* prices for services: *your charges are too high*
  5 *n.* command: *I am in charge of . . .*
  6 *n.* electrical load
  6 *v.* accuse of: *he was charged with murder*
4 **charm**
  4 *n.* attraction: *a woman's charm*
  5 *v.* fascinate
  6 *n.* magic spell, amulet
5 **chart**
  5 *n.* paper with diagrammatic information: *a temperature chart*
  6 *n.* map used by sailors
  7 *v.* keep record of development: *chart progress*
5 **charter**
  5 *v.* book transport for group: *charter a flight to Las Palmas*
  6 *n.* aeroplane: *there's a charter leaving next Friday*
  7 *n.* written or printed statement of rights
4 **chase**
  4 *v.* hunt by running after: *dogs like to chase rabbits*

4 *v.* hurry after: *the children chased after the procession*
5 *n.* act of hurrying after
6 *n.* act of hunting
1 **cheap**
  1 *adj.* low in price
  3 *adj.* of poor quality
  7 *adj.* despicable: *feel cheap*
4 **cheat** *v.*
3 **check**
  3 *v.* examine in order to verify: *check a bill*
  4 *v.* hold back, slow down, stop: *check their advance*
  5 *n.* pattern of crossed lines
  6 *n.* cheque (US)
  6 *n.* bill (US)
  7 *v.* move in chess
3 **check in** *v.* register (at a hotel)
3 **check out** *v.* leave (hotel)
4 **check over** *v.* see if all is in order
4 **check up** *v.* verify, see if something is correct
4 **cheek**
  4 *n.* part of face
  6 *n.* impudence
4 **cheer**
  4 *v.* comfort and encourage: *this news cheers me*
  5 *v.* applaud, shout: *they cheered the Queen*
  6 *int.* (when drinking): *cheers!*
4 **cheerful** *adj.* bright, happy: *a cheerful worker/room*
1 **cheese** *n.*
4 **chemical** *n./adj.*
3 **chemist**
  3 *n.* expert in chemistry
  4 *n.* pharmacist
3 **cheque** *n.*
5 **chest**
  5 *n.* part of body
  6 *n.* box, trunk
5 **chew** *v.* masticate
3 **chicken** *n.* fowl
4 **chief**
  4 *adj.* main, principal: *chief clerk; chief difficulty*

6 *n.* headman: *chief of a tribe*
1 **child/children**
  1 *n.* human offspring
  7 *n.* outcome: *a child of the revolution*
4 **childhood** *n.*
5 **childish** *adj.*
3 **chimney** *n.* structure through which smoke passes
3 **chin** *n.*
2 **China** *n.*
3 **Chinese** *n./adj.*
5 **chip**
  5 *n.* piece of potato
  5 *n.* small piece broken or cut off something: *a wood chip*
  5 *n.* tiny electronic device
  6 *v.* knock off small piece
5 **chips** *n.(pl.)*
2 **chocolate**
  2 *n.* substance: *a bar of chocolate*
  3 *n./adj.* colour
3 **choice**
  3 *n.* act of selection: *make a choice*
  4 *n.* thing selected: *this one is my choice*
  5 *n.* the range of selection: *there's no choice in this shop*
  7 *adj.* high quality: *choice flowers*
5 **choke**
  5 *v.* fail to swallow normally: *choke over one's food*
  6 *v.* throttle: *choke someone*
  7 *n.* control on fuel/air mixture in car
2 **choose**
  2 *v.* select from alternatives: *choose one of these*
  5 *v.* wish, decide: *I'll do as I choose*
5 **chop**
  5 *v.* cut into pieces: *chop wood*
  6 *n.* thick slice of meat with bone
  7 *v.* alter: *chop and change; chop about*
4 **christian** *n./adj.*
5 **christianity** *n.*
1 **Christmas** *n.*
1 **church**
  1 *n.* building for christian worship
  4 *n.* organisation: *the christian church*

6 *n.* the clerical profession: *go into the church*
7 *n.* the parish unit, i.e. the congregation, the service
2 **cigar** *n.*
1 **cigarette** *n.*
1 **cinema**
    1 *n.* place for showing films
    6 *n.* the art form or the industry
2 **circle**
    2 *n.* shape: *draw a circle*
    5 *v.* move round in a ring: *circling the airfield*
    6 *n.* social group: *Lady Astor's circle*
3 **circular** *adj.*
4 **circumstance**
    4 *n.* condition/fact connected with an event or person: *don't judge till you know all the circumstances*
    7 *n.* financial condition: *what are his circumstances?*
4 **circus**
    4 *n.* show involving performing acrobats, animals and clowns
    7 *n.* open space where streets converge: *Piccadilly Circus*
4 **citizen**
    4 *n.* person who has full rights in a state
    6 *n.* person who lives in a town: *the citizens of Leeds*
2 **city**
    2 *n.* large and important town
    7 *n.* the financial centre of London
4 **civilisation** *n.*
5 **civilise**
    5 *v.* bring from savagery
    7 *v.* improve, educate, refine
3 **claim**
    3 *v.* demand as due: *I claim my wages*
    5 *v.* assert: *I claim these figures are correct*
    5 *n.* demand for one's rights: *I put in a claim against . . .*
    6 *n.* right to demand: *she has no claim on him*
3 **clap**
    3 *v.* applaud
    4 *v.* strike on the body in friendship

7 *n.* loud sound: *a clap of thunder*
1 **class**
    1 *n.* group of students in a school or college
    3 *v.* assign to a group
    4 *v.* level of society: *the upper class*
    5 *adj.* idea of quality: *a first-class carriage; a low-class hotel*
    6 *n.* group of all the same sort: *the class of people living there*
5 **classification** *n.*
5 **classify**
    5 *v.* put into groups
    7 *v.* declare as secret: *this information is classified*
1 **classroom** *n.*
5 **clay** *n.*
1 **clean**
    1 *adj.* not soiled: *a clean shirt*
    1 *adj.* uncontaminated: *clean water*
    2 *v.* remove dirt
    5 *adj.* morally good: *a clean record*
2 **clear**
    2 *adj.* easily distinguished or understood: *clear writing/thinking*
    3 *adj.* transparent: *a clear day*
    4 *v.* free from obstruction: *clear the garden path*
    4 *adj.* unobstructed: *a clear road*
    5 *adv.* out of the way: *stand clear*
    6 *v.* clarify: *clear one's ideas about*
    6 *adj.* untroubled: *a clear conscience*
    7 *v.* obtain agreement on a matter: *clear it with the President*
5 **clear off** *v.* disappear (person)
4 **clear out** *v.* empty (a room)
3 **clear up**
    3 *v.* tidy up
    4 *v.* stop raining, turn sunny
5 **clearing** *n.*
3 **clerk**
    3 *n.* person employed in an office
    6 *n.* shop assistant (US)
2 **clever**
    2 *adj.* quick at learning, skilful: *he's clever at mathematics*
    3 *adj.* skilfully done: *a clever speech*
    6 *adj.* nimble: *clever fingers*
    6 *adj.* smart: *he was too clever for us*

3 **cliff** *n.*

4 **climate**
    4 *n.* weather conditions
    6 *n.* abstract conditions: *the political climate*

2 **climb**
    2 *v.* mount, ascend
    5 *n.* height climbed: *a stiff climb*

4 **cloakroom**
    4 *n.* place for hanging coats
    4 *n.* toilet

1 **clock**
    1 *n.* instrument for measuring time
    6 *n.* idea of the inexorable passage of time: *work around/against the clock*
    7 *v.* register arrival at and departure from work: *to clock in/out*

5 **clockwork** *n./adj.*

2 **close**
    2 *v.* shut: *close the gate*
    3 *adv.* near: *keep close to*
    5 *adj.* opposite of open: *a close secret*
    6 *adj.* oppressive: *the weather is very close*
    7 *n.* end: *at the close of play*

3 **cloth** *n.*

5 **clothe** *v.*

2 **clothes** *n.(pl.)* garments: *summer clothes*

4 **clothing** *n.*

2 **cloud**
    2 *n.* feature of weather
    4 *n.* mass of things moving in the air: *a cloud of locusts*
    5 *n.* threat: *under a cloud of suspicion*
    6 *n.* vague patch on or in a liquid or transparent object
    7 *v.* become opaque/duller

2 **cloudy**
    2 *adj.* (partly) covered with clouds: *cloudy sky*
    6 *adj.* dull, opaque (of a translucent liquid or solid): *cloudy water*

4 **club**
    4 *n.* society
    4 *n.* premises of society
    6 *n.* a heavy stick
    6 *v.* strike with heavy stick: *the police clubbed down the demonstrators*

7 *n.* suit in cards

5 **clue** *n.*

4 **coach**
    4 *n.* carriage (railway, motor)
    5 *n.* sports trainer: *he's the coach for our local team*
    5 *v.* train others in sports

3 **coal** *n.*

2 **coast**
    2 *n.* land bordering the sea
    6 *v.* ride or slide without power: *we coasted all the way downhill on our bikes*

1 **coat**
    1 *n.* garment
    5 *v.* cover: *coated with mud*
    5 *n.* covering: *a coat of paint*

5 **cock**
    5 *n.* farmyard fowl
    7 *n.* tap or trigger mechanism

1 **coffee**
    1 *n.* drink
    4 *adj.* colour

2 **coffee-pot** *n.*

5 **coil**
    5 *v.* wind or twist
    5 *n.* twist (of rope)
    6 *n.* electrical apparatus
    7 *n.* contraceptive device

3 **coin**
    3 *n.* metal money
    6 *v.* produce metal money
    7 *v.* invent: *coin a phrase*

1 **cold**
    1 *adj.* opposite of hot
    2 *n.* illness: *I've got a cold in my nose*
    4 *n.* coldness: *I feel the cold*
    5 *adj.* lacking in warm feelings: *a cold heart*

3 **collar**
    3 *n.* part of a garment
    5 *n.* attachment on animal: *a dog's collar*
    7 *n.* metal band joining machine parts

5 **colleague** *n.*

3 **collect**
    3 *v.* bring together: *collect materials for the house*

5 *v.* come together: *the people collected in the market place*
6 *v.* get subscriptions: *she collects for several charities*
4 **collection**
  4 *n.* set of items collected: *a stamp collection*
  5 *n.* gathering: *a collection of dust*
  6 *n.* money taken at a meeting
  7 *n.* clearing of mail from pillar box: *postal collection*
3 **college** *n.* educational institution and its buildings
1 **colour**
  1 *n.* hue, pigment
  2 *v.* apply colour
  5 *n.* race: *what colour is he?*
  6 *n.* political allegiance
4 **column**
  4 *n.* tall/upright pillar
  5 *n.* division of a printed page
  5 *n.* a series of numbers
  7 *n.* a line of ships/men
2 **comb**
  2 *n.* instrument for ordering hair
  2 *v.* use a comb
  7 *v.* search thoroughly: *comb the countryside*
5 **combination**
  5 *n.* joining or putting together
  5 *n.* state of being joined
  6 *n.* number of persons or things joined: *the college is supported by a combination of fees and grants*
4 **combine**
  4 *v.* use jointly, bring together: *he combines taste and skill in his work*
  5 *v.* act jointly: *the unions combined to oppose the move*
1 **come**
  1 *v.* move towards speaker: *come here*
  1 *v.* arrive at: *they came to a river*
  2 *v.* arrive with purpose: *they've come to work here*
  3 *v.* occur: *May comes between April and June*
  4 *v.* become: *my shoelaces have come undone*

4 **come across**
  4 *v.* find/meet accidentally
  5 *v.* be understood: *his argument came across well*
5 **come by** *v.* pass
3 **come down** *v.* be reduced (price)
4 **come forward** *v.* present oneself
5 **come off** *v.* succeed in happening
4 **come on** *v.* appear (on stage etc.)
3 **come out**
  3 *v.* bloom (flowers, leaves)
  5 *v.* solve itself (sum, problem)
3 **come round**
  3 *v.* visit
  4 *v.* recur on a regular basis
  5 *v.* regain consciousness
5 **come up against** *v.* be faced with (a problem)
3 **comfort**
  3 *n.* ease: *this hotel is known for its comfort*
  4 *n.* solace in grief or pain: *she gave him comfort*
  4 *v.* give solace
2 **comfortable**
  2 *adj.* pleasant to be in: *a comfortable house*
  3 *adj.* in a state of comfort: *are you feeling more comfortable now?*
3 **command**
  3 *n.* control: *in command of the fleet*
  3 *v.* control: *command an army*
  4 *n.* order: *give a command*
  5 *v.* order: *the King commands and we obey*
4 **commerce** *n.*
4 **commercial**
  4 *adj.* of trade/business
  5 *n.* advertisement on TV/radio
4 **committee** *n.*
2 **common**
  2 *adj.* often found or experienced: *a common flower; a common event*
  4 *adj.* shared by all of a group: *common interests*
  5 *adj.* undistinguished: *common salt*
  6 *n.* a piece of ground: *Clapham Common*

6 *n.(pl.)* lower house in Parliament: *the House of Commons*
7 *adj.* lacking good taste: *she's rather common*

5 **commonsense** *adj.*

5 **communicate**
  5 *v.* pass on information: *I will communicate that to my superiors*
  6 *v.* be in contact: *they communicate daily*
  7 *v.* lead from one place to another: *this room communicates with the garden*

4 **communication**
  4 *n.* act of communicating
  4 *n.* that which is communicated
  5 *n.* means of communication: *TV/road communications*

5 **communism** *n.*

5 **communist** *n./adj.*

5 **community**
  5 *n.* people living in one place
  6 *n.* group of people with a common pattern of life: *a community of monks*
  7 *n* condition of sharing and having things in common: *a community of feeling on the matter*

3 **companion** *n.* friend, associate

2 **company**
  2 *n.* a business
  3 *n.* companionship: *in company with*
  5 *n.* any group but especially of soldiers/actors

5 **comparatively** *adv.*

3 **compare**
  3 *v.* discover similarities (or differences)
  5 *v.* equal, rival: *the results compare well*

5 **comparison**
  5 *n.* presence of similarities: *there's a close comparison between them*
  5 *n.* act of comparing

5 **compass**
  5 *n.* device for finding North
  6 *n.* drawing instrument

4 **compete** *v.*

4 **competition**
  4 *n.* organised contest: *a boxing competition*
  5 *n.* commercial rivalry: *competition lowers prices*

3 **complain** *v.*

5 **complaint**
  5 *n.* statement of/grounds for dissatisfaction
  7 *n.* illness, disease

2 **complete**
  2 *adj.* utter: *the complete destruction of the city*
  3 *adj.* total: *the complete works of Shakespeare*
  4 *v.* bring to an end, finish: *complete the course*
  4 *v.* fill in: *complete the form*

2 **completely** *adv.*

5 **completion** *n.*

4 **complex**
  4 *adj.* having many parts in relationship: *a complex argument*
  7 *n.* inferiority complex
  7 *n.* set of buildings: *a housing complex*

4 **complicate** *v.*

5 **compose**
  5 *v.* combine to form: *six tribes compose the nation*
  6 *v.* make up speech/poetry/music
  7 *v.* calm: *compose yourself*

5 **composer** *n.*

4 **composition**
  4 *n.* the thing written
  4 *n.* the act of writing
  6 *n.* combination of things: *the composition of white light is . . .*
  7 *n.* arrangement in a picture

5 **compound**
  5 *n.* something made up of two or more parts
  6 *adj.* multiple: *a compound sentence; a compound fracture*
  7 *n.* an enclosed area with buildings

3 **computer** *n.*

4 **concentrate**
  4 *v.* focus: *concentrate on your work*

5 *v.* gather densely: *concentrate
soldiers in a town*
7 *n.* liquid in dense form: *acid
concentrates*
4 **concern**
   4 *v.* have relation to: *this concerns
you*
   6 *n.* a business
   6 *n.* responsibility: *this is no concern
of mine*
4 **concerning** *prep.*
4 **concert**
   4 *n.* musical entertainment
   7 *n.* agreement, harmony: *working in
concert*
5 **conclude**
   5 *v.* come/bring to an end: *conclude a
speech*
   6 *v.* reason, deduce: *the jury
concluded from the evidence*
4 **conclusion**
   4 *n.* end: *at the conclusion of his reign*
   5 *n.* finalisation: *the conclusion of a
peace treaty*
   6 *n.* reasoned view: *come to the
conclusion that . . .*
5 **concrete**
   5 *n.* building material
   6 *v.* cover with concrete: *he concreted
the pathway*
   6 *adj.* definite/positive: *concrete
proposals*
   7 *adj.* opposite of abstract
2 **condition**
   2 *n.* state: *that car is in good
condition*
   4 *n.(pl.)* environment: *under existing
conditions*
   5 *n.* stipulation: *lay down conditions*
5 **conditional** *adj.* form of the verb
4 **conduct**
   4 *n.* behaviour
   5 *v.* guide: *the guard conducted
visitors round the museum*
   6 *v.* manage: *he conducts his business
affairs in a careless way*
   6 *v.* control an orchestra
   7 *v.* allow electric current to pass
4 **conference** *n.*

4 **confess**
   4 *v.* declare one's faults: *he confessed
that he did it*
   5 *v.* admit: *I confess I don't like him
much*
   6 *v.* declare before God
5 **confession**
   5 *n.* the thing confessed
   5 *n.* act of admitting a fault: *I have
two confessions to make to you*
   7 *n.* confession to a priest
4 **confidence**
   4 *n.* trust: *I have great confidence in
you*
   5 *n.* assurance: *he is full of confidence*
   6 *n.* secrecy: *in strict confidence*
4 **confident**
   4 *adj.* assured: *confident of victory*
   5 *adj.* trusting: *a confident friendship*
5 **confidential** *adj.* secret, private
4 **confuse** *v.* mix up
4 **confusion** *n.*
5 **congratulate** *v.*
5 **congratulation** *n.*
5 **congress**
   5 *n.* law-making body
   6 *n.* conference: *our third
international congress*
3 **connect**
   3 *v.* join things: *connect two wires*
   4 *v.* join in act or in mind: *I don't
wish to be connected with this
affair*
3 **connection**
   3 *n.* abstract link: *connection between
A and B*
   4 *n.* physical link: *an electrical
connection*
   6 *n.* personal or family relation
5 **conquer** *v.*
5 **conqueror** *n.*
4 **conscience** *n.*
4 **conscious**
   4 *adj.* aware: *conscious of his own
importance*
   5 *adj.* not unconscious: *he was
conscious during the operation*
5 **consciousness** *n.*
5 **conservation** *n.*

5 **conservative**
    5 *adj.* opposed to sudden change
    6 *adj.* cautious, moderate
    6 *n.* member of conservative party, holder of conservative political views
3 **consider**
    3 *v.* hold opinion: *I consider him a fool*
    5 *v.* reflect: *consider before you choose*
    6 *v.* have regard to: *consider her feelings*
3 **considerable** *adj.*
4 **considerably** *adv.*
4 **consideration**
    4 *n.* something to be taken into account: *time is an important consideration in this case*
    5 *n.* act of thinking about: *please give the matter your careful consideration*
    6 *n.* quality of being considerate: *he has great consideration for others*
    7 *n.* reward: *he'll do anything for a consideration*
4 **consist**
    4 *v.* be composed of: *the committee consists of ten members*
    6 *v.* be essentially: *happiness consists in personal freedom*
4 **constant**
    4 *adj.* continuous/frequently recurring
    7 *adj.* faithful, unchanging: *a constant friend*
4 **construct** *v.*
4 **construction**
    4 *n.* making: *the construction of new roads*
    5 *n.* something put together
    6 *n.* structure: *a construction of words*
    7 *n.* interpretation: *don't put the wrong construction on his action*
4 **contact**
    4 *v.* get in touch with: *where can I contact Mr Green?*
    5 *n.* state of being in touch: *our troops are in contact with the enemy*
    6 *n.* social/professional/business connection (person): *useful contacts*
    7 *n.* electricity point
2 **contain**
    2 *v.* have in its hold: *the wine contained in the bottle; this box contains 1 kilo of sugar*
    3 *v.* have as part of itself: *these rocks contain gold; this book contains a chapter on Portugal*
    4 *v.* be equal to: *a gallon contains 8 pints*
    7 *v.* limit: *contain your enthusiasm*
5 **container**
    5 *n.* holder
    7 *n.* large box for transportation of goods
5 **contemporary**
    5 *adj.* belonging to the same time: *a contemporary record*
    7 *adj.* modern: *contemporary art*
3 **content**
    3 *adj.* pleased, happy: *I should be content to live here all my life*
    6 *n.* substance contained: *a high sugar content*
3 **contents** *n.(pl.)* the elements contained
4 **continent**
    4 *n.* large land mass
    6 *n.* mainland Europe
5 **continental**
    5 *adj.* typical of a continent: *a continental climate*
    6 *adj.* typical of mainland Europe: *continental breakfast*
2 **continue**
    2 *v.* go further, go on: *the desert continued for miles*
    4 *v.* go on to say: *'But,' he continued, 'there is . . .'*
4 **continuous** *adj.*
4 **contract**
    4 *n.* binding agreement
    5 *v.* make or become smaller
    6 *v.* agree upon formally
    7 *v.* succumb to: *contract an illness*
4 **contrast**
    4 *v.* discover differences between: *contrast the two speakers*

5 *n.* difference seen between partly unlike things: *the contrast of light and shade*
6 *v.* show differences: *his actions contrasted sharply with his promises*
3 **control**
  3 *n.* direction, check: *control over staff*
  4 *v.* govern: *he controlled his temper*
  5 *n.* management and guidance: *traffic control; birth control*
  6 *n.* set for comparison: *group 2 were used as a control*
4 **convenience**
  4 *n.* usefulness: *the convenience of having the kitchen near to the dining room*
  6 *n.* personal suitability: *at your earliest convenience*
  7 *n.* appliance: *every modern convenience*
4 **convenient** *adj.*
2 **conversation** *n.*
4 **convince** *v.*
1 **cook**
  1 *n.* man or woman who cooks
  1 *v.* heat food for eating
  5 *v.* undergo cooking: *those apples cook well*
3 **cooker**
  3 *n.* a stove
  7 *n.* type of apple (for cooking)
2 **cool**
  2 *adj.* nearer cold than hot: *a cool wind/drink*
  3 *v.* become colder
  5 *v.* cause to be cool
  7 *adv.* under control (of the emotions or manner): *keep cool*
5 **co-operate** *v.*
5 **co-operation** *n.*
5 **copper**
  5 *n.* metal
  7 *n.* coin
  7 *n.* (colloq.) policeman
1 **copy**
  1 *n.* another version of the same thing
  1 *v.* reproduce: *copy this document for me*

4 *n.* one of (a published work): *I want a copy of Stevenson's 'Treasure Island'*
7 *n.* counterfeit: *that isn't a Titian, it's a copy*
5 **cord**
  5 *n.* length of twisted strand
  6 *n.* part of the body: *spinal cord; vocal cords*
5 **cork**
  5 *n.* the stopper of a bottle
  6 *v.* close with a cork
  7 *n.* material: *mats made of cork*
3 **corn**
  3 *n.* cereal grain or crop
  7 *n.* lump of hard skin on foot
1 **corner**
  1 *n.* angle of a building/room/tablecloth
  6 *n.* place hard to escape from: *his argument drove me into a corner*
  7 *v.* monopolise: *corner the market*
2 **correct**
  2 *adj.* according to fact: *a correct statement*
  3 *v.* mark errors: *he corrected the proofs*
  6 *adj.* appropriate: *correct behaviour and dress*
  7 *v.* rectify, adjust: *the pilot corrected the compass reading*
4 **correction**
  4 *n.* act of correcting: *the correction of essays*
  5 *n.* correct versions: *the corrections are in red ink*
4 **correspond**
  4 *v.* exchange letters
  6 *v.* be in harmony with: *this house corresponds to my needs*
  6 *v.* be equivalent to: *50° Fahrenheit corresponds to 10° Centigrade*
5 **correspondence**
  5 *n.* letter writing
  7 *n.* agreement, similarity
5 **corridor** *n.*
2 **cost**
  2 *n.* price: *cost of production*

2 *v.* can be bought for: *it costs £5*
5 *n.* sacrifice: *at any cost*
6 *n.(pl.)* expenses of process/project
7 *v.* estimate the price: *cost a scheme*
5 **costly** *adj.*
3 **cottage** *n.*
2 **cotton**
  2 *n.* material
  4 *n.* thread
5 **cottonwool** *n.*
5 **couch** *n.*
3 **cough** *n./v.* act or sound
of coughing
2 **could**
  2 *modal* past ability: *at 15 I could run 5 miles*
  3 *modal* could (in requests): *could you tell me?*
  4 *modal* were able to: *if you could meet him now*
  5 *modal* might: *that could be Jackson over there*
1 **count**
  1 *v.* number: *count from one to a hundred*
  3 *n.* reckoning: *keep count; lose count*
  4 *v.* include: *there are 6 if you count the children*
  5 *v.* rely on: *you can't count on him*
  7 *v.* consider: *count your blessings*
  7 *v.* amount to: *that counts for very little*
  7 *n.* title of nobility: *Count Dracula*
4 **count in** *v.* include
5 **count on** *v.* rely on
3 **count up** *v.* find the total
5 **counter**
  5 *n.* table or flat surface for transactions in a shop or café
  6 *n.* token for keeping count
  6 *v.* oppose: *he countered my argument with . . .*
2 **country**
  2 *n.* nation, motherland: *serve one's country*
  2 *n.* opposite of town: *country people*
  3 *n.* area of land: *open country; the West Country*

7 *n.* the people of a nation: *to appeal to the country*
5 **countryside** *n.*
4 **couple**
  4 *n.* two persons or things seen together or associated: *a couple of rabbits*
  6 *n.* a married pair
  7 *n.* dancing pair: *ten couples took the floor*
  7 *v.* link: *couple two railway coaches*
3 **courage** *n.* bravery
3 **course**
  3 *adv.* naturally: *of course*
  4 *n.* series: *a course of lessons*
  5 *n.* passage of time: *in the course of time*
  6 *n.* a line of action: *take an unexpected course*
4 **court**
  4 *n.* place of law: *police court*
  5 *n.* place for sport: *a tennis court*
  6 *n.* address: *he lives at Bolt Court*
  7 *v.* try to win someone in marriage
2 **cousin** *n.*
2 **cover**
  2 *v.* conceal: *cover it with sand*
  3 *n.* lid, blanket etc.: *put a cover over that fruit*
  5 *n.* binding of a book: *the cover needs renewing*
  6 *v.* protect, screen: *artillery covered the advance*
  7 *v.* extend over: *his authority does not cover this case*
  7 *n.* wrapper or envelope: *under separate cover*
  7 *n.* place set at table: *cover charge*
5 **covering** *n.*
1 **cow**
  1 *n.* domestic animal
  6 *n.* she of certain animals: *cow elephant*
  7 *v.* render fearful: *he was cowed into submission*
4 **coward** *n.*
4 **crack**
  4 *n.* partial breakage or fissure

5 *n.* break or hit with a noise: *to crack a nut*

5 *n.* noise: *a loud crack*

6 *n.* make a noise: *the whips cracked*

3 **crash**

  3 *n.* destruction, collapse: *a nasty car crash*

  3 *v.* break (thoroughly): *crash through the fence*

  4 *n.* noise: *he fell with a crash*

  7 *n./v.* collapse in business: *a crash of prices; his business has crashed*

4 **crawl**

  4 *v.* move slowly, pulling the body along the ground: *the baby crawled across the room*

  5 *n.* a stroke in swimming: *the crawl*

  6 *v.* move slowly (of transport): *the train crawled into the station*

  6 *n.* slow movement: *the traffic was reduced to a crawl*

  7 *v.* be full of small moving creatures: *the ground was crawling with ants*

  7 *v.* ingratiate: *he crawled for a favour*

3 **crazy**

  3 *adj.* mentally disordered

  4 *adj.* wildly excited: *she is crazy about that group*

2 **cream**

  2 *n.* fat from milk: *pour off the cream*

  3 *n.* substance: *face cream*

  4 *adj.* colour: *the walls are cream*

  7 *n.* the best part of: *the cream of the crop*

  7 *v.* take the best only: *he creamed the best recruits for his regiment*

3 **create**

  3 *v.* bring something into existence: *God created the world*

  4 *v.* give rise to, produce: *his behaviour created a bad impression*

  7 *v.* be invested with a rank: *he was created a Baron*

4 **credit**

  4 *n.* trust regarding payment of debts or keeping promises: *no credit is given at this shop*

  4 *adj.* (same sense): *credit card*

5 *n.* money in bank account: *to your credit*

5 *n.* money advanced: *the bank refused him further credit*

6 *n.* record of payments: *credits and debits*

6 *v.* believe: *I don't credit him with such intelligence*

7 *n.* honour, approval: *he gained credit through his action in . . .*

7 *n.* belief: *the rumour is gaining credit*

5 **creep**

  5 *v.* move like a reptile

  6 *v.* move gradually (plants): *the plants crept up the wall*

2 **crew** *n.*

3 **crime**

  3 *n.* offence against the law: *burglary is a crime*

  4 *n.* a foolish or wrong act: *it would be a crime to send her abroad now*

3 **criminal** *n.*

4 **crisis** *n.*

5 **critical**

  5 *adj.* fault-finding: *critical remarks*

  7 *adj.* of the work of a critic: *a critical review*

  6 *adj.* of or at a crisis: *the patient's condition is critical*

5 **crockery** *n.*

3 **crop**

  3 *n.(pl.)* plants in the field: *get the crops in*

  5 *n.* yearly produce from soil

  5 *n.* large number: *his statement produced a crop of questions*

  6 *v.* graze: *the sheep cropped the grass*

  6 *v.* cut short: *he had his hair cropped*

  7 *v.* occur: *something has cropped up*

2 **cross**

  2 *n.* mark or shape: *put a cross against your name*

  2 *v.* traverse: *cross the sea*

  5 *v.* intersect: *where two roads cross*

  5 *v.* place across each other: *she crossed her arms*

6 *n*. mixed breed: *a cross between a spaniel and terrier*
7 *n*. trial: *we all have our crosses to bear*
3 **cross out** *v*. remove (from list/record)
3 **cross-roads** *n.(pl.)*
5 **crossing** *n*.
1 **crowd**
   1 *n*. a large number of people together
   4 *v*. gather densely: *they crowded about him*
3 **crown**
   3 *n*. royal headdress
   5 *v*. invest as monarch: *crown the king*
   6 *n*. kingship, government: *the Crown*
   7 *v*. add the best part of all: *he crowned his work by . . .*
   7 *n*. top of a head/hill
2 **cruel**
   2 *adj*. liking to inflict pain: *a cruel person*
   2 *adj*. act so done: *cruel deeds*
3 **cruelty**
   3 *n*. readiness to give pain: *cruelty to animals*
   7 *n*. cruel acts: *you will not be forgiven for these cruelties*
5 **crush**
   5 *v*. compress and break: *crush the leaves*
   6 *v*. break the spirit/force: *he crushed the opposition*
5 **crust** *n*. hard surface on a pie or loaf
1 **cry**
   1 *v*. weep: *the baby often cries*
   2 *v*. shout: *don't cry out before you're hurt*
   3 *n*. weep: *have a good cry*
   4 *n*. shout: *cries of joy*
   5 *n*. call: *the cry of a bird*
3 **cultivate**
   3 *v*. till: *cultivate the soil*
   5 *v*. nurture: *cultivate a friendship/the arts*
5 **cultural** *adj*.
4 **culture**
   4 *n*. education and taste: *a centre of culture*

6 *n*. civilisation: *the culture of the Bantu peoples; Greek culture*
7 *n*. cultivation: *he has five acres devoted to tulip culture*
1 **cup**
   1 *n*. bowl: *cups in the cupboard*
   1 *n*. contents of cup: *two cups of flour*
   5 *n*. prize: *the Football Association Cup*
   6 *v*. form into bowl: *cup one's hands*
1 **cupboard** *n*.
4 **cure**
   4 *v*. heal: *this medicine has cured my disease*
   5 *n*. healing: *I can't promise a complete cure*
   6 *n*. remedy: *hard work is a cure for boredom*
3 **curiosity**
   3 *n*. being curious
   7 *n*. a strange or rare object
3 **curious**
   3 *adj*. eager to know about
   5 *adj*. inquisitive: *don't be so curious*
   7 *adj*. strange: *a curious silence*
5 **curl**
   5 *n*. curved lock of hair
   5 *v*. induce wave: *he curled his hair*
5 **curly** *adj*.
3 **current**
   3 *n*. flow: *electric current; current of water*
   5 *adj*. topical, ongoing: *current events/opinion*
4 **curse**
   4 *v*. swear at: *he cursed the driver*
   5 *n*. swearing expression: *a volley of curses*
   6 *n*. evil fate: *he laid a curse upon the family*
   6 *v*. consign to evil: *the priests cursed those who had burned the temple*
   7 *v*. afflict: *curse with a bad temper*
3 **curtain**
   3 *n*. cloth covering window
   6 *v*. provide with curtains
2 **curve**
   2 *n*. bend: *a curve in the road*
   3 *v*. bend: *the road curves round*

3 **cushion**
  3 *n.* article of furnishing
  7 *v.* protect against shocks: *cushion against inflation*
  7 *n.* protective layer: *a cushion of air*
2 **custom** *n.* accepted behaviour: *social customs*
4 **customs** *n.(pl.)* search at airport etc.
3 **customer** *n.* person who buys things
1 **cut**
  1 *n.* act and result of incision
  1 *v.* incise, sever, divide
  2 *v.* shorten, decrease: *cut prices*
  6 *n.* share
4 **cut across** *v.* take shorter way to destination
5 **cut back** *v.* reduce (expense, manpower)

4 **cut down** *v.* reduce (expenses, consumption)
5 **cut in** *v.* push suddenly into stream (of traffic, speech)
4 **cut off** *v.* stop flow (of supplies, communication)
5 **cut out**
  5 *v.* delete (from a set)
  5 *v.* give up (habit)
3 **cut up** *v.* divide into small pieces
3 **cycle**
  3 *n.* bicycle
  5 *v.* to travel on bicycle
  6 *n.* cyclical series of events: *the cycle of the seasons*
5 **cyclist** *n.*
5 **cylinder**
  5 *n.* chamber in car engine
  5 *n.* shape

D

4 **dad** *n.*
4 **daddy** *n.*
4 **daily** *adj./adv.* happening every day
5 **dam**
  5 *n.* barrier
  7 *v.* erect barrier
3 **damage**
  3 *v.* harm, injure: *the attack damaged his reputation*
  3 *n.* harm: *the storm caused great damage*
  7 *n.(pl.)* penalty for harm caused: *they paid damages*
5 **damn**
  5 *int./n.*
  6 *v.* curse
3 **damp**
  3 *adj.* moist: *damp air*
  6 *n.* moisture: *there is rising damp in the wall*
  7 *v.* make sad or dull: *don't damp their hopes*

1 **dance**
  1 *v.* move rhythmically to music
  1 *n.* a set of steps: *a country dance*
  2 *n.* social occasion: *a dance at the Lyceum*
1 **dancer** *n.*
4 **dancing** *n.*
2 **danger**
  2 *n.* state: *he is in great danger*
  4 *n.* cause of danger: *he is a danger to the public*
2 **dangerous** *adj.*
3 **dare**
  3 *v.* have the courage to: *spend as much as I dare*
  5 *v.* have the temerity to: *he would not dare to meet me*
  6 *v.* challenge: *I dared him to do it*
1 **dark**
  1 *adj.* not emitting light: *a dark night*
  1 *n.* night-time: *cats can see in the dark*

2 *adv.* shade in colour: *dark blue*
6 *adj.* secret: *keep it dark*
7 *adj.* bad: *dark deeds*
5 **darken** *v.*
4 **darkness** *n.*
5 **darling** *n.* person/object much loved
4 **dash**
    4 *v.* rush: *they dashed to safety*
    4 *n.* run: *make a dash for freedom*
    5 *v.* smash: *the waves dashed against the rocks*
    5 *n.* punctuation mark
    7 *n.* sprint: *the 100 metres dash*
2 **date**
    2 *n.* time: *date of birth*
    3 *v.* put date on: *date your letter*
    5 *n.* present time: *be out of date*
    6 *v.* go out with someone of opposite sex: *they've been dating for months*
    6 *n.* fruit
    7 *v.* estimate time of origin: *date a coin*
    7 *n.* person of opposite sex in rendezvous
1 **daughter** *n.*
5 **dawn**
    5 *n.* period between night and day
    5 *v.* begin to grow light
    7 *v.* begin to appear: *it dawned on him that . . .*
1 **day**
    1 *n.* 24 hours
    1 *n.* period of light: *day and night*
3 **days** *n.(pl.):* *in the days of the Romans*
4 **daylight** *n.*
4 **daytime** *n.*
2 **dead**
    2 *adj.* no longer alive: *a dead man*
    3 *adj.* without sensation: *my fingers are dead*
    5 *adj.* no longer used: *a dead language*
    6 *n.* dead persons: *the dead may return as ghosts*
    7 *adj./adv.* complete: *dead silence; he stopped dead*
3 **deaf**
    3 *adj.* unable to hear: *a deaf man*

6 *adj.* unwilling to hear: *he was deaf to all her prayers*
5 **deafen** *v.*
3 **deal**
    3 *v.* treat: *the victims were dealt with roughly*
    3 *v.* attend to: *he dealt with the problem*
    4 *n.* a lot: *there's a great deal of it about*
    5 *n.* transaction: *that's a good deal (business)*
    6 *n.* agreement: *we made a deal*
    7 *v.* share: *deal the cards*
5 **dealer**
    5 *n.* business man: *a dealer in antiques*
    7 *n.* giver out of cards
1 **dear**
    1 *adj.* expensive: *it's too dear*
    3 *adj.* form of address: *Dear Sir*
    5 *int.* disappointment: *Oh dear!*
    5 *adj.* precious: *life is very dear to him*
    7 *adj.* much loved: *a dear friend of ours*
3 **death**
    3 *n.* decease: *his mother's death was a blow*
    4 *n.* end: *the death of this enterprise*
4 **debt**
    4 *n.* money/service owed
    6 *n.* indebtedness: *Aristotle's debt to Plato was great*
5 **decay**
    5 *v.* crumble, rot
    6 *n.* state/process of decaying
5 **deceive** *v.*
1 **December** *n.*
5 **decent**
    5 *adj.* modest: *decent behaviour*
    5 *adj.* respectable: *they live in decent style*
    6 *adj.* considerable: *he left her a decent sum*
    7 *adj.* likeable: *a decent fellow*
2 **decide**
    2 *v.* resolve: *I have decided to go*
    5 *v.* settle: *decide a dispute*

5 **decidedly** *adv.*

5 **decimal** *n. /adj.*

3 **decision**
   3 *n.* judgement, selection: *that was a fair decision*
   6 *n.* determination: *he is a man of decision*

2 **deck**
   2 *n.* surface/floor of a ship, bus etc.
   6 *n.* pack of cards
   7 *v.* decorate: *deck it out with flags*

4 **declaration** *n.*

3 **declare**
   3 *v.* say emphatically: *I declare that I am innocent*
   4 *v.* make known publicly: *Bermuda declared its independence*
   7 *v.* make clearly known: *he declared himself a partisan of . . .*

5 **decorate**
   5 *v.* adorn with ornaments
   6 *v.* paint (a house)
   7 *v.* honour: *decorate with a medal*

4 **decrease**
   4 *v.* become less/smaller: *exports have decreased*
   6 *n.* diminution: *a decrease in population*

3 **deed** *n.*

1 **deep**
   1 *adj.* far down: *a deep hole*
   1 *adv.:* *they sank deep into the mud*
   4 *adv.* colour, sound: *deep blue*
   5 *adj.* low (musical scale): *a deep note*
   6 *adj.* profound (abstract): *deep emotion*

5 **deepen** *v.*

3 **deeply** *adv.* intensely: *she loves him deeply*

5 **deer** *n.*

5 **defeat**
   3 *n.* conquering: *the defeat of the enemy*
   3 *v.* beat: *the French were defeated*
   6 *v.* prevent realisation of: *his hopes were defeated*

3 **defence**
   3 *n.* act of defending: *the defence of a castle*
   4 *n.* instrument of defence: *the castle's defences*
   6 *n.* speech for person/cause: *the defence of the prisoner*

3 **defend**
   3 *v.* protect: *defend oneself with a stick*
   6 *v.* speak for: *defend a prisoner in a court*
   6 *v.* guard in sport (football)

4 **definite** *adj.*

3 **degree**
   3 *n.* measure of an angle: *90 degrees*
   3 *n.* measure of heat: *at 50 degrees centigrade*
   5 *n.* academic qualification: *the degree of Master of Arts*
   6 *n.* steps of intensity/quality/progress: *by degrees*

3 **delay**
   3 *n.* pause: *without any delay*
   4 *v.* defer, lose time: *don't delay*
   5 *v.* detain: *the work delayed me at the office*

4 **delicate**
   4 *adj.* finely made: *a delicate piece of silk*
   4 *adj.* fragile: *handle this delicate glass carefully*
   6 *adj.* needing great tact: *a delicate mission*
   6 *adj.* not easily perceived: *delicate colours*
   6 *adj.* sensitive: *a delicate touch*
   7 *adj.* not robust: *a delicate child*

5 **delicious** *adj.*

4 **delight**
   4 *n.* great pleasure: *I read it with delight*
   6 *v.* please greatly: *music delights me*

4 **delighted** *adj.* very happy: *I'm delighted at the news*

2 **deliver**
   2 *v.* hand over: *deliver letters*
   6 *v.* give forth: *deliver an attack/a speech*
   7 *v.* help to bring to birth: *deliver a baby*

7 *v.* set free: *deliver the prisoners from the enemy*
5 **delivery**
  5 *n.* postal service: *there are three deliveries a day*
  7 *n.* bringing to birth: *the delivery of a baby*
2 **demand**
  2 *v.* claim: *I demand my rights*
  3 *v.* ask forcefully: *he demanded to know my name*
  3 *n.* claim: *the landlord's demand seems reasonable*
  5 *n.* public need: *supply and demand*
  6 *v.* call for, require: *it demands your immediate attention*
5 **democracy**
  5 *n.* system of government (power to change rulers by voting)
  6 *n.* a country which operates such a system
  7 *n.* society based on equality: *is there more democracy in Australia than in Great Britain?*
5 **democratic**
  5 *adj.* supporting democracy
  7 *adj.* with similar rights for all, fair all round
4 **dense**
  4 *adj.* thick (liquids, vapour): *a dense fog*
  6 *adj.* thick (people, things): *a dense forest/crowd*
4 **dentist** *n.*
3 **deny**
  3 *v.* say that something is not true: *he denied the charge*
  5 *v.* disown: *he denied signing it*
  7 *v.* prevent from getting: *he denied his family enough to eat*
4 **department** *n.* administrative division of a ministry/business/university etc.: *Department of Education*
4 **departure**
  4 *n.* leaving (transport): *arrivals and departures*
  6 *n.* going away (persons): *his departure was unexpected*

7 *n.* variation: *a new departure in physics*
3 **depend**
  3 *v.* be related to: *the price depends on the size*
  4 *v.* be supported by: *depend on charity*
  5 *v.* trust: *I depend on you to do it*
5 **dependant** *n.*
5 **dependence**
  5 *n.* state of being supported: *his dependence upon his parents*
  7 *n.* reliability: *you can't put much dependence on him*
5 **dependent** *adj.*
4 **depress**
  4 *v.* make/be sad, low in spirits
  6 *v.* press, push or pull down: *depress a lever*
  7 *v.* make less active: *a depressed market*
3 **depth**
  3 *n.* vertical measurement: *what is the depth of the well?*
  6 *n.* profundity: *this book shows a depth of scholarship*
  7 *n.(pl.)* deepest regions: *the depths of despair*
5 **deputy**
  5 *n.* assistant with authority to act for superior
  7 *n.* member of parliament (e.g. France)
4 **descend**
  4 *v.* come or go down: *the road descended steeply*
  6 *v.* have as ancestors: *to be descended from*
  7 *v.* sink in level of behaviour: *descend to fraud*
5 **descendant** *n.*
5 **descent**
  5 *n.* coming or going down: *a gradual descent into the valley*
  6 *n.* ancestry and inheritance: *he is of French descent*
2 **describe**
  2 *v.* give a picture of in words: *please describe what you saw*

6 *v.* characterise: *I'd describe it as a failure*
7 *v.* draw: *describe a circle with your compasses*

3 **description**
  3 *n.* word picture: *give a description of the thief*
  4 *n.* act of describing: *beautiful beyond description*
  7 *n.* kind: *there were cars of every description*

4 **desert**
  4 *n.* sterile (sandy) land: *the Sahara desert*
  6 *v.* abandon: *he deserted her and emigrated to Brazil*

3 **deserve** *v.* merit: *you deserve to win*

4 **design**
  4 *v.* draw plan: *he designed the first jet engine*
  4 *n.* drawing or outline: *a dress design*
  4 *n.* pattern: *the design on the wallpaper*

5 **desirable**
  5 *adj.* to be wished for: *silence is desirable during meditation*
  6 *adj.* arousing passion for possession

4 **desire**
  4 *v.* wish intensely: *she has always desired to visit Egypt*
  4 *n.* strong wish: *a desire to see his parents again*
  6 *n.* lust: *animal desires*
  6 *n.* object desired: *to be heard was the desire of everyone present*
  7 *v.* request: *I desire you to inform me*

1 **desk**
  1 *n.* piece of furniture
  5 *n.* reception counter in a hotel
  7 *n.* post of responsibility in an organisation: *the Southern Africa desk*

4 **despair**
  4 *n.* hopelessness: *I gave up in despair*
  6 *v.* give up hope: *I despair of ever seeing him*

4 **desperate**
  4 *adj.* filled with despair and ready to do anything: *desperate in their attempts to escape*
  5 *adj.* lawless, violent: *a desperate criminal*
  6 *adj.* extremely serious: *the state of the country is desperate*
  7 *adj.* giving little hope of success: *desperate remedies*

5 **dessert** *n.*

5 **destination**
  5 *n.* final stop: *when you reach your destination, ask . . .*
  7 *n.* addressee: *the destination of this note isn't clear*

2 **destroy**
  2 *v.* ruin: *the storm destroyed my crops*
  6 *v.* kill: *that dog ought to be destroyed*

3 **detail**
  3 *n.* piece of information: *give me all the details*
  5 *n.* minutiae: *explain something in detail*
  6 *v.* describe fully: *everything has been fully detailed*
  7 *n.* small features: *the picture has too much detail*

2 **detective** *n.*

4 **determination**
  4 *n.* will power: *she is a woman of great determination*
  6 *n.* resolve: *he came with the determination of staying a week*
  7 *n.* fixing limits, finding exact position

5 **determine**
  5 *v.* resolve: *I am determined to go*
  6 *v.* decide: *determine the rights and wrongs of the case*
  7 *v.* fix accurately: *determine the position of a star*

3 **develop**
  3 *v.* cause to grow or evolve: *develop a business*
  4 *v.* grow: *a child develops rapidly between the ages of 2 and 4*

3 **development**
  3 *n.* gradual unfolding: *development of mind and body*
  4 *n.* growth measured: *the development of the chest*
  5 *n.* events: *the latest developments in Israel*
  6 *n.* innovations: *the latest developments in science*
4 **devil**
  4 *n.* Satan, any evil spirit, a bad man
  7 *n.* term of pity: *queer devil; poor devil*
5 **diagram** *n.*
5 **dial**
  5 *v.* telephone: *I've dialled them three times*
  6 *n.* face of a measuring device: *the dial on a radio*
5 **diameter** *n.*
3 **diamond**
  3 *n.* precious stone
  5 *n.* shaped in parallelogram: *diamond-pattern quilt*
4 **diary** *n.*
4 **dictate** *v.* speak for recording: *dictate to a secretary*
5 **dictation** *n.* passage that is dictated, activity of dictating
2 **dictionary** *n.*
1 **die**
  1 *v.* decease
  5 *v.* become weak: *interest in it died*
  6 *v.* long: *dying for a drink*
4 **differ**
  4 *v.* be unlike: *they differ in their tastes*
  6 *v.* not agree: *I differ from you about that*
2 **difference**
  2 *n.* unlikeness: *there's a big difference in attitude*
  4 *n.* gap: *there's a difference of nearly a kilo*
2 **different**
  2 *adj.* unlike: *this pencil is different from mine*
  3 *adj.* other: *this is a different way we are taking*

  5 *adj.* various: *different people have different ideas*
2 **difficult**
  2 *adj.* not easy: *a difficult problem*
  6 *adj.* hard to handle (of persons): *he's a difficult child*
3 **difficulty**
  3 *n.* being hard to handle: *the difficulty of the subject*
  5 *n.* occasion of problems: *to be in difficulties*
2 **dig**
  2 *v.* work the soil
  7 *v.* like, enjoy (colloq.)
5 **digest**
  5 *v.* process food in stomach
  7 *n.* information in easily assimilable form: *the Reader's Digest*
5 **digs** *n.(pl.)* rented accommodation
4 **dine**
  4 *v.* have dinner
  7 *v.* give dinner to: *he wined and dined her*
1 **dinner** *n.*
5 **dip**
  5 *v.* put into liquid: *dip your pen in the ink*
  6 *v.* penetrate lightly/briefly: *he dipped into Jacobean drama*
  7 *v.* go down a little: *birds dipping in their flight*
  7 *n.* slight hollow: *a dip in the ground*
5 **diploma** *n.*
3 **direct**
  3 *adj.* straight/in a straight line: *the direct way to London*
  4 *v.* guide and control: *direct a business*
  5 *v.* point/aim: *direct a beam of light*
  5 *adj.* not through an intermediary: *in direct contact*
  6 *v.* order: *I was directed to make this report*
  7 *adj.* forthright: *he's a very direct person*
3 **direction**
  3 *n.* course: *go in the wrong direction*
  4 *n.* instruction: *directions are on the packet*

3 **directly**
   3 *adv.* straight: *coming directly towards us*
   5 *adv.* without an intermediary: *apply directly to the skin*
   6 *adv.* very soon/at once: *I'll do it directly*
   7 *conj.* as soon as: *directly I saw him, I left*
3 **director** *n.*
5 **directory** *n.*
2 **dirt**
   2 *n.* unclean matter: *dirt under your fingernails*
   6 *n.* earth: *a dirt road*
   7 *n.* immoral matter
1 **dirty**
   1 *adj.* soiled: *dirty clothes*
   4 *v.* make unclean: *dirty one's hands*
   5 *adj.* immoral: *dirty stories*
   6 *adj.* causing uncleanness: *a dirty job*
   7 *adj.* impure: *dirty coal*
3 **disadvantage**
   3 *n.* unfavourable condition: *his lack of English is a disadvantage*
   6 *n.* loss, injury: *rumours to his disadvantage*
3 **disagree**
   3 *v.* differ in view: *I disagree with what you say*
   7 *v.* not suit (allergies): *cucumber disagrees with me*
4 **disagreement**
   4 *n.* difference of view: *I am in disagreement with my bank*
   6 *n.* minor quarrel: *they often had disagreements*
3 **disappear** *v.* vanish suddenly, go gradually away
4 **disappearance** *n.*
3 **disappoint**
   3 *v.* fail to satisfy: *please don't disappoint me*
   6 *v.* prevent hope etc. from being realised: *I'm sorry to disappoint your expectations*

4 **disappointment**
   4 *n.* being disappointed: *to her great disappointment it rained all day*
   5 *n.* somebody or something that disappoints: *he'd had many disappointments in life*
5 **disapproval** *n.*
5 **disaster** *n.*
4 **discipline**
   4 *n.* result of training in habits of obedience: *perfect discipline under fire*
   5 *n.* training in habits of obedience: *some teachers practise discipline more strictly than others*
   6 *v.* control: *he disciplined his behaviour in company*
   7 *v.* punish
5 **discomfort**
   5 *n.* absence of comfort
   6 *n.* something that causes hardship: *the discomforts endured in the Arctic*
5 **discotheque** *n.*
5 **discount**
   5 *n.* reduction of money: *get it at the discount shop*
   7 *v.* disregard: *you can discount what he says*
2 **discover** *v.*
4 **discovery** *n.*
3 **discuss** *v.*
3 **discussion** *n.*
3 **disease** *n.*
5 **disembark** *v.*
4 **disgust** *n./v.*
2 **dish**
   2 *n.* vessel
   6 *n.* food: *it's his favourite dish*
   7 *v.* distribute (colloq.): *dish out*
   7 *n.(pl.)* crockery after use: *wash the dishes*
4 **dishwasher** *n.*
3 **dislike** *n./v.*
5 **dismiss**
   5 *v.* terminate employment: *the servant was dismissed*
   6 *v.* allowed to go: *the teacher dismissed the class*

41

7 *v.* decide not to consider: *he dismissed it from his mind*

5 **dismissal** *n.*

5 **disorder**
5 *n.* disarray: *the burglars left the room in disorder*
7 *n.* disturbances, riots: *the disorders in the capital*
7 *n.* malfunctioning: *disorders of the mind/digestive system*

4 **display**
4 *v.* show to catch attention: *department stores display their goods*
4 *n.* show: *fashion display*
6 *v.* exhibit: *don't display your ignorance*

5 **displease** *v.*

5 **dissatisfaction** *n.*

5 **dissatisfy** *v.*

4 **dissolve**
4 *v.* turn from solid to liquid: *salt dissolves in water*
7 *v.* bring to an end: *they dissolved the partnership in 1972*

3 **distance**
3 *n.* measure of space: *the distance from here to London*
6 *n.* long period of time: *when I look back over a distance of fifty years*

3 **distant**
3 *adv.* away from: *three miles distant from the station*
3 *adj.* from far away: *a distant view of Mt Everest*
7 *adj.* opposite to close: *she is a distant cousin*

4 **distinct**
4 *adj.* easily perceived: *distinct pronunciation*
5 *adj.* distinguished: *keep the two ideas distinct*

4 **distinction**
4 *n.* point of difference: *the distinction between poetry and prose is obvious*
7 *n.* standing: *the President spoke to everyone of distinction*
7 *n.* honour: *a mark of distinction*

4 **distinguish**
4 *v.* make/see as different: *you can distinguish him by his scar*
6 *v.* see clearly: *with good eyesight you can distinguish distant objects*
7 *v.* make eminent: *he distinguished himself as a soldier*

4 **distribute**
4 *v.* give or send out: *they distributed food to the starving*
6 *v.* spread out: *distribute manure over a field*

3 **district** *n.*

3 **disturb**
3 *v.* change the correct or normal condition of: *that might disturb his plans*
5 *v.* break in on: *don't disturb him, he's asleep*
6 *v.* agitate: *I'm very disturbed by your news*

3 **ditch**
3 *n.* narrow channel
7 *v.* (colloq.) throw aside

3 **dive**
3 *v.* plunge: *dive into the sea*
5 *v.* submerge: *the submarine dived*
6 *v.* go suddenly lower or out of sight: *he dived into a doorway*

5 **diver** *n.*

3 **divide**
3 *v.* cut into parts or shares: *divide it up into 4*
4 *v.* separate: *the channel divides England from France*
6 *v.* classify: *divide the books according to subject*

4 **division**
4 *n.* part of a whole: *the upper division of the school*
5 *n.* act of dividing: *division of labour*
5 *n.* mathematical process: *multiplication and division*
6 *n.* class: *a division of submarine plants*
7 *n.* large army unit: *the 50th Division*

4 **divorce**
4 *v.* separate from married partner: *they divorced 10 years ago*

4 *n.* end of a marriage

7 *n.* any other ending implying separation

7 *v.* dissociate completely

1 **do**

   1 *aux.: does he want it? I don't think so*

   1 *v.* carry out action: *what are you doing now?*

   1 *v.* complete: *I've done the housework*

   2 *v.* make, produce: *she's done you six copies of the report*

   2 *v.* make tidy: *go and do your hair*

   3 *v.* study: *he's doing chemistry at school now*

   3 *v.* suffice: *this room will do quite well*

   4 *v.* solve: *here's a crossword for you to do*

   5 *v.* cook: *is the meat well done?*

   5 *v.* be connected with: *it all has to do with his childhood*

   6 *v.* cheat: *I'm sure I was done at the garage*

5 **do away with** *v.* get rid of

5 **do out of** *v.* stop someone from having

3 **do without** *v.* manage in the absence of

1 **doctor**

   1 *n.* medical practitioner

   7 *n.* academic title: *Doctor of Laws*

5 **document**

   5 *n.* written or printed record

   7 *v.* to document: *to keep a detailed record*

1 **dog** *n.* the animal

5 **doll**

   5 *n.* model of baby or person

   7 *n.* pretty but empty-headed woman

2 **dollar** *n.*

3 **domestic**

   3 *adj.* of the home: *domestic service*

   5 *adj.* of the family: *he has severe domestic troubles*

   6 *adj.* tamed: *cows are domestic animals*

5 **donkey** *n.*

1 **door**

   1 *n.* that which closes an entrance

4 *n.* house: *next door; a few doors down*

7 *n.* proximity: *at death's door*

3 **doorstep** *n.*

4 **doorway** *n.*

5 **dose**

   5 *n.* amount of medicine to be taken

   6 *v.* administer medicine: *he dosed himself with aspirin*

5 **dot**

   5 *n.* a small round mark

   6 *v.* make a small round mark

3 **double**

   3 *adj.* having two parts or layers: *double doors; a double meaning*

   4 *adj.* twice as much: *a double share*

   5 *v.* increase by as much again: *the sales doubled*

   6 *v.* fold: *double the paper*

   7 *v.* retrace route: *double back*

   7 *n.* exact likeness: *he's my double*

3 **doubt**

   3 *n.* uncertainty: *I have my doubts*

   3 *v.* be uncertain: *I doubt the truth of it*

   5 *v.* mistrust: *I doubt his honesty*

4 **doubtful** *adj.*

5 **doubtless** *adv.*

1 **down**

   1 *adv.* to/in a lower position: *sit down*

   1 *prep.* along: *go down the street*

   3 *adv.* low on a scale: *from the richest down to the poorest*

   6 *adv.* smaller in size or activity: *grind down; die down*

   7 *adv.* to a place considered lower/less important: *go down from London to the country*

   7 *adv.* idea of illness: *down with influenza*

2 **downstairs** *adv.*

5 **downwards** *adv.*

4 **dozen**

   4 *n.* twelve

   7 *n.* lots of: *I've been here dozens of times*

3 **drag**

   3 *v.* pull a heavy thing along: *dragging a great branch*

5 *v.* move slowly and laboriously: *the meeting dragged on*
6 *v.* involve: *don't drag me into it*
drain
3 *n.* a pipe or channel for waste water
4 *v.* cause unwanted water to flow away
6 *n.* diminution: *a great drain on our resources*
7 *v.* empty: *drain a glass of beer*
4 **dramatic**
4 *adj.* of drama: *dramatic works*
6 *adj.* striking: *a dramatic change in the situation*
6 *n.(pl.)* stage activities
1 **draw**
1 *v.* make line, depict: *draw a picture*
2 *v.* pull, pull after one: *this horse draws the cart*
5 *v.* extract: *draw water; draw conclusions*
6 *v.* move: *the train drew out*
6 *n.* equal outcome to a match: *the match ended in a draw*
6 *v.* end a match with equal score: *the teams drew 2 all*
7 *v.* attract, like a magnet: *draw a crowd*
7 *v.* extend: *draw out a discussion*
7 *v.* set out in order: *draw up a document*
5 **draw in**
4 *v.* slow down and stop (train, taxi)
5 *v.* become shorter (daytime)
3 **draw out**
3 *v.* take money out of bank account
3 *v.* set out on journey (train, ship)
5 *v.* become longer (daytime)
4 **draw up**
4 *v.* come to a stop (vehicle)
5 *v.* prepare a written statement (report, document)
3 **drawer** *n.* part of piece of furniture: *chest of drawers*
2 **dream**
2 *v.* imagine during sleep: *I dreamt all night*
7 *v.* fancy: *I never dreamt he'd do that*

1 **dress**
1 *n.* article of clothing: *she put on her new dress*
1 *v.* clothe oneself
2 *v.* clothe someone else: *she dressed the baby*
5 *n.* apparel in general: *in local dress*
4 **dressmaking** *n.*
4 **drill**
4 *n.* exercise: *repeat these drills*
5 *v.* exercise: *the soldiers were drilled at the barracks*
6 *v.* bore: *drill a hole*
6 *n.* instrument for boring: *electric drill*
1 **drink**
1 *n.* amount of liquid: *a drink of beer*
1 *v.* quench thirst: *something to drink*
6 *v.* soak: *blotting paper drinks up water*
7 *v.* take alcohol: *he drinks too much*
4 **drive**
4 *n.* journey by car
7 *n.* private roadway to a house: *leave your car in the drive*
1 **drive**
1 *v.* steer a car: *drive to the station*
6 *v.* cause to go: *drive cattle along the road*
6 *v.* direct force onto a thing: *drive in a nail*
7 *v.* force to work: *he drove his workers very hard*
5 **drive-in** *adj.*: *drive-in cinema*
4 **driver**
4 *n.* person steering
6 *n.* person forcing movement/action: *slave-driver*
1 **drop**
1 *v.* fall: *fruit dropped from the tree*
3 *v.* allow to fall: *he dropped it like a hot coal*
4 *n.* fall: *a drop in temperature*
4 *v.* lower: *he dropped his voice*
5 *n.* globule: *a drop of oil*
6 *n.* small amount of liquid: *just a drop*
3 **drop back** *v.* fall behind

4 **drop by** v. visit casually
4 **drop in on** v. visit someone casually
4 **drop off**
    4 v. allow someone to alight from vehicle
    5 v. doze off
5 **drop out** v. withdraw from (a group, society)
5 **drop-out** n.
2 **drown**
    2 v. die by submersion: *he fell overboard and was drowned*
    4 v. kill by submersion
    5 v. obliterate: *the record drowned the teacher's voice*
    6 v. bathe: *her face was drowned in tears*
3 **drug**
    3 n. habit-forming substance: *LSD is a drug*
    4 n. medicine
    6 v. render unconscious by drugs: *they drugged the caretaker*
3 **drum**
    3 n. musical instrument: *beat the drum*
    4 n. cylindrical vessel: *an oil drum*
    7 v. instil: *drum some sense into him*
    7 v. gather forcefully: *drum up support*
2 **drunk** n. a (habitually) drunk person
1 **dry**
    1 adj. opposite of wet: *a dry cloth*
    3 v. remove moisture: *dry your hands*
    6 adj. thirsty: *I'm dry*
    6 adj. of taste: *dry martini/wine*
    7 adj. of character: *in a dry voice*
5 **dryness** n.

3 **due**
    3 adj. owed: *money due to me*
    4 adj. concerning times: *the train is not due yet*
    6 adj. proper, right: *with due ceremony*
5 **due to** prep.: *our late arrival was due to fog*
4 **dull**
    4 adj. boring: *a dull book*
    5 adj. lacking sparkle: *a dull boy; dull sky*
    6 adj. lacking movement: *trade is dull*
    6 adj. not sharp: *a dull edge to this knife*
    7 v. render insensitive: *my senses were dulled*
5 **dullness** n.
4 **dumb**
    4 adj. unable to speak
    5 adj. temporarily silent: *the class fell dumb*
    7 adj. stupid
2 **during** prep.
5 **dusk** n.
3 **dust**
    3 n. dry/fine dirt
    4 v. remove dust
    7 v. sprinkle: *dust the cake lightly with sugar*
5 **duster** n. cloth for cleaning
5 **dustman** n.
3 **dusty** adj.
3 **duty**
    3 n. service/action morally due: *my duty to the children*
    4 n. tasks: *the headmaster's duties*
    6 n. obligatory payment: *customs duty*

E

2 **each**
    2 adj. every: *for each child*
    3 adv. individually: *he gave them 50p each*

    3 pron.: *they like each other*
3 **eager** adj.
1 **ear**
    1 n. organ of body

7 *n.* grain-bearing part of corn etc.

1 **early**
  1 *adv.: he gets up early*
  3 *adj.: an early start*

3 **earn** *v.* gain by working: *earn one's living*

5 **earnest**
  5 *adj.* assiduous: *an earnest pupil*
  6 *adv.* seriously: *in earnest*

5 **earnings** *n.(pl.)* wages, intake of money gained

1 **ear-ring** *n.*

2 **earth**
  2 *n.* planet
  4 *n.* soil: till the earth
  4 *n.* ground: *he felt the earth beneath his feet again*

5 **earthenware** *n./adj.: earthenware pottery*

5 **earthquake** *n.*

4 **ease**
  4 *v.* lessen: *to ease the pain*
  6 *n.* comfort, rest: *take your ease*
  7 *v.* move gently: *he eased himself into the chair*

1 **east** *n./adj.*

3 **Easter** *n.*

5 **eastern** *adj.*

5 **eastward** *adv./adj.: we sailed in an eastward direction*

1 **easy**
  1 *adj.* not difficult
  5 *adj.* comfortable: *not an easy life*
  5 *adv.* comfortably: *not to take it easy*

1 **eat** *v.*

4 **economic**
  4 *adj.* concerning economics
  6 *adj.* balancing the true cost: *an economic rent*

4 **economy**
  4 *n.* avoidance of waste of money
  7 *n.* theory and practice of government: *political economy*

2 **edge**
  2 *n.* the edge of a knife, city, cliff
  6 *v.* move gradually: *to edge away/ahead*

4 **editor** *n.*

3 **educate** *v.*

3 **education**
  3 *n.* systematic training and instruction
  6 *n.* development of character and intellectual powers: *moral/aesthetic education*

4 **educational** *adj.*

4 **effect**
  4 *n.* result, outcome: *the effect of drugs*
  6 *v.* cause: *effect a cure*

5 **effective**
  5 *adj.* having result
  6 *adj.* making a striking impression

5 **efficiency** *n.*

4 **efficient**
  4 *adj.* capable: *an efficient manager*
  5 *adj.* producing the required result: *an efficient method*

3 **effort** *n.*

1 **egg** *n.*

1 **eight** *n./adj.*

1 **eighteen** *n./adj.*

2 **eighth** *adj.*

1 **eighty** *n./adj.*

2 **either**
  2 *conj.* one of: *that man must be either blind or drunk*
  4 *pron./adj.* any one of: *take either (half), they're exactly the same*
  5 *adv.* also: *I don't like that wine either*
  7 *adv.* moreover: *and not so long ago either*

5 **elastic**
  5 *adj.* that can be stretched: *elastic band*
  5 *n.* material: *a piece of elastic*
  7 *adj.* flexible: *elastic rules*

5 **elbow**
  5 *n.* joint in arm
  6 *v.* push one's way: *to elbow through the crowd*

5 **elder** *adj.*

5 **eldest** *adj.*

4 **elect**
  4 *v.* choose someone for public function
  7 *adj.* chosen

4 **election** *n.* act of choosing person(s) for public office

2 **electric**
  2 *adj.* worked by electricity: *an electric kettle*
  2 *adj.* charged with electricity: *electric current*

3 **electrical** *adj.* for handling electricity: *electrical equipment*

5 **electrician** *n.*

2 **electricity** *n.* current: *switch the electricity off at the mains*

5 **electronic** *adj.*

5 **element**
  5 *n.* substance not so far split up into simpler form
  6 *n.* necessary feature: *an essential element*

4 **elementary**
  4 *adj.* basic
  6 *adj.* simple

3 **elephant** *n.*

1 **eleven** *n./adj.*

2 **eleventh** *adj.*

2 **else**
  2 *adv.* in addition: *no-one else*
  5 *adv.* otherwise: *how else can I manage?*

4 **elsewhere** *adv.*

5 **embarrass** *v.* disconcert

4 **emergency** *n.* sudden serious happening: *in an emergency, call the guard*

4 **emotion** *n.* strong feeling

5 **emotional** *adj.* of the emotions: *an emotional parting*

4 **emphasise** *v.* put stress on

3 **employ**
  3 *v.* give work to: *he employs 10 men*
  7 *v.* make use of: *how do you employ your time?*

4 **employee** *n.* person employed for wages

3 **employer** *n.* person who employs others

3 **employment** *n.* regular work or occupation

1 **empty**
  1 *adj.* containing nothing

3 *v.* rid of contents: *empty the bucket*
  6 *adj.* without substance: *an empty threat*

5 **enclose**
  5 *v.* put a wall, fence around: *the duke enclosed the park*
  6 *v.* put something in an envelope, parcel

3 **encourage**
  3 *v.* give hope/confidence/support: *he encouraged me to apply*
  6 *v.* fill with courage: *encouraged by this success, they . . .*

5 **encouragement** *n.*

1 **end**
  1 *n.* furthest point, last point
  3 *n.* small piece remaining: *the end of the cigar*
  3 *v.* come to a finish

5 **ending** *n.*

5 **endless** *adj.*

2 **enemy**
  2 *n.* adversary in war: *fight against the enemy*
  4 *n.* person who wishes to harm or attack: *he has many enemies*

5 **energetic** *adj.*

4 **energy**
  4 *n.* force, vigour: *she seems to have lost all her energy*
  5 *n.* material power: *nuclear energy*

5 **engage**
  5 *v.* employ: *they engaged a typist*
  7 *v.* undertake, promise: *I engaged to manage the business*
  7 *v.* military: *engage in battle*

4 **engaged**
  4 *adj.* having agreed to marry
  4 *adj.* occupied, in use: *the telephone is engaged*

2 **engine**
  2 *n.* machine developing power: *the engine in my car's still cold*
  4 *n.* locomotive: *the engine has broken down*

3 **engineer**
  3 *n.* designer of bridges etc.
  4 *n.* skilled person in control of a power unit

7 *v.* arrange indirectly: *she engineered that meeting*

5 **engineering**
  5 *n.* form of technology
  5 *n.* work or profession of an engineer

3 **English Channel** *n.*

2 **enjoy**
  2 *v.* get pleasure from
  7 *v.* have advantage, benefit: *enjoy good health*

5 **enjoyable** *adj.*

5 **enjoyment**
  5 *n.* pleasure, joy
  6 *n.* activity that gives joy/pleasure
  7 *n.* possession and use of something

5 **enlarge**
  5 *v.* make, become larger: *he's enlarged those photos*
  7 *v.* say or write more about: *enlarge upon the topic*

3 **enormous** *adj.*

2 **enough**
  2 *adj.* sufficient: *isn't there enough bread?*
  3 *n.* sufficiently: *enough has been said*
  4 *adv.* sufficiently: *not quick enough*

5 **ensure**
  5 *v.* guarantee: *please ensure that your safety belts are fastened*
  7 *v.* make safe: *ensure against loss of heat*

3 **enter**
  3 *v.* come or go into a space: *they entered the museum*
  7 *v.* become a member of, join: *enter Parliament*

4 **entertain**
  4 *v.* receive as guests
  5 *v.* amuse, interest
  7 *v.* be ready to consider: *entertain ideas/doubts*

4 **entertainment**
  4 *n.* entertaining or being entertained: *a hotel famous for its entertainment*
  5 *n.* public performance

4 **entire** *adj.* whole, complete

3 **entirely** *adv.* completely

3 **entrance**
  3 *n.* opening by which one enters

5 *n.* coming or going in: *to make an entrance*
7 *adj.* qualifying: *entrance examination*

4 **entry**
  4 *n.* coming or going in
  4 *n.* entrance: *no entry*
  7 *n.* item in a list: *dictionary entry*
  7 *n.* list/number of persons entering a competition

3 **envelope**
  3 *n.* covering of a letter
  6 *v.* cover on all sides: *the fog enveloped us*

5 **environment**
  5 *n.* surroundings
  7 *n.* circumstances, influences

5 **envy**
  5 *v.* feel jealous of
  5 *n.* feeling of jealousy: *his car was the envy of his friends*
  6 *n.* feeling of disappointment and ill-will: *he was filled with envy at my success*

3 **equal**
  3 *adj.* same in size/amount
  6 *adj.* capable of having strength/ability for: *he is equal to the job*
  6 *n.* match: *no man is his equal*
  6 *v.* make: *two + two equals four*

5 **equality** *n.*

5 **equator** *n.*

3 **equipment**
  3 *n.* things needed for a purpose: *modern equipment*
  6 *n.* equipping or becoming equipped: *the equipment of his laboratory took a long time*

4 **erect**
  4 *v.* build, set up: *erect a building*
  7 *v.* set upright: *erect a mast*
  7 *adj.* upright, standing on end

5 **erotic** *adj.* of sexual love or desire

4 **error** *n.* mistake

3 **escape**
  3 *n.* act of getting free
  3 *v.* get free/away
  6 *v.* avoid: *escape punishment*

7 *v.* not be available for recall: *his name escapes me*
3 **especially**
   3 *adv.* in particular: *he likes apples, especially Granny Smiths*
   3 *adv.* to an exceptional degree: *it's especially cold today*
4 **essential**
   4 *adj.* necessary: *essential equipment*
   6 *adj.* fundamental: *his essential dishonesty*
4 **establish**
   4 *v.* set up: *to establish new procedures*
   6 *v.* settle in a position: *he is now established in his new job*
   7 *v.* cause people to accept a claim: *Newton established the law of gravity*
4 **estimate**
   4 *v.* form a judgement about cost/size etc.
   6 *n.* approximate calculations: *the estimate for that building is £25,000*
1 **Europe** *n.*
2 **European** *adj.*
2 **even**
   2 *adv.* for emphasis: *even he couldn't tell you*
   5 *adj.* level, flat
   7 *adj.*: *even/odd numbers*
1 **evening** *n.*
4 **event**
   4 *n.* happening (usually something important)
   6 *n.* case: *in any event*
2 **ever**
   2 *adv.* at any time: *have you ever been to Los Angeles?*
   4 *adv.* after comparative/superlative: *harder than ever*
   5 *adv.* at all times: *ever after*
5 **everlasting** *adj.*
1 **every** *adj.*
2 **everybody** *pron.*
5 **everyday** *adj.*: *it's not an everyday occurrence*
2 **everyone** *pron.*

2 **everything** *pron.*
3 **everywhere** *adv.*
4 **evidence**
   4 *n.* traces: *evidence of his presence*
   4 *n.* reason for believing something: *the evidence lies in the position of the gun*
5 **evident** *adj.*
4 **evil**
   4 *adj.* wicked, sinful, bad
   6 *n.* sin, wrong-doing
3 **exact**
   3 *adj.* correct: *the exact time*
   6 *adj.* accurate: *an exact scholar*
   7 *v.* demand, insist on: *they exacted payment from us on the hour*
3 **exam** *n.*
3 **examination**
   3 *n.* test
   6 *n.* scrutiny: *a medical examination*
3 **examine**
   3 *v.* scrutinise: *examine the goods before you pay*
   5 *v.* test: *he examined me on my spoken Persian*
5 **examiner** *n.*
1 **example**
   1 *n.* fact/thing illustrating a general rule: *for example*
   5 *n.* model: *set an example*
3 **excellent** *adj.*
2 **except**
   2 *prep.* not including
   5 *prep.* apart from the fact: *fine – except that he can't*
   6 *v.* set apart from: *if you except Charles, then there are 8 of us*
5 **except for** *prep.*: *your essay is good except for the spelling*
4 **exception**
   4 *n.* something or somebody that is not included: *no exception; an exception to the rule*
   7 *n.* objection: *take exception to*
4 **excess**
   4 *adj.* more than needed/proper: *excess baggage*
   6 *n.* superabundance: *an excess of enthusiasm*

4 **exchange**
  4 *v.* take one thing for another: *exchange a book*
  5 *v.* convert: *exchange marks for lire*
  6 *v.* give and receive: *exchange views*
  6 *v.* swop: *an exchange of stamps*
  6 *n.* currency equivalences: *rate of exchange*
3 **excite**
  3 *v.* stimulate: *skating excites her*
  5 *v.* provoke emotions: *the strain has excited him alarmingly*
4 **excitement** *n.*
4 **exclamation**
  4 *n.* punctuation mark: *exclamation mark*
  7 *n.* shout: *they received the proposals with exclamations of anger*
5 **exclude**
  5 *v.* keep out: *women are excluded from that club*
  7 *v.* prevent: *exclude possibility of doubt*
5 **excursion** *n.*
2 **excuse**
  2 *v.* forgive: *excuse me for being late*
  4 *n.* pretended reason: *I don't believe his excuse*
  5 *v.* allow not to do: *excuse him from attending classes*
5 **executive**
  5 *n.* business man
  6 *adj.* having to do with managing
  7 *adj.* having authority to carry out decisions
1 **exercise**
  1 *n.* school task
  3 *n.* muscular activity: *he doesn't take enough exercise*
  5 *v.* cause to be active: *exercise horses/the mind*
  7 *n.* form of training: *a military exercise*
  7 *v.* employ, make use of: *exercise authority*
5 **exhaust**
  5 *v.* weary: *I'm exhausted*
  6 *v.* make empty: *exhaust an oil well*
  6 *n.* outlet: *car exhaust*

7 *v.* say everything: *exhaust a subject*
5 **exhibition**
  5 *n.* collection shown publicly
  7 *n.* art of showing
4 **exist**
  4 *v.* be: *does the kiwi still exist?*
  4 *v.* live: *you can't exist on £2 a day*
5 **existence**
  5 *n.* fact of being: *only eight of these are in existence*
  5 *n.* state/manner of existence: *they lead a mean existence*
4 **exit**
  4 *n.* way out
  6 *n.* departure: *make an exit*
  7 *v.* goes out: *exit Macbeth*
5 **expand**
  5 *v.* make/become larger
  6 *v.* unfold, spread out: *he expanded on the idea*
5 **expansion**
  5 *n.* *the expansion of metal*
  6 *n.* growth: *this estate was built during the expansion of the 1960s*
3 **expect**
  3 *v.* think something will happen
  4 *v.* be pregnant: *expect a baby*
  5 *v.* believe: *I expect you already know*
  6 *v.* rely on: *I expect you to attend*
5 **expense**
  5 *n.* spending, cost
  7 *n.* bringing discredit/contempt: *we laughed at his expense*
3 **expensive** *adj.*
3 **experience**
  3 *n.* event/activity that affects one: *an unusual experience*
  4 *n.* process of gaining skill: *three years' experience*
  6 *n.* acquaintance: *have experience of travel in Thailand*
  6 *v.* undergo: *I experienced a strange event last week*
4 **experiment**
  4 *n.* test (in piece of research), trial
  5 *v.* research by testing
5 **experimental** *adj.*

4 **expert**
  4 *n.* person with special knowledge
  6 *adj.* trained by practice, skilful
2 **explain**
  2 *v.* make clear
  6 *v.* account for: *please explain your behaviour*
4 **explanation** *n.*
3 **explode**
  3 *v.* blow up
  6 *v.* show anger
2 **exploit**
  2 *v.* discover/map new territory
  6 *v.* investigate: *will you explore the possibilities*
5 **exploration** *n.*
4 **explorer** *n.*
3 **explosion** *n.*
5 **explosive**
  5 *adj.* likely to explode
  5 *n.* substance which explodes: *the explosives are in that case*
4 **export**
  4 *v.* send goods abroad
  4 *n.* thing exported: *exports are up in value this month*
  4 *n.* act/practice of exporting: *goods for export*
4 **express**
  4 *v.* make known: *to express my meaning*
  5 *n.* fast train: *the express to Edinburgh*
  7 *adj.* clearly stated: *it was his express instruction that . . .*
4 **expression**
  4 *n.* showing attitude: *an expression of love*
  5 *n.* form of words: *a vulgar expression*

  7 *n.* symbol in maths denoting a quantity
4 **extend**
  4 *v.* enlarge, make longer: *you can extend your holiday*
  5 *v.* stretch out: *London extends for miles*
4 **extension**
  4 *n.* additional part: *we built the extension five years ago*
  6 *n.* subsidiary system: *extension telephone*
4 **extent**
  4 *n.* area: *to its full extent*
  6 *n.* degree: *to a certain extent*
5 **external** *adj.*
3 **extra**
  3 *adj.* additional
  5 *n.* additional charge: *there are no hidden extras to this offer*
4 **extraordinary** *adj.*
5 **extraordinarily** *adv.*
3 **extreme**
  3 *adj.* uttermost: *the extreme limit of the property*
  6 *adj.* intense: *extreme opinions*
  6 *n.* greatest degree: *annoying in the extreme*
4 **extremely** *adv.*
1 **eye**
  1 *n.* organ of body
  5 *n.* part of instrument: *the eye of a needle*
  6 *v.* observe, watch: *he eyed the stranger with suspicion*
5 **eyebrow** *n.*
5 **eyelid** *n.*
5 **eyesight** *n.*

F

1 **face**
  1 *n.* part of body
  3 *n.* sign of emotion: *angry face*
  5 *v.* direction: *facing this way*
  6 *n.* presence: *say it to his face*
  6 *n.* surface: *face of the circle*
  6 *v.* meet confidently: *face the enemy/danger*
  6 *n.* confronting: *face to face*
  7 *adj.* apparent: *face value*
5 **face up to** *v.* accept a challenge
2 **fact**
  2 *n.* something that has happened
  2 *n.* something known to be true: *it's a fact that . . .*
  5 *n.* reality: *fact not fiction*
3 **factory** *n.*
5 **fade**
  5 *v.* lose colour, freshness: *the curtains faded*
  5 *v.* go out of hearing/view
2 **fail**
  2 *v.* be unsuccessful
  5 *v.* reject: *the examiners failed the candidate*
  6 *v.* be not enough: *the crops failed*
  6 *v.* become weak: *his health was failing*
  6 *v.* omit: *he failed to turn up*
  7 *v.* become bankrupt: *several banks failed*
4 **failure**
  4 *n.* failing: *failure in an exam*
  5 *n.* instance of failing: *he was a failure as a teacher*
  6 *n.* state of being inadequate: *harvest failure*
  6 *n.* neglect: *his failure to help*
5 **faint**
  5 *adj.* weak: *a faint voice*
  5 *adj.* vague: *a faint hope*
  5 *v.* lose consciousness
  6 *adj.* giddy: *she felt faint*
  6 *adj.* weak, exhausted: *faint with hunger*

2 **fair**
  2 *adj.* just: *it's not fair*
  3 *adj.* average: *a fair amount of sense*
  3 *adj.* (of the weather) not wet
  4 *adj.* blond: *fair hair*
  4 *n.* market: *sheep fair*
  4 *n.* entertainment: *fun fair*
  6 *n.* commercial exhibition: *the World Fair*
  7 *adj.* clean, neat: *a fair copy*
3 **fairly** *adv.*
5 **faith**
  5 *n.* trust
  5 *n.* religious belief
5 **faithful**
  5 *adj.* loyal, true: *a faithful friend*
  6 *adj.* true to the facts: *a faithful account*
  7 *n.(pl.)* true believers
2 **fall**
  2 *v.* collapse/tumble
  3 *v.* come or go down: *the temperature fell*
  5 *v.* hang down: *her hair fell to her shoulders*
  6 *v.* become: *he fell silent*
5 **fall back on** *v.* rely on for support
4 **fall behind** *v.* be attracted to
5 **fall in with**
  5 *v.* meet by chance
  5 *v.* agree to a proposal
5 **fall out** *v.* stop being friends with
5 **fall through** *v.* fail to materialise
3 **false**
  3 *adj.* wrong
  4 *adj.* artificial: *false teeth*
  6 *adj.* deceptive: *false witness*
  7 *adj.* disloyal: *false to his vows*
4 **fame** *n.*
3 **familiar**
  3 *adj.* having good knowledge of
  4 *adj.* well known
  4 *adj.* common
  6 *adj.* close, intimate, personal
1 **family**
  1 *n.* parents and children

1 *n.* children
3 *n.* all people descended from common ancestor
6 *n.* group of things with common characteristics: *family of languages*
7 *n.* famous or distinguished ancestry
2 **famous** *adj.*
3 **fan**
  3 *n.* object moved to make a current of air
  5 *n.* fanatical supporter
  6 *n.* send current of air on to
5 **fancy**
  5 *adj.* not plain or ordinary: *fancy dress*
  6 *v.* imagine
  6 *v.* want
  6 *n.* fondness, liking for: *a fancy for food/wine*
  7 *v.* have too high an opinion of: *fancy oneself*
5 **fantastic**
  5 *adj.* wild, strange
  5 *adj.* impossible to carry out
  5 *adj.* marvellous, wonderful
2 **far**
  2 *adv.* distant
  2 *conj.*: *as far as*
  4 *adv.* until now: *so far*
  4 *adv.* with other preps/advs: *far off/away/out/back etc.*
  5 *adj.* distant: *Far East*
  6 *adv./adj.*: *far and away*
4 **fare**
  4 *n.* charge for journey
  6 *n.* food: *traveller's fare*
3 **Far East** *n.*
1 **farm**
  1 *n.* land for agriculture or stock, buildings so used
  3 *v.* use land
  6 *v.* distribute work: *farm out*
1 **farmer** *n.*
4 **farmhouse**
  4 *n.* building for farmer and family
  6 *adj.* shape of loaf of bread
5 **farther** *adv.*
5 **farthest** *adv.*
5 **fascinate** *v.* attract, charm

4 **fashion**
  4 *n.* prevailing customs in clothes etc.
  6 *n.* manner of doing something
4 **fashionable** *adj.*
2 **fast**
  2 *adv./adj.*: quick, quickly
  3 *adj.* showing time later than the true time
  6 *adj.* firmly fixed: *stuck fast*
  7 *v.* refrain from eating
2 **fasten** *v.* fix firmly, tie together
1 **fat**
  1 *adj.* not thin
  4 *n.* substance for cooking
  5 *adj.* thick, well filled: *a fat purse*
5 **fatal**
  5 *adj.* causing death
  7 *adj.* of destiny: *the fatal day*
4 **fate**
  4 *n.* what is destined to happen
  6 *n.* death, destruction: *his fate*
  7 *n.* power controlling events
1 **father**
  1 *n.* parent
  5 *n.* religious title
  6 *n.(pl.)* ancestors
3 **fault**
  3 *n.* being wrong: *it's his fault*
  6 *n.* blemish, flaw: *its only fault was . . .*
  7 *v.* find fault with: *you couldn't fault him*
5 **faultless** *adj.*
5 **faulty** *adj.*
5 **favour**
  5 *n.* act of kindness
  6 *n.* aid, support: *in favour of*
  6 *n.* friendly regard, willingness: *win a person's favour*
  6 *v.* support: *fortune favours the brave*
  6 *v.* treat with partiality
4 **favourable** *adj.*
3 **favourite**
  3 *adj.* preferred thing: *her favourite song*
  3 *n.* competitor expected to win in contest
  5 *n.* person receiving favours

3 **fear**
  3 *n.* emotion
  6 *v.* be afraid of
  7 *n.* in case: *for fear that*
5 **fearful**
  5 *adj.* extreme: *it's a fearful nuisance*
  6 *adj.* causing horror: *the shipwreck was a fearful experience*
  7 *adj.* frightened, apprehensive
5 **fearless** *adj.*
5 **feast**
  5 *n.* religious anniversary or festival
  5 *n.* splendid meal
  6 *v.* take part in a feast
  7 *n.* something that greatly satisfies the mind
3 **feather**
  3 *n.* bird's skin covering
  5 *adj.* made of feathers: *feather bed*
5 **feature**
  5 *n.* characteristic part: *the main feature of Iran is its elevation*
  6 *n.* article in newspaper (not news)
1 **February** *n.*
4 **fee** *n.* charge, payment
5 **feeble** *adj.*
2 **feed**
  2 *v.* give food to: *feed the rabbits*
  5 *v.* eat: *the cows were feeding in the meadow*
  6 *v.* supply with materials or fuel
  7 *n.* meal
2 **feel**
  2 *v.* be in certain state: *she felt ill*
  3 *v.* explore by touching: *it feels soft*
  3 *v.* be aware of, perceive: *can you feel the heat?*
  5 *v.* consider
  5 *v.* experience: *feel as if*
  7 *n.* sensation: *the feel of this material*
2 **feel like** *v.* be in the mood for
4 **feel up to** *v.* judge oneself capable of
3 **feeling**
  3 *n.* emotions
  6 *n.* power and capacity to feel sympathy/understanding
  6 *n.* taste: *a feeling for music*
5 **female** *n./adj.*

3 **fence**
  3 *n.* barrier
  7 *v.* fight with swords
5 **fertile**
  5 *adj.* producing much (of lands, people)
  6 *adj.* able to produce young
5 **festival**
  5 *n.* public celebrations
  5 *n.* series of performances
2 **fetch**
  2 *v.* go for and bring back
  6 *v.* cause to come out: *fetch tears to the eyes*
  7 *v.* bring in, sell for: *the books fetched £10*
5 **fever**
  5 *n.* high temperature: *a high fever*
  6 *n.* disease with high temperature: *rheumatic fever*
  7 *n.* nervous agitation: *in a fever of impatience*
5 **feverish** *adj.*
2 **few**
  2 *adj.* (with 'a') a small number of: *a few people*
  4 *adj.* not many, not so many as expected
4 **fiction**
  4 *n.* branch of literature
  7 *n.* something invented or imagined
1 **field**
  1 *n.* piece of land
  6 *n.* (usually in compounds) wide area or expanse: *sports field*
  6 *n.* (usually in compounds) area of land from which minerals are obtained: *coal-field*
  6 *v.* catch or stop: *he fielded the ball*
  6 *v.* put into play: *they are fielding a strong team*
  7 *n.* area of study or activity: *the field of politics*
3 **fierce**
  3 *adj.* violent, cruel: *a fierce ruler*
  4 *adj.* intense: *fierce heat*
1 **fifteen** *n./adj.*
2 **fifth** *adj.*
1 **fifty** *n./adj.*

2 **fight**
  2 *v.* use physical force
  2 *n.* struggle: *a good fight*
  6 *n.* desire or ability for fighting:
    they had lots of fight left in
    them
5 **fighter** *n.* person or thing that fights
3 **figure**
  3 *n.* shape of the body: *she has a*
    good figure
  4 *n.* symbol for a number: *figure 5*
  5 *n.* human form: *she saw a figure in*
    the shadows
  5 *n.* diagram: *a geometrical figure*
  6 *v.* have part in: *he figured in the*
    argument
  7 *n.* person in social setting: *an*
    important figure
  7 *n.* expression: *figure of speech*
5 **file**
  5 *n.* metal tool: *a nail file*
  5 *n.* container: *a file of papers*
  6 *v.* smooth: *file your nails*
  7 *v.* place on record: *file a complaint*
  7 *n.* line of people: *walk in file*
2 **fill**
  2 *v.* make full
  6 *n.* full supply: *eat one's fill*
2 **fill in** *v.* complete (a form)
4 **filling**
  4 *n.* contents: *pie filling*
  5 *n.* dental treatment: *she's to have*
    two fillings done
  6 *adj.* making full: *a filling meal*
2 **film**
  2 *n.* motion picture
  3 *n.* roll for use in photography
  5 *v.* make motion picture
  6 *n.* thin coating or covering: *a film of*
    dust
  7 *v.* cover: *her eyes filmed over*
4 **film-star** *n.*
5 **filter**
  5 *n.* straining device: *coffee filter*
  7 *v.* cause to flow through: *he filtered*
    the solution
  7 *v.* make a way: *the idea filtered*
    through
  7 *v.* (traffic) be allowed to pass

4 **final**
  4 *adj.* last in series: *the final chapter*
  4 *adj.* conclusive: *a final decision*
  5 *n.* last in series of contests: *the Cup*
    Final
  7 *n.* newspaper edition
4 **financial** *adj.*
1 **find**
  1 *v.* get back after a search: *did you*
    find your pen?
  2 *v.* discover: *he found a new*
    restaurant
  6 *v.* arrive at naturally: *water finds its*
    own level
  6 *v.* become aware of: *he was found*
    to be dishonest
  6 *n.* something found: *a great find*
3 **fine**
  3 *adj.* (of weather) bright: *a fine day*
  4 *adj.* enjoyable: *a fine view*
  5 *adj.* delicate: *fine silk*
  5 *adj.* of very fine particles: *fine*
    dust
  5 *adj.* slender, thin: *fine thread*
  5 *n.* penalty: *a parking fine*
  5 *v.* impose a penalty: *she was fined*
    £5
1 **finger**
  1 *n.* part of hand
  4 *v.* touch
  6 *n.* shape of finger: *fish fingers*
1 **finish**
  1 *v.* end, complete
  4 *n.* last part: *the finish of a race*
  6 *v.* make perfect: *the woodwork is*
    beautifully finished
  6 *n.* state of being perfect: *a smooth*
    finish
1 **fire**
  1 *n.* element: *fire and water*
  3 *v.* shoot: *fire a gun*
  6 *n.* strong emotion: *eyes full of fire*
  7 *v.* set fire to: *fire a haystack*
  7 *v.* use fuel: *fire a boiler*
5 **fireman** *n.*
5 **fireplace** *n.*
3 **firm**
  3 *adj.* not yielding: *firm ground*
  4 *n.* company, business

5 *adj.* showing strength of character: *a firm father*
5 **firmness** *n.*
1 **first**
  1 *adj.* leading in space or time
  7 *n.* class of degree: *a first in Maths*
3 **first-class** *adj.: first-class carriage*
5 **First World War** *n.*
1 **fish**
  1 *n.* cold-blooded animal
  2 *v.* catch fish: *go fishing*
5 **fisherman** *n.*
5 **fist** *n.*
2 **fit**
  2 *v.* be right size: *that coat doesn't fit*
  4 *v.* put in place: *to fit a lock*
  4 *adj.* right and proper: *fit for a King*
  5 *adj.* suitable: *not fit to eat*
  5 *adj.* in good health: *fit and well*
5 **fitness** *n.*
1 **five** *adj./n.*
1 **fix**
  2 *v.* make firm or fast
  4 *v.* decide: *they fixed the rent at . . .*
  4 *v.* arrange: *she's fixed a meeting for Friday*
  6 *v.* direct: *he fixed his attention on me*
5 **fixture**
  5 *n.* something fixed in place: *fixtures and fittings*
  7 *n.* date and time fixed for event: *a sporting fixture*
3 **flag**
  3 *n.* piece of cloth: *the British flag*
  6 *v.* become weak: *his strength flagged*
4 **flame**
  4 *n.* product of burning: *candle flame*
  5 *n.* blaze of light: *flames of sunset*
  6 *n.* passion: *flames of desire*
  6 *v.* blaze: *his anger flamed up again*
5 **flap**
  5 *v.* beat: *ducks flapping their wings*
  5 *n.* part for folding: *tuck the flap into the envelope*

3 **flash**
  3 *n.* sudden burst of flame or light: *flash of lightning*
  3 *v.* give out sudden bright light: *lightning flashed*
  5 *v.* come suddenly: *the idea flashed into his mind*
  5 *v.* send: *flash a signal*
  7 *n.* brief item of news: *a news flash*
  7 *v.* send or reflect: *her eyes flashed defiance*
5 **flash** *n.*
1 **flat**
  1 *adj.* smooth and level: *a flat top*
  3 *n.* suite of rooms
  4 *adj.* lying at full length: *flat on his back*
  5 *adj.* dull, uninteresting: *life is flat*
  5 *n.* flat part of anything: *the flat of his hand*
  6 *adj.* needing to be recharged: *the battery's flat*
  6 *adj.* having lost bubbles: *this soda's flat*
  7 *n.* not sharp: *the sonata in B flat*
  7 *adj.* absolute: *a flat refusal*
5 **flatten**
  5 *v.* destroy: *the village was flattened in the bombardment*
  7 *v.* vanquish: *her argument flattened him*
4 **flavour**
  4 *n.* distinctive taste: *a flavour of garlic*
  5 *n.* special quality or characteristic: *a flavour of romance*
  5 *v.* give a flavour to
5 **fleet** *n.* number of ships
5 **flesh**
  5 *n.* muscular tissue
  7 *n.* pulpy parts of fruit and vegetables
3 **flight**
  3 *n.* journey made by air
  5 *n.* flying through the air: *the art of flight*
  6 *n.* series of stairs: *a flight of stairs*
  7 *n.* number of objects moving together through the air: *a flight of arrows*

7 *n.* escape: *the Flight from Egypt*
3 **float**
   3 *v.* not sink: *to float on water/in air*
   4 *v.* cause to float: *float a raft*
   6 *v.* allow exchange value of currency
      to vary
   7 *v.* start with finance: *float a*
      company
   7 *n.* low platform on wheels used in
      processions
5 **flock**
   5 *n.* number of birds or animals
   6 *n.* crowd of people
   7 *v.* gather together
3 **flood**
   3 *n.* great quantity of water
   4 *v.* submerge an area
1 **floor**
   1 *n.* lower surface of rooms
   4 *n.* level of a building: *the 2nd floor*
   6 *v.* knock down: *he floored him in*
      the second round
   7 *n.* part of an assembly hall
3 **flour**
   3 *n.* fine meal made from grain
   6 *v.* cover or sprinkle with flour
3 **flow**
   3 *v.* move smoothly
   5 *v.* hang down loosely
   6 *v.* come from: *wealth flows from*
      industry
   7 *n.* quantity that flows: *the flow of*
      work
1 **flower**
   1 *n.* plant
   3 *v.* produce flowers (trees, plants)
4 **flue** *n.*
5 **fluent** *adj.*
1 **fly**
   1 *n.* insect
   1 *v.* move through the air
   3 *v.* control aircraft, transport
      goods/people by air
   6 *v.* go quickly: *time flies*
   7 *n.* flap of cloth on trousers: *your*
      fly's undone
4 **fog** *n.*
3 **fold**
   3 *v.* bend

4 *v.* cover, wrap
5 *n.* part that is folded: *the folds of a*
   dress
7 *v.* (cooking) mix: *fold the eggs into*
   the flour
5 **folksong** *n.*
1 **follow**
   1 *v.* come/go after: *he followed me*
   2 *v.* go along: *follow this road*
   4 *v.* understand: *I followed his*
      argument
   4 *v.* take, accept as a guide: *I followed*
      his advice
   6 *v.* be necessarily true: *it doesn't*
      follow that
   7 *v.* engage in as business or trade:
      follow the sea
5 **follower** *n.*
2 **fond**
   2 *adj.* keen: *he's fond of*
   4 *adj.* loving and kind: *a fond mother*
   7 *adj.* unlikely to be realised: *fond*
      hopes of a new job
1 **food** *n.*
2 **fool**
   2 *n.* person without much sense
   5 *v.* behave like a fool: *he fooled with*
      the gun
   5 *v.* cheat, deceive: *you don't fool*
      me
   6 *n.* jester
   7 *adj.* silly: *some fool politician*
   7 *n.* creamy dessert: *gooseberry fool*
4 **foolish** *adj.*
1 **foot/feet**
   1 *n.* part of body
   4 *n.* measure of length: *a foot high*
   6 *n.* lowest part: *foot of the page*
   6 *n.* lower end of a bed
   7 *n.* step: *light of foot*
   7 *n.* unit of verse
   7 *v.* pay: *I'll foot the bill*
1 **football** *n.*
4 **footpath** *n.*
4 **footstep** *n.*
1 **for**
   1 *prep.* direction: *set out for home*
   1 *prep.* eventual possession: *some*
      letters for you

1 *prep.* purpose: *get ready for an examination; what for?*

2 *prep.* purpose (with infinitive): *it's useless for him to go on*

2 *prep.* extent in time: *we'll be away for the whole of August*

2 *prep.* extent in space: *we walked for about 10 miles*

2 *prep.* representing: *C. for Christopher*

3 *prep.* aptitude, liking: *an ear for music*

3 *prep.* to the extent of: *put me down for £5*

4 *prep.* supporting: *are you for this party or not?*

4 *prep.* as a result of: *better for your long sleep*

5 *prep.* in view of: *it's quite warm for January*

5 *prep.* with regard to: *hard up for money*

5 *conj.* since: *the book isn't ready yet, for the revision has still to be done*

3 **forbid** *v.*

3 **force**
   3 *n.* strength: *the force of the explosion*
   4 *n.* armed body of men: *Air Force*
   4 *v.* compel
   5 *n.* pressure exerted at a point
   6 *n.* person/thing that makes great changes: *a force for good*
   6 *n.* authority: *put a law into force*
   7 *v.* produce under stress: *he forced a smile*

5 **forecast** *v./n.*

5 **forehead** *n.*

2 **foreign**
   2 *adj.* from another country
   5 *adj.* not natural to: *foreign to his nature*
   6 *adj.* coming from outside: *a foreign body*

3 **foreigner** *n.*

2 **forest**
   2 *n.* area covered with trees
   6 *n.* (fig.): *a forest of masts*

1 **forget**
   1 *v.* not remember
   5 *v.* put out of mind: *forget our quarrels*
   6 *v.* behave thoughtlessly: *he forgot himself*

5 **forgetful** *adj.*

3 **forgive**
   3 *v.* pardon
   7 *v.* not demand payment: *he forgave the debt*

1 **fork**
   1 *n.* utensil for eating
   3 *n.* gardening tool
   5 *n.* place where road divides
   5 *v.* divide into branches: *the road forks after a mile*
   6 *v.* move with a fork: *fork hay*

2 **form**
   2 *n.* printed paper to be filled in: *income tax form*
   3 *n.* diagram: *in the form of a triangle*
   4 *v.* organise: *form a class*
   4 *n.* variant: *this verb has two forms*
   4 *v.* give shape to, make: *form a sentence*
   5 *v.* build up: *she formed his character*
   6 *n.* condition of health or training: *in good form*
   6 *n.* class in school: *sixth form*
   6 *v.* come into existence: *the idea formed in his mind*
   7 *n.* manner of behaviour: *good form*
   7 *n.* long wooden bench

5 **formal**
   5 *adj.* in accordance with custom: *formal dress*
   6 *adj.* geometric in design: *a formal garden*
   7 *adj.* of outward shape or appearance: *a formal resemblance*

3 **former**
   3 *adj.* of an earlier period
   5 *adj.* the first mentioned of two

4 **formula**
   4 *n.* statement of rule in signs or numbers

6 *n.* form of words: *the formula used in the treaty*

3 **fortnight** *n.*

3 **fortunately** *adv.*

5 **fortune**
  5 *n.* chance, good or bad
  5 *n.* great sum of money

1 **forty** *adj./n.*

5 **forward/s**
  5 *adj.* directed towards the front: *a forward movement*
  5 *adv.* onwards: *move forwards*
  6 *v.* send a letter on to a new address: *she forwarded my mail*
  7 *v.* help to advance: *forward someone's plans*

4 **foundation**
  4 *n.* something that is founded: *the Ford Foundation*
  5 *n.* establishing: *the foundation of the school*
  5 *n.* strong base of a building
  6 *n.* underlying principle: *the foundation of his belief*
  7 *adj.* support: *foundation garment*
  7 *adj.* basic: *foundation cream*

3 **fountain**
  3 *n.* spring of water
  7 *n.* (fig.) source or origin: *the fountain of knowledge*

1 **four** *adj./n.*

1 **fourteen** *adj./n.*

2 **fourth** *adj.*

3 **fox** *n.*

5 **frame**
  5 *n.* border: *picture frame*
  5 *v.* put border around: *frame a picture*
  6 *n.* skeleton or main structure
  7 *n.* structure to protect plants from bad weather
  7 *n.* single exposure on a roll of film

5 **framework** *n.*

1 **France** *n.*

4 **frank**
  4 *adj.* open
  6 *v.* mark stamp: *it franks the letters*

2 **free**
  2 *adj.* preserving freedom

3 *adj.* not fixed/held back: *feel free*

4 *adj.* without: *free from blame*

4 *adj.* available without payment: *free entry*

4 *adj.* not occupied or engaged: *a free room*

4 *v.* set at liberty

7 *adj.* lavish: *he is free with his advice*

7 *adj.* without constraint: *he is free in his conversation*

4 **freedom** *n.*

3 **freeze**
  3 *v.* become ice: *the lake froze*
  4 *v.* feel very cold: *I'm freezing*
  4 *v.* preserve by freezing (food)
  6 *n.* period of frozen weather
  7 *n.* severe control of movement in economics or politics
  7 *v.* (economic) make assets unrealisable

5 **freezer** *n.*

1 **French** *n./adj.*

2 **Frenchman** *n.*

5 **French Revolution, the** *n.*

5 **frequency** *n.*

3 **frequent** *adj.*

2 **fresh**
  2 *adj.* newly made/grown: *fresh vegetables*
  3 *adj.* food not salted/tinned/frozen: *fresh food*
  5 *adj.* new, different: *fresh news*
  5 *adj.* (of weather) cool, refreshing: *a fresh breeze*
  6 *adj.* bright and pure: *fresh colours*

5 **freshen** *v.*

5 **friction**
  5 *n.* rubbing one thing against another
  7 *n.* difference of opinion

1 **Friday** *n.*

2 **fridge** *n.*

1 **friend**
  1 *n.* person liked
  3 *n.* helper: *a friend of the poor*
  6 *n.* helpful things: *a pipe is a man's best friend*

2 **friendly** *adj.*

3 **friendship**
  3 *n.* being friends

5 *n.* period of being friends: *a friendship of twenty years*
5 **fright** *n.* a great fear
3 **frighten** *v.*
5 **frightful**
  5 *adj.* causing fear: *a frightful accident*
  5 *adj.* awful: *a frightful journey*
5 **frightfully** *adv.* very
1 **from**
  1 *prep.* movement from: *go from London to Rome*
  1 *prep.* distance from: *be away from home*
  1 *prep.* interval in time: *from twelve o'clock to two*
  1 *prep.* point of origin: *a letter from my sister*
  2 *prep.* lower limit: *cheese from 80p per pound*
  3 *prep.* deprivation, release: *take that knife (away) from the baby*
  4 *prep.* distinction: *tell a mouse from a rat*
  4 *prep.* cause: *suffer from disease*
1 **front**
  1 *adj.* foremost: *the front page*
  1 *prep.:* *in front of*
  1 *n.* foremost side: *the front of the building*
  2 *n.* foremost part: *front of the train*
  5 *n.* (war) place where fighting is taking place: *western front*
  5 *v.* face: *hotels that front the sea*
  6 *n.* road facing the sea: *sea front*
  7 *n.* boundary between masses of cold and warm air: *cold front*
4 **frontier**
  4 *n.* border: *the frontier between Spain and France*
  6 *n.* (fig.) extreme limit: *frontiers of knowledge*
5 **frost**
  5 *n.* weather conditions: *10 degrees of frost*
  5 *n.* powder-like covering: *white frost*
  6 *v.* become covered with frost
  7 *v.* give roughened surface to the glass

4 **frown** *n./v.*
1 **fruit**
  1 *n.* food from trees/bushes
  7 *n.* plants in general used for food: *the fruits of the earth*
  7 *n.* (fig.) rewards: *the fruits of labour*
5 **fruitful** *adj.*
3 **fry** *v.*
3 **fuel**
  3 *n.* material for producing energy
  6 *v.* supply with or obtain fuel
5 **fulfil** *v.*
1 **full**
  1 *adj.* completely filled
  5 *adj.* occupied with: *full of the news*
  5 *adj.* reaching maximum: *in full bloom*
  5 *adj.* complete: *the full amount*
  6 *adj.* rounded: *a full face*
  6 *adj.* having material arranged in wide folds: *a full skirt*
5 **fully** *adv.*
3 **fun**
  3 *n.* amusement: *what fun!*
  5 *n.* amusing: *your friend is great fun*
  7 *adj.* used for amusement: *a fun hat*
4 **function**
  4 *n.* activities or purpose of person or thing: *the functions of a judge*
  6 *n.* public ceremony
4 **funds** *n.(pl.)*
4 **funeral**
  4 *n.* burial or cremation
  5 *adj.* of or for a funeral: *funeral music*
1 **funny**
  1 *adj.* causing amusement
  4 *adj.* strange
3 **fur**
  3 *n.* soft hair of animals
  5 *n.* animal skin with the fur on
  7 *n.* coating on tongue
4 **furnish** *v.*
3 **furniture** *n.*
3 **further**
  3 *adv.* farther: *go further*
  4 *adj.* more: *further information*
  5 *adj.* another: *a further point to be made*

6 *adv.* moreover
6 *v.* promote: *he furthered his interests*
3 **furthest** *adj./adv.*
5 **fuse**
    5 *n.* part of electric circuit
    5 *v.* be broken: *the light fused*
    7 *n.* cord to explosive

7 *v.* join two pieces of wire together using heat
7 *v.* (fig.) make into one whole: *these ideas fused in the revolution*
3 **future**
    3 *adj.* to come
    3 *n.* what is to come

G

3 **gain**
    3 *v.* obtain: *gain experience/time/money*
    4 *v.* increase: *she's gained 5 kilos*
    5 *v.* go fast: *his watch gained 10 minutes*
    6 *v.* reach with effort: *Labour gained all their objectives*
    7 *n.* increase in possessions: *the love of gain*
4 **gallon** *n.*
1 **game**
    1 *n.* fun: *it's just a game*
    2 *n.* form of play with rules: *the game of tennis*
    5 *n.* athletic contest: *Olympic games*
    5 *n.* single round in contest: *he won four games in the first set*
    6 *n.* scheme, plan: *what is his game?*
    7 *n.* animals and birds hunted for sport: *big game*
5 **gang**
    5 *n.* group of people associating together
    6 *n.* group of workmen: *a road gang*
5 **gangway**
    5 *n.* passage between row of seats
    6 *n.* bridge from ship to shore
5 **gap**
    5 *n.* opening in space: *a gap in the fence*
    6 *n.* time interval: *a gap in the conversation*

7 *n.* conceptual interval: *credibility/generation gap*
3 **garage**
    3 *n.* building to keep a car in
    4 *n.* service station
    5 *v.* put a car in a garage
1 **garden**
    1 *n.* piece of ground for growing flowers or vegetables
    3 *v.* cultivate
2 **gardener** *n.*
3 **gas**
    3 *n.* substance used for heating and lighting
    6 *n.* (US) petrol
    7 *v.* make unconscious with gas, kill by so doing
5 **gasp**
    5 *v.* struggle for breath
    6 *v.* utter in a breathless way: *he gasped out a few words*
2 **gate** *n.*
5 **gate-post** *n.*
5 **gateway**
    5 *n.* way in or out
    7 *n.* (fig.) means of approach
3 **gather**
    3 *v.* collect: *she gathered flowers/books*
    4 *v.* join together: *a crowd gathered*
    5 *v.* obtain gradually: *she gathered experience*

7 *v.* understand: *I gathered he was unhappy*

3 **gay**
    3 *adj.* cheerful
    4 *adj.* (colloq.) homosexual
    6 *adj.* loose: *a gay life*

5 **gear**
    5 *n.* part of a car: *change gear*
    6 *n.* mechanism: *landing gear*
    7 *n.* equipment in general: *hunting gear*

3 **general**
    3 *adj.* affecting everyone: *the general interest*
    4 *adj.* not detailed/specific: *a general outline/degree*
    5 *n.* soldier

3 **generous**
    3 *adj.* given freely: *generous with money*
    5 *adj.* plentiful: *a generous helping*

3 **gentle**
    3 *adj.* not rough: *a gentle voice*
    7 *adj.* with a good social position

3 **gentleman**
    3 *n.* any man of any social position: *a gentleman called to see you*
    4 *n.* man of wealth and social position
    5 *n.* honourable man: *a true gentleman*
    6 *n.* (old use) man attached to the court

5 **gentleness** *n.*

5 **gents**
    5 *n.* WC
    6 *adj.* male: *a gents outfitters*

4 **genuine** *adj.*

5 **geographical** *adj.*

4 **geography** *n.*

5 **geometrical** *adj.*

5 **geometry** *n.*

1 **German** *n./adj.*

2 **German** *n.* (nat.)

1 **Germany** *n.*

1 **get**
    1 *v.* become: *they got wet*
    1 *v.* receive: *he got that for Christmas*
    2 *v.* possess: *we've got an old Volvo*
    3 *v.* arrive: *when did you get here?*

3 *v.* bring to a condition: *she got the children ready*

4 *v.* reach a stage: *get to know the manager; get it done*

4 *v.* move: *can you get over that wall?*

5 *v.* cause (with infinitive): *you won't get him to understand*

4 **get across** *v.* communicate

3 **get along with** *v.* manage to live together with

4 **get (a)round**
    4 *v.* overcome, circumvent (a problem)
    4 *v.* become known (within a group)

3 **get at**
    3 *v.* reach, gain access to
    5 *v.* suggest

3 **get away** *v.* leave

4 **get away with**
    4 *v.* escape with stolen goods
    5 *v.* go unpunished

2 **get back**
    2 *v.* return
    3 *v.* recover possession of

3 **get by**
    3 *v.* manage to pass
    4 *v.* survive

2 **get down**
    2 *v.* descend
    3 *v.* write quickly
    3 *v.* leave the table (of children): *may I get down, please?*
    5 *v.* demoralise: *this wet weather gets me down*

2 **get in**
    2 *v.* enter (vehicle)
    4 *v.* collect

2 **get off**
    2 *v.* alight from
    3 *v.* remove (clothing)
    4 *v.* (cause to) leave
    5 *v.* (cause to) escape injury/punishment

2 **get on**
    2 *v.* put on (clothing)
    3 *v.* progress

3 **get on with**
    3 *v.* make progress with
    4 *v.* manage to work/live with

4 **get out** *v.* leave (bounded space)
4 **get out of**
   4 *v.* leave (place, situation)
   4 *v.* derive
   5 *v.* avoid
4 **get over**
   4 *v.* recover from
   5 *v.* make clear
5 **get round to** *v.* have time for
4 **get through**
   4 *v.* pass (a test)
   4 *v.* make contact (by phone)
   5 *v.* consume, master
3 **get together** *v.* meet, assemble
2 **get up**
   2 *v.* rise (from bed)
   3 *v.* climb
3 **get up to** *v.* reach
4 **giant**
   4 *adj.* of great size or force: *a giant caterpillar*
   5 *n.* man of great height
4 **gift**
   4 *n.* something given: *a Christmas gift*
   6 *n.* natural ability or talent: *a gift for music*
1 **girl**
   1 *n.* female
   4 *n.* maidservant: *a girl to work in the house*
   4 *n.* worker in a shop: *a salesgirl*
1 **give**
   1 *v.* hand over to keep: *I gave him a book for his birthday*
   1 *v.* entrust for a time: *give the porter your bag*
   2 *v.* exchange, pay: *he paid £100 for that painting*
   3 *v.* emit: *she gave a long sigh*
   6 *v.* yield under pressure: *that chair gives under my weight*
   6 *n.* quality of elasticity
5 **give away** *v.* betray, reveal
2 **give back** *v.* return
4 **give in**
   2 *v.* hand in
   4 *v.* yield
2 **give out** *v.* distribute

4 **give up**
   4 *v.* stop doing (smoking)
   5 *v.* surrender
3 **glad**
   3 *adj.* pleased: *I'm glad*
   6 *adj.* causing joy: *glad news*
2 **glance**
   2 *v.* look at
   2 *n.* quick look
   7 *v.* shine: *their helmets glanced in the sunlight*
1 **glass**
   1 *n.* brittle substance
   1 *n.* container
2 **glasses**
   2 *n.(pl.)* spectacles
   7 *n.(pl.)* binoculars
4 **glimpse** *n. /v.*
5 **glory**
   5 *n.* honour, something deserving honour
   6 *v.* rejoice in
3 **glove** *n.*
4 **glow**
   4 *v.* send out brightness
   5 *v.* (fig.) be warm, flushed
   5 *n.* glowing state
4 **glue** *n. /v.*
1 **go**
   1 *v.* move in space: *go by train; go home*
   2 *v.* be placed: *where do the coats go?*
   3 *v.* fit inside: *this box won't go in the boot*
   3 *v.* work: *this watch won't go any more*
   4 *v.* extend: *money doesn't go far these days*
   4 *v.* become: *the apples have gone bad*
   5 *v.* fail: *my hearing is going*
   6 *n.* energy: *there's plenty of go in him still*
2 **go after** *v.* pursue
2 **go by** *v.* pass
5 **go down with** *v.* become ill with
3 **go for** *v.* go to fetch
5 **go in for**
   5 *v.* practise (profession)

5 *v.* enter (a competition)
3 **go off**
   3 *v.* leave, start
   3 *v.* stop working (power supplies)
   3 *v.* explode (gun, fireworks)
   4 *v.* go bad (milk, meat)
2 **go on**
   2 *v.* continue
   2 *v.* happen: *what's going on?*
   2 *v.* be lit
   5 *v.* be spent on
2 **go out**
   2 *v.* stop burning (fire)
   5 *v.* ebb
4 **go over** *v.* examine
5 **go through**
   5 *v.* endure
   5 *v.* examine
3 **go under** *v.* sink
3 **go with**
   3 *v.* be part of
   4 *v.* match, suit
5 **go without** *v.* endure lack of, manage
3 **goal**
   3 *n.* point scored in game
   4 *n.* posts
   6 *n.* object of ambition
3 **goat** *n.*
2 **God** *n.*
5 **goddess** *n.*
2 **gold**
   2 *n.* precious metal
   4 *adj.* colour of metal
   5 *n.* brilliant or precious thing
5 **golden**
   5 *adj.* of gold: *golden hair*
   6 *adj.* precious: *a golden opportunity*
5 **goldsmith** *n.*
5 **golf** *n.*
1 **good**
   1 *adj.* pleasing, suitable etc.
   4 *adj.* skilful: *good at drawing*
5 **Good Friday** *n.*
1 **goodbye** *int.*
3 **goodness**
   3 *n.* quality
   5 *int.* of mild surprise
1 **goodnight** *int.*

3 **goods** *n.(pl.)*
5 **goose/geese** *n.*
4 **gossip**
   4 *v.* talk about local matters
   6 *n.* hearsay
4 **govern**
   4 *v.* rule: *govern the state*
   6 *v.* control: *he governed his temper*
   7 *v.* determine, influence: *he is governed by the opinions of others*
2 **government**
   2 *n.* method of rule: *democratic government*
   4 *n.* ministry: *his son is in the Government*
4 **grace**
   4 *n.* gracefulness: *she danced with grace*
   5 *n.* favour, goodwill: *an act of grace*
   6 *n.* behaviour: *do something with good/bad grace*
   7 *n.* prayer: *he said grace*
5 **graceful** *adj.*
4 **grade**
   4 *n.* degree in rank/value
   4 *n.* mark: *he got an A grade in Maths*
   5 *v.* arrange in graded order
3 **grain**
   3 *n.* food plant: *a cargo of grain*
   4 *n.* single seed of such plant: *a few grains of rice*
   5 *n.* small particle: *a grain of sand*
   6 *n.* (fig.) element: *a grain of truth*
   7 *n.* pattern of lines in e.g. wood: *a beautiful grain*
5 **gram/gramme** *n.*
4 **grammar**
   4 *n.* rule of language
   6 *adj.* type of curriculum: *grammar school*
4 **grammatical** *adj.*
5 **gramophone** *n.*
4 **grand**
   4 *adj.* fine: *they had a grand holiday*
   4 *adj.* magnificent: *a grand dinner*
   5 *adj.* most important: *the Grand Finale*
   6 *adj.* self-important: *grand airs*

6 *adj.* full, complete: *the grand total*
3 **grandchild** *n.*
3 **granddaughter** *n.*
1 **grandfather** *n.*
1 **grandmother** *n.*
4 **grandparent** *n.*
3 **grandson** *n.*
4 **grant**
  4 *v.* consent: *she granted his request*
  6 *v.* agree: *I grant he is honest*
  6 *n.* money: *university grant*
5 **grape** *n.*
5 **graph** *n.*
4 **grasp**
  4 *v.* seize firmly
  5 *v.* understand
  5 *n.* hold, grip: *in the grasp of the enemy*
1 **grass** *n.*
5 **grassy** *adj.*
3 **grateful** *adj.*
4 **grave**
  4 *n.* burial plot
  6 *adj.* serious
5 **grease**
  5 *n.* melted animal fat
  5 *v.* smear
  6 *n.* an oily substance
3 **great**
  3 *adj.* of remarkable ability / character: *a great man*
  4 *adj.* above average: *a great friend*
  4 *adj.* (colloq.) good, enjoyable: *a great time*
  6 *adj.* noted, important: *a great lady*
3 **greatly** *adv.*
4 **greatness** *n.*
5 **greed** *n.*
4 **greedy**
  4 *adj.* wanting too much food
  6 *adj.* desirous: *greedy for power*
1 **green**
  1 *adj.* colour
  4 *n.(pl.)* vegetables
  5 *adj.* (of fruit) not yet ripe
  7 *adj.* (fig.) inexperienced: *he's still green at his job*
4 **greengrocer** *n.*

3 **greet**
  3 *v.* say words of welcome
  7 *v.* (of sights and sounds) meet the eyes and ears: *the view that greeted us*
3 **greeting** *n.*
1 **grey** *n. / adj.*
5 **grill**
  5 *n.* part of a cooker
  5 *v.* cook: *grill steak*
  6 *n.* dish of meat cooked by grilling: *a mixed grill*
  6 *n.* a place where grills are served: *the Grill Room*
  7 *v.* question closely: *he was grilled by the police*
5 **grind**
  5 *v.* crush: *he ground the coffee*
  6 *v.* oppress: *people ground by taxation*
  7 *v.* polish: *grind a lens*
  7 *v.* work hard: *grind for his exam*
  7 *n.* long monotonous task: *the daily grind*
4 **grip**
  4 *v.* hold tightly
  5 *n.* bag
1 **grocer** *n.*
1 **ground**
  1 *n.* surface of the earth: *lie on the ground*
  3 *n.* soil, earth: *the frost has made the ground hard*
  4 *n.* area of land for special purpose: *cricket ground*
  5 *n.(pl.)* land / gardens round a building: *school grounds*
  6 *n.* (fig.) area: *they covered a lot of ground*
  6 *n.(pl.)* reason: *on what grounds?*
  6 *v.* force to stay on the ground: *the plane was grounded*
  6 *v.* provide basis of knowledge: *the teacher grounded them in algebra*
  7 *n.* surface on which a design is painted: *pink roses on a white ground*
1 **group**
  1 *n.* collection

3 *v.* form into collection
1 **grow**
    1 *v.* develop, increase: *how you've grown*
    4 *v.* become: *it grew dark*
    5 *v.* cause to grow: *he grows roses*
5 **growl**
    5 *v.* make a low, threatening sound: *the dog growled*
    5 *n.* low sound
    6 *v.* say in a growling manner: *don't growl at me*
5 **grown-up** *n./adj.*
4 **growth**
    4 *n.* growing, development: *the growth of the economy*
    5 *n.* cultivation: *the growth of apples*
    6 *n.* something that has grown: *a thick growth of weeds*
    7 *n.* diseased formation in the body: *a cancerous growth*
5 **guarantee**
    5 *n.* undertaking
    5 *v.* promise: *I guarantee to finish by noon*
    7 *n.* responsibility for a debt: *he gave a guarantee on behalf of his friend*
3 **guard**
    3 *n.* soldier, sentry
    4 *v.* protect
    4 *n.* warder in prison

4 *n.* official on a train
5 *n.* apparatus designed to prevent injury: *mud-guard; fire-guard*
6 *n.* state of watchfulness: *be on your guard*
3 **guess** *n./v.*
3 **guest** *n.*
2 **guide**
    2 *n.* person showing the way
    3 *n.* book: *a Guide to London*
    4 *v.* direct
    5 *n.* something that directs or influences: *instinct is not always a good guide*
5 **guilt** *n.*
3 **guilty**
    3 *adj.* having done wrong: *the guilty man*
    4 *adj.* showing or feeling guilt: *a guilty look*
5 **guitar** *n.*
5 **gulf**
    5 *n.* part of sea: *Gulf of Mexico*
    7 *n.* (fig.) division: *the gulf between the estranged couple*
4 **gum**
    4 *n.* type of sweet: *chewing gum*
    5 *n.* sticky substance from some trees
    6 *n.* flesh where teeth are
    6 *n.* rubber: *gum-boots*
1 **gun** *n.*
5 **gunpowder** *n.*

H

3 **habit**
    3 *n.* settled practice: *the habit of smoking*
    5 *n.* usual behaviour: *habit is second nature*
    7 *n.* (old) condition: *a cheerful habit of mind*
1 **hair** *n.*
4 **hairbrush** *n.*
2 **haircut** *n.*

4 **hairdresser** *n.*
3 **hairdrier** *n.*
1 **half**
    1 *adj.* one of two equal parts: *half a pound*
    2 *n.* one of two equal parts: *a half of my apple*
    3 *adv.* to the extent of a half: *half cooked*

3 **hall**
  3 *n.* passage where main entrance of a building opens
  4 *n.* large room for meetings/concerts etc.: *Town Hall*
  6 *n.* country house: *Hindlesham Hall*
  7 *n.* building for university students: *St George's Hall*
1 **hallo** *int.*
5 **halt**
  5 *n.* stop, pause: *he called a halt*
  5 *v.* come to a stop
  6 *v.* hesitate: *halt between two opinions*
4 **halve**
  4 *v.* divide into two equal parts
  5 *v.* lessen by a half
2 **hammer**
  2 *n.* tool
  4 *v.* strike or beat
  6 *n.* part of the piano
  7 *n.* part of firing device of a gun
  7 *n.* mallet used by auctioneer
  7 *v.* (fig.) produce by hard work: *they hammered out a scheme*
1 **hand**
  1 *n.* part of the body
  4 *v.* pass
  5 *n.* person from whom news etc. comes: *at first hand*
  5 *n.* pointer on a clock: *the second hand*
  6 *n.* person good at something: *an old hand at this*
  6 *n.* workman: *all hands on deck*
  6 *n.* share in an activity: *he had a hand in this proposal*
  6 *n.* position or direction: *on either hand*
  7 *n.* (in cards) number of cards dealt to a player
3 **hand in** *v.* submit
4 **hand on** *v.* pass to next person/group/generation
2 **hand out** *v.* distribute
4 **hand over** *v.* surrender something/someone
4 **handbag** *n.*

5 **handful**
  5 *n.* what can be held in the hand
  6 *n.* small number: *only a handful of people attended the meeting*
3 **handkerchief** *n.*
2 **handle**
  2 *n.* lever: *a door handle*
  4 *v.* touch: *explosives are dangerous to handle*
  5 *v.* control: *the teacher can't handle the class*
  6 *v.* treat: *she handled him badly*
  7 *v.* (commercial) buy and sell: *they don't handle those goods*
3 **handout** *n.*
4 **handshake** *n.*
4 **handsome**
  4 *adj.* goodlooking: *a handsome man*
  6 *adj.* generous: *a handsome present*
4 **handwriting** *n.*
4 **handy**
  4 *adj.* useful: *a handy present*
  5 *adv.* not far away: *keep a plaster handy*
  6 *adj.* good with his hands: *a handyman*
2 **hang**
  2 *v.* support: *hang a picture*
  4 *v.* put to death: *he was hanged for murder*
  6 *v.* equivalent of damn: *I'll be hanged if I know*
  7 *v.* put up: *hang wallpaper/a door etc.*
4 **hang about** *v.* wait idly
5 **hang back** *v.* hesitate
3 **hang on**
  3 *v.* wait
  4 *v.* grip firmly
4 **hang on to** *v.* retain
3 **hang up** *v.* end telephone conversation
2 **happen**
  2 *v.* take place: *what happened?*
  4 *v.* chance: *I happened to meet him*
1 **happy**
  1 *adj.* feeling/giving pleasure
  3 *adj.* fortunate, lucky

5 *adj.* pleased: *I am happy to accept the invitation*
6 *adj.* well-suited: *a happy thought*
4 **happiness** *n.*
3 **harbour**
  3 *n.* port
  6 *n.* any place of shelter
  7 *v.* protect, conceal
1 **hard**
  1 *adj.* not soft
  3 *adj.* difficult
  4 *adj.* causing pain/unhappiness: *a hard time*
  4 *adv.* with great energy: *work hard*
  4 *adv.* severely: *it is raining hard*
  5 *adj.* severe, harsh: *a hard father*
  6 *adv.* with a struggle: *hard-earned money*
5 **harden** *v.*
2 **hardly**
  2 *adv.* only just: *she could hardly walk*
  3 *adv.* almost not: *hardly ever*
  5 *adv.* severely: *hardly treated*
  6 *adv.* (suggesting improbability): *you can hardly mean that*
  7 *conj.* scarcely: *hardly had she entered when the child began . . .*
5 **hardness** *n.*
5 **hardware** *n.*
5 **harm**
  5 *n.* damage, injury
  5 *v.* cause injury
5 **harmful** *adj.*
5 **harmless** *adj.*
4 **harmony**
  4 *n.* pleasing combination of sounds/colours
  5 *n.* agreement of interests
3 **harvest**
  3 *n.* gathering in of crops
  3 *v.* gather in crops
  6 *n.* (fig.) consequences of action or behaviour: *reap the harvest of hard negotiations*
5 **hasty**
  5 *adj.* quick: *a hasty decision*
  7 *adj.* quick-tempered
1 **hat** *n.*
3 **hate** *v./n.*

5 **hateful** *adj.*
1 **have**
  1 *aux.*: *I haven't seen him; he hasn't gone yet*
  1 *v.* possess: *they have a house in Woking*
  2 *modal* obligation: *do you have to go already?*
  2 *v.* take: *have a drink*
  3 *v.* undergo: *he usually has colds in winter*
  4 *v.* cause: *have your hair cut*
3 **have back** *v.* have something returned
3 **have in** *v.* have people in one's home
2 **have on** *v.* be dressed in
4 **have round** *v.* have visitors to one's home
4 **hay** *n.*
1 **he** *pron.*
1 **head**
  1 *n.* part of the body
  2 *v.* use the head in sport: *head the ball*
  3 *n.* top: *at the head of the page*
  3 *v.* be at the top: *his name headed the list*
  3 *n.* leading position: *the head of this organisation*
  3 *v.* lead: *he headed the athletics team*
  4 *n.* talent: *a good head for figures*
  4 *v.* moving in direction: *they were heading south*
  5 *n.* unit (people and animals): *cattle cheap at £80 a head*
4 **headache** *n.*
4 **heading** *n.*
4 **headline** *n.*
5 **headlong**
  5 *adv.* with the head first: *to fall headlong*
  7 *adj.* hasty: *a headlong decision*
5 **headmaster** *n.*
5 **headquarters** *n.*
4 **heal**
  4 *v.* (of wounds) become healthy
  5 *v.* cure
2 **health** *n.*
3 **healthy**
  3 *adj.* having good health

4 *adj.* likely to produce good health: *a healthy climate*
5 *adj.* showing good health: *a healthy appetite*
4 **heap** *v./n.*
1 **hear**
  1 *v.* perceive sound
  3 *v.* be told, informed: *have you heard the news?*
  6 *v.* listen to: *hear what he has to say*
2 **heart**
  2 *n.* part of the body
  3 *n.* centre of the emotions: *a man with a kind heart*
  4 *n.* central part: *the heart of the matter*
  6 *n.* suit of playing cards
2 **heat**
  2 *n.* hotness
  4 *v.* make hot
  5 *n.* (fig.) intense feeling: *in the heat of argument*
  6 *n.* competition: *preliminary heats*
  7 *n.* period of condition of sexual excitement in animals: *on heat*
4 **heater** *n.*
4 **heating** *n.*
3 **heaven**
  3 *n.* opposite of hell
  5 *n.* state of extreme happiness
  6 *n.* the firmament: *the broad expanse of heaven*
  7 *n.* god, providence: *heaven forbid*
1 **heavy**
  1 *adj.* not light (weight)
  4 *adj.* more than usual: *heavy rain*
  6 *adj.* slow, tedious: *he found the going heavy*
3 **hedge**
  3 *n.* bush forming a boundary
  4 *v.* put a barrier around
  7 *n.* (fig.) defence against possible loss: *a hedge against inflation*
  7 *v.* secure oneself against loss
5 **heel**
  5 *n.* part of the human foot
  7 *n.* cad
3 **height**
  3 *n.* measurement: *what is his height?*

5 *n.* high part: *the heights of the mountain*
6 *n.* utmost degree: *the height of fashion*
5 **heighten** *v.*
3 **hell**
  3 *n.* (in religion) place of punishment
  4 *n.* (colloq.) to intensify a meaning: *what the hell do you want?*
  5 *n.* place/condition of great suffering: *that journey was hell*
1 **hello** *int.*
1 **help**
  1 *n.* act of helping
  2 *n.* something that helps
  3 *v.* aid
  4 *v.* desist from: *she can't help crying*
  6 *n.* remedy: *there's no help for it*
  6 *n.* girl who helps in the house: *a home help*
4 **helper** *n.*
3 **helpful** *adj.*
5 **helping** *n.* portion: *a second helping of pudding*
5 **helpless** *adj.*
5 **hen** *n.*
1 **her** *pron.*
1 **here**
  1 *adv.* in/at this point, hither
  3 *adv.* (in initial position): *here comes the bus*
3 **hero**
  3 *n.* boy or man respected for bravery
  5 *n.* chief man in poem, play etc.
2 **hers** *pron.*
2 **herself**
  2 *pron.* (reflexive): *she hurt herself*
  3 *pron.* (emphatic): *she herself told me*
  5 *pron.* in normal state: *she's not quite herself*
4 **hesitate** *v.*
5 **hesitation** *n.*
5 **hey** *int.*
2 **hi** *int.*
2 **hide**
  2 *v.* conceal
  5 *n.* animal skin
  7 *n.* place to observe birds
5 **hi-fi** *n.*

1 **high**
  1 *adj./adv.* extending far upwards: *a kite high in the sky*
  3 *adj.* at one end of scale: *high prices; a high note*
  5 *adj.* elevated: *a high official; high ideals*
  6 *adj.* intoxicated (alcohol or drugs)
5 **highland** *n.*
3 **highly** *adv.*
5 **highroad** *n.*
5 **highway** *n.*
5 **hijack** *n./v.*
1 **hill**
  1 *n.* small mountain: *the Chiltern hills*
  3 *n.* slope: *a steep hill*
5 **hillside** *n.*
1 **him** *pron.*
2 **himself**
  2 *pron.* (reflexive): *he cut himself*
  3 *pron.* (emphatic): *he says so himself*
  5 *pron.* normal state: *he's not quite himself*
5 **hinder** *v.*
5 **hindrance** *n.*
5 **Hindu** *n./adj.*
3 **hire**
  3 *v.* rent
  4 *n.* hiring: *for hire; hire purchase*
1 **his** *pron.*
5 **historical** *adj.*
3 **history**
  3 *n.* branch of knowledge dealing with past events
  4 *n.* orderly descriptions of past events: *a history of Europe*
  5 *n.* train of events: *life history*
2 **hit**
  2 *v.* strike
  4 *v.* find, reach: *hit the headlines*
  5 *n.* stroke in game: *8 hits at the ball*
  5 *n.* successful attempt or performance: *a hit song; the hit parade*
  6 *v.* score: *he hit 70 before lunch*
  7 *n.* criticism: *that was a hit at me*
5 **hitch-hike** *v.*
5 **hobby** *n.*

1 **hold**
  1 *v.* grasp: *holding an umbrella*
  2 *v.* maintain position: *hold your arms up*
  3 *v.* contain: *this carton holds one litre*
  4 *v.* restrain: *the police couldn't hold the crowd*
  4 *v.* support: *this hook won't hold such a weight*
  4 *n.* control: *she lost her hold over him*
  5 *n.* store: *a ship's hold*
  6 *v.* maintain grip: *that car holds the road well*
4 **hold back** *v.* restrain, withhold
5 **hold in** *v.* restrain
3 **hold on** *v.* wait, keep in position
3 **hold on to** *v.* keep, keep hold of
4 **hold out** *v.* last, remain
4 **hold up** *v.* delay
3 **holder**
  3 *n.* gadget: *cigarette holder*
  5 *n.* possessor: *the holder of a British passport*
1 **hole**
  1 *n.* opening or hollow place
  3 *n.* animal burrow
  4 *n.* (golf) place where ball must go
  6 *n.* unpleasant situation: *I was in rather a hole*
  6 *v.* get a ball in a hole (golf, billiards)
2 **holiday** *n.*
4 **hollow**
  4 *adj.* not solid: *a hollow pipe*
  5 *adj.* as if coming from inside something hollow: *a hollow voice*
  5 *n.* hole, a place in the ground
  5 *v.* make a hollow
  6 *adj.* (fig.) unreal: *a hollow laugh*
  6 *adj.* sunken: *hollow cheeks*
3 **holy**
  3 *adj.* of God: *the Holy Bible*
  3 *adj.* devoted to religion: *a holy man*
1 **home**
  1 *n.* place where one lives
  3 *adv.*: *is he home yet?*
  4 *adj.*: *home comforts; home town*

5 *n.* institution: *a children's home*
6 *n.* habitat: *the home of the tiger*
7 *adv.* to the point aimed at: *he drove the point home*
5 **homeless** *adj.*
3 **home-made** *adj.*
2 **honest**
  2 *adj.* not telling lies: *an honest man*
  4 *adj.* showing character: *an honest face*
5 **honesty** *n.*
4 **honey** *n.*
3 **honour**
  3 *n.* great respect: *in honour of the dead*
  5 *n.* person bringing credit: *he is an honour to his family*
  6 *v.* respect highly
  7 *n.* good personal character: *on my honour*
3 **honourable** *adj.*
5 **hook**
  5 *n.* bent piece of metal: *a clothes hook*
  5 *v.* fasten catch
2 **hope**
  2 *v.* expect and desire
  3 *n.* feeling of expectation and desire
  5 *n.* person/thing on which hope is based: *it's my only hope*
3 **hopeful**
  3 *adj.* having hope: *he feels hopeful*
  5 *adj.* giving hope: *a hopeful sign*
3 **hopeless**
  3 *adj.* giving no hope: *a hopeless prospect*
  5 *adj.* incurable: *a hopeless idiot*
4 **horizon**
  4 *n.* line where sky and earth meet
  7 *n.* (fig.) limit of one's knowledge etc.
5 **horizontal** *adj.*
5 **horn**
  5 *n.* on cattle/goats
  5 *n.* substance of outgrowths on cattle
  7 *n.* musical instrument
5 **horoscope** *n.*
1 **horse** *n.*
4 **horseback** *n.: travel on horseback*

4 **horseman** *n.*
2 **hospital** *n.*
3 **host**
  3 *n.* person who entertains guests
  4 *n.* inn-keeper
  5 *n.* great number: *host of friends*
  6 *v.* entertain guests
5 **hostage** *n.*
3 **hostess**
  3 *n.* air-stewardess
  4 *n.* woman who entertains
  6 *n.* woman inn-keeper
1 **hot**
  1 *adj.* having heat: *a hot day*
  4 *adj.* spicy (food): *a hot curry*
  5 *adj.* intense, violent: *a hot temper*
  7 *adj.* (of stolen goods) difficult to dispose of: *hot goods/money*
  7 *adj.* recent: *hot off the press*
1 **hotel** *n.*
5 **hothouse** *n.*
1 **hour**
  1 *n.:* sixty minutes
  3 *n.(pl.):* office hours
  5 *n.* fixed point in time
1 **house**
  1 *n.* building
  5 *v.* provide shelter for
  5 *v.* store goods
  6 *n.* institution: *publishing house*
5 **household** *adj.* of the home: *household goods*
4 **housekeeper** *n.*
3 **housekeeping** *n.*
1 **housewife** *n.*
3 **housework** *n.*
1 **how** *adj.*
3 **however** *conj.*
4 **huge** *adj.*
1 **hullo** *int.*
3 **human**
  3 *adj.* of man or mankind: *a human being*
  5 *adj.* characteristic for man: *human kindness*
4 **humble**
  4 *adj.* having a modest opinion of oneself
  5 *v.* make humble

6 *adj.* low in rank: *of humble birth*
4 **humorous** *adj.*
4 **humour**
    4 *n.* amusement: *a story full of humour*
    5 *n.* state of mind: *in good/bad humour*
    6 *v.* gratify: *she humoured him*
2 **hundred** *n./adj.*
3 **hunger**
    3 *n.* need/desire for food
    5 *n.* (fig.) any desire
1 **hungry** *adj.*
4 **hunt**
    4 *n.* act of hunting
    4 *v.* go after for food or sport
    5 *v.* search for: *he hunted for his key*

5 **hunter** *n.*
3 **hurrah/y** *int.*
2 **hurry**
    2 *v.* do something quickly
    3 *n.* eager haste: *in a hurry*
2 **hurt**
    2 *v.* suffer injury or pain: *he hurt his back*
    4 *v.* injure a person/his feelings: *he was hurt by their criticisms*
    6 *v.* come to harm: *it won't hurt to post it tomorrow*
    6 *n.* harm, injury
1 **husband**
    1 *n.* spouse
    7 *v.* use sparingly: *husband one's strength*
3 **hut** *n.*

I

1 **I** *pron.*
2 **ice**
    2 *n.* frozen water
    4 *n.* frozen sweet: *water ice*
    4 *v.* make very cold: *iced coffee*
    5 *v.* cover with sugar icing
2 **ice-cream** *n.*
5 **icy** *adj.*
2 **idea** *n.*
4 **ideal**
    4 *adj.* satisfying one's idea of perfection: *ideal weather*
    5 *adj.* existing only in the imagination: *ideal happiness*
    5 *n.* idea, example of perfection
4 **identify**
    4 *v.* show/prove the identity
    7 *v.* feel you belong: *she identifies with that group*
5 **idle**
    5 *adj.* lazy
    6 *v.* tick over: *the engine is idling*
    7 *adj.* useless: *idle tales*

    7 *v.* waste time
5 **idleness** *n.*
2 **if** *conj.*
4 **if only** *conj.*: *if only we had a map, we could get there*
1 **ill**
    1 *adj.* sick
    5 *adj.* bad: *ill luck*
    7 *adv.* badly: *we could ill afford the time*
2 **illness**
    2 *n.* specific malady
    3 *n.* state of being ill
4 **image**
    4 *n.* likeness, copy: *an image of a saint*
    5 *n.* reflection seen through the lens of a camera
    6 *n.* mental picture of person or thing
    7 *n.* simile, metaphor: *he spoke in images*
4 **imagination** *n.*
3 **imagine** *v.*

4 **imitate**
    4 *v.* copy behaviour, take as example
    5 *v.* mimic
    6 *v.* be like: *wood painted to imitate marble*
5 **imitation**
    5 *n.* behaviour: *they learn by imitation*
    5 *n.* act: *he gave an imitation of the Prime Minister*
    6 *n.* not real: *imitation leather*
3 **immediate**
    3 *adj.* occurring at once: *an immediate answer*
    6 *adj.* nearest: *his immediate family*
3 **immense** *adj.*
5 **immigrant** *n./adj.*
5 **immoral** *adj.*
4 **impatient** *adj.*
4 **import**
    4 *v.* move goods
    4 *n.* act of importing goods
    6 *n.* implied meaning: *what was the import of his words?*
    6 *v.* signify: *what do his words import?*
    7 *n.* formal importance: *questions of great import*
2 **importance** *n.*
1 **important**
    1 *adj.* of great influence: *important decisions*
    3 *adj.* (of a person) having authority
3 **impossible**
    3 *adj.* not possible
    6 *adj.* that cannot be endured: *an impossible situation*
4 **impress**
    4 *v.* strike forcibly: *we were impressed by the view*
    5 *v.* emphasise: *I impressed on him the urgency*
4 **impression**
    4 *n.* effect on the mind or feelings: *he made a good impression*
    5 *n.* vague or uncertain belief: *I get the impression . . .*
    6 *n.* mark made by pressing
    7 *n.* product of one printing: *a first impression of 500 copies*

4 **impressive** *adj.*
5 **imprison** *v.*
5 **improper**
    5 *adj.* not suited to the situation
    5 *adj.* indecent
    6 *adj.* incorrect: *an improper diagnosis*
3 **improve**
    3 *v.* get better: *his health improved*
    4 *v.* make better: *he improved his performance*
    5 *v.* make good use of: *to improve on the situation*
3 **improvement**
    3 *n.* increase in quality: *a noticeable improvement in his English*
    5 *n.* something which adds value: *he carried out improvements to his property*
1 **in**
    1 *prep.* location: *in my house*
    1 *prep.* situation: *in the army*
    1 *prep.* position in time: *in winter*
    2 *prep.* within period of time: *do it in a day*
    2 *adv.* available: *will you be in on Monday?*
    3 *adv.* arrived: *is the plane in yet?*
    4 *prep.* of activity: *succeed in the attempt; weak in maths*
    5 *adv.* fashionable, in season: *long skirts are in; peaches are in*
    6 *adv.* in power: *the Tories were in then*
4 **in addition to** *prep.*: *a special certificate is required for entry, in addition to the usual documents*
4 **in all**
1 **in bed**
3 **in any case**
3 **in case** *conj.*: *take your coat in case it rains*
4 **in common**
2 **in danger**
4 **in debt**
4 **in difficulties**
1 **in the end**
2 **in fact**

1 **in front of** *prep.: don't stand in front of the fire*
4 **in general**
3 **in half**
3 **in a hurry**
2 **in ink**
2 **in love**
3 **in order**
5 **in order that** *conj.: the traffic halted in order that the President might pass*
4 **in order to** *conj.: we stopped the car in order to watch the procession*
4 **in particular**
2 **in pencil**
2 **in pieces**
3 **in place**
4 **in prison**
3 **in private**
3 **in public**
4 **in secret**
3 **in sight**
3 **in stock**
4 **in tears**
2 **in time**
3 **in town**
3 **in turn**
3 **in two**
4 **in a way**
5 **in other words**
2 **inch**
   2 *n.* measure of length
   6 *n.* small amount: *inch by inch*
   7 *v.* move by small degrees: *he inched forward to the cliff edge*
4 **incident**
   4 *n.* event: *a frontier incident*
   5 *n.* piece of action in a poem, play etc.
2 **include** *v.*
4 **including** *prep.*
4 **income** *n.*
3 **incorrect** *adj.*
3 **increase**
   3 *v.* make bigger
   4 *n.* increasing, growth
5 **incredible** *adj.*
5 **indeed**
   5 *adv.* in fact: *I was happy, indeed delighted*

   6 *adv.* greatly: *I was indeed pleased*
5 **independence** *n.*
3 **independent**
   3 *adj.* not controlled by other people/things: *she became independent of her parents at 18*
   4 *adj.* free from influence by others: *an independent thinker*
   5 *adj.* self-governing: *the colony became independent*
3 **index**
   3 *n.* list of names, etc. at the end of a book
   5 *adj.* pointer: *index finger*
   6 *v.* construct index: *this book is well indexed*
   7 *n.* number taken as a standard: *the cost of living index*
2 **India** *n.*
3 **Indian** *n./adj.*
4 **indicate** *v.*
5 **indirect**
   5 *adj.* not straight (statement): *an indirect reference*
   6 *adj.* not direct (system): *indirect taxation*
3 **individual**
   3 *n.* any particular human being
   4 *adj.* specifically for one person: *individual attention*
   6 *adj.* characteristic of one single person: *an individual style of speech and dress*
5 **indoor/s** *adj./adv.*
3 **industrial** *adj.*
3 **industry**
   3 *n.* trade or manufacture
   6 *n.* quality of being hard-working
5 **infect** *v.*
5 **infectious**
   5 *adj.* infecting with disease
   7 *adj.* (fig.) influencing others: *infectious humour*
3 **influence**
   3 *n.* power to affect: *a good influence*
   4 *v.* affect
   6 *n.* power due to wealth/position
   7 *n.* action of natural forces: *the influence of the moon*

5 **influential** *adj.*
3 **inform**
  3 *v.* give knowledge to
  5 *v.* provide evidence against
3 **information** *n.*
3 **inhabitant** *n.*
3 **initial**
  3 *n.* first letter of a name
  4 *adj.* of or at the beginning
  5 *v.* mark: *he initialled the letter*
5 **injection** *n.*
5 **injure** *v.*
4 **injury**
  4 *n.* harm to body
  6 *n.* damage to reputation
2 **ink** *n.*
5 **inn**
  5 *n.* public house
  7 *n.* law college in London: *Inn of Court*
4 **inner** *adj.*
4 **innocent**
  4 *adj.* not guilty
  5 *adj.* harmless: *innocent fun*
  5 *adj.* knowing nothing of evil or wrong: *an innocent child*
  6 *adj.* foolishly simple: *don't be so innocent as to believe him*
4 **inquire** *v.*
5 **inquiry** *n.*
3 **insect** *n.*
3 **inside**
  3 *adj./adv.* not outside
  3 *n.* inner side: *the inside of a box*
  5 *n.* part of track: *he overtook on the inside*
  6 *n.* stomach: *a pain in his inside*
3 **insist** *v.*
5 **inspect** *v.*
5 **inspector** *n.*
4 **instal**
  4 *v.* place in position for use: *he installed a new TV*
  6 *v.* settle in a place: *she is comfortably installed in her new home*
  7 *v.* place someone in position of authority, with a ceremony: *the new dean was installed*

5 **instance**
  5 *n.* example: *for instance*
  7 *v.* give as an example
4 **instant**
  4 *adj.* coming at once: *instant relief*
  4 *adj.* (of food) made easily and quickly: *instant coffee*
  5 *adj.* urgent: *in instant need of help*
2 **instead** *adv.*
3 **instead of** *prep.*: *can I go instead of you?*
4 **institute**
  4 *n.* society or its offices
  7 *v.* establish: *he instituted an enquiry*
4 **institution**
  4 *n.* organisation working for educational or other purposes
  6 *n.* long-established custom
5 **instruct**
  5 *v.* teach
  6 *v.* give orders to: *instruct him to start early*
  7 *v.* inform: *I have been instructed that you still owe £50*
4 **instruction**
  4 *n.(pl.)* directions: *operating instructions*
  5 *n.* tuition: *instruction is given in music*
3 **instrument**
  3 *n.* thing which makes music
  5 *n.* implement for delicate work: *surgical instruments*
  6 *n.* system or procedure: *an instrument for evaluation*
5 **instrumental**
  5 *adj.* of or for musical instruments: *instrumental music*
  6 *adj.* serving as a means: *he was instrumental in my getting the job*
4 **insult** *n./v.*
4 **insurance**
  4 *n.* safeguard against loss
  5 *n.* payment made to or by such a company: *they paid £20,000 insurance*
  6 *n.* any measure taken against loss or failure
5 **insure** *v.*

5 **intake** *n.*
4 **intelligence**
    4 *n.* mental ability
    7 *n.* news/information regarding secret
    events: *the Intelligence Department*
3 **intelligent** *adj.*
3 **intend**
    3 *v.* have purpose or plan: *he intended*
    to leave
    6 *v.* mean: *what do you intend by*
    those words?
5 **intense**
    5 *adj.* high in degree: *intense heat*
    5 *adj.* (of feelings) ardent, violent,
    emotional
4 **intention** *n.*
5 **intentional** *adj.*
2 **interest**
    2 *n.* knowing or wanting to learn: *a*
    great interest in politics
    3 *v.* cause someone to be interested
    3 *n.* activity or field of concern: *his*
    chief interest is horses
    4 *n.* object arousing concern or
    curiosity: *a matter of interest*
    5 *n.* money charged on a loan: *6 %*
    interest
5 **interfere**
    5 *v.* break in upon: *don't interfere in*
    my affairs
    6 *v.* meddle, tamper: *don't interfere*
    with this machine
    7 *v.* hinder, prevent: *does pleasure*
    ever interfere with duty?
5 **interference**
    5 *n.* breaking in upon
    7 *n.* unwanted radio signal
4 **interior**
    4 *adj.* situated inside
    5 *adj.* home, domestic
    5 *n.* the inside
    6 *adj.* inland
    6 *n.* inland area
    7 *n.* domestic affairs of the country:
    Department of the Interior
5 **intermediate** *adj.*
5 **internal**
    5 *adj.* of the inside: *internal bleeding*
    6 *adj.* domestic: *internal affairs*

3 **international** *adj.*
4 **interpret**
    4 *v.* translate into another language
    6 *v.* consider as the meaning: *we*
    interpreted his silence as a refusal
    7 *v.* make clear the meaning of: *the*
    actor interpreted Hamlet well
3 **interrupt**
    3 *v.* break in upon: *don't interrupt*
    when I'm speaking
    5 *v.* break the continuity of: *his*
    schooling was interrupted by the
    war
4 **interruption** *n.*
4 **interval**
    4 *n.* time between two acts of a play
    6 *n.* space between objects: *arranged*
    at intervals of 10 feet
    7 *n.* (music) difference in pitch
    between 2 notes
4 **interview** *n./v.*
1 **into** *prep.*
5 **intonation** *n.*
3 **introduce**
    3 *v.* present, make known by name:
    he introduced John to Gillian
    4 *v.* bring into use or operation: *he*
    introduced many new ideas
    6 *v.* bring into a debate: *he introduced*
    a Bill
4 **introduction**
    4 *n.* introducing of persons to one
    another
    5 *n.* opening section: *the introduction*
    to this article
    6 *n.* an elementary stage: *'An*
    Introduction to Greek Philosophy'
5 **invalid**
    5 *n.* disabled person
    6 *adj.* not valid
    6 *adj.* weak through illness or injury
    7 *adj.* suitable for invalids: *an invalid*
    chair
4 **invent**
    4 *v.* create, design: *invent a new*
    machine
    5 *v.* make up, think of: *invent a story*
4 **invention** *n.*
5 **inventor** *n.*

5 **investigate** *v.*
5 **investigation** *n.*
5 **investment**
   5 *n.* investing money
   5 *n.* money which is invested
3 **invitation** *n.*
3 **invite**
   3 *v.* ask: *she invited him in*
   6 *v.* ask for: *the chairman invited questions*
5 **invoice** *n.*
4 **involve**
   4 *v.* cause to be mixed up in: *they were involved in crime*
   6 *v.* entail: *the job involved my living in London*
5 **inward/s** *adj./adv.*
4 **Ireland** *n.*
4 **Irish** *adj.*
5 **Irishman** *n.*
2 **iron**
   2 *n.* metal

4 *n.* tool for ironing
4 *v.* smooth clothes with iron
1 **is** *v.*
5 **Islam** *n.*
2 **island**
   2 *n.* land with water all around
   5 *n.* pavement in mid street
4 **issue**
   4 *v.* produce, publish
   5 *n.* publication: *a new issue*
   6 *n.* question for discussion: *an important issue*
   7 *n.* outgoing: *the place of issue*
1 **it** *pron.*
5 **item**
   5 *n.* single thing in a list
   5 *n.* detail of news
1 **its** *pron.*
2 **itself** *pron.*

J

4 **jacket**
   4 *n.* coat
   5 *n.* skin (of a potato)
   6 *n.* cover of a hardback book
   7 *n.* covering around a tank
5 **jail** *n./v.*
5 **jam**
   5 *n.* fruit boiled and preserved in sugar: *strawberry jam*
   5 *n.* number of things together making movement difficult: *a traffic jam*
   6 *v.* become fixed: *the brakes jammed*
   7 *v.* block a broadcast
1 **January** *n.*
2 **Japan** *n.*
3 **Japanese** *n./adj.*
2 **jar**
   2 *n.* glass container

   6 *n.* harsh sound
   7 *n.* shock: *his fall gave him a nasty jar*
5 **jaw**
   5 *n.* either of the bone structures containing the teeth
   5 *n.* lower part of the face
4 **jazz**
   4 *n.* form of popular music
   6 *v.* enliven: *jazz up the party*
3 **jealous**
   3 *adj.* envious
   6 *adj.* feeling or showing fear of loss: *a jealous husband*
   7 *adj.* taking watchful care: *jealous of his possessions*
5 **jeans** *n.(pl.)*
3 **jet**
   3 *n.* aeroplane

5 *n.* fast stream of liquid: *a jet of water*

6 *n.* narrow opening: *a gas jet*

5 **jewel**

    5 *n.* precious stone

    6 *n.* artificial diamonds: *a 15-diamond watch*

    7 *n.* (fig.) anything highly valued

5 **jewellery** *n.*

5 **Jewish** *n./adj.*

1 **job**

    1 *n.* employment: *what's his job?*

    3 *n.* piece of work: *some week-end jobs to do*

    6 *n.* hard task: *it's a job to get by on so little*

5 **jockey**

    5 *n.* on radio: *disc jockey*

    5 *n.* horse-rider

4 **jog** *v.* run slowly for exercise: *go jogging*

2 **join**

    2 *v.* come together: *the roads join here*

    2 *v.* become a member of: *he joined the army*

    3 *v.* put together

    5 *v.* come into someone's company: *I'll join you soon*

    5 *n.* place where two pieces are joined

3 **join in** *v.* participate

4 **join up** *v.* unite

4 **joint**

    4 *n.* piece of meat

    5 *n.* place where parts are joined

    6 *n.* device joining things: *finger joints*

    6 *adj.* held by two or more people together: *a joint account*

3 **joke** *n./v.*

5 **jolly** *adj.*

4 **journalist** *n.*

2 **journey** *n.*

4 **joy** *n.*

5 **joyful** *adj.*

3 **judge**

3 *n.* officer who decides cases in a law court

4 *n.* person who decides in a contest

5 *n.* person qualified to give an opinion: *a good judge of horses*

5 *v.* estimate, form an opinion about: *I can't judge the truth of what he said*

6 *v.* give a decision

4 **judgement**

    4 *n.* decision of a judge or court

    5 *n.* good sense: *he shows good judgement*

    6 *n.* process of judging: *his judgement was at fault*

4 **jug** *n.* container

3 **juice**

    3 *n.* fluid part of fruits

    6 *n.* fluid in the organs of the body: *gastric juices*

    7 *n.* (colloq.) electricity, petrol or similar source of power

1 **July** *n.*

1 **jump**

    1 *v.* move quickly: *jump about*

    2 *v.* pass over: *jump a fence*

    3 *v.* start: *she made me jump*

    4 *n.* act of jumping: *the high jump*

    4 *n.* sudden rise in prices: *a jump in the cost of living*

    5 *v.* rise suddenly in value: *gold shares jumped on the Stock Market*

4 **jumper**

    4 *n.* sweater

    5 *n.* one who jumps

5 **junction** *n.* place where roads etc. meet

1 **June** *n.*

5 **jury** *n.* group of people in court

1 **just**

    1 *adv.* exactly: *it's just eleven o'clock*

    2 *adv.* very recently: *I've just had breakfast*

    4 *adv.* merely: *he just sits there and does nothing*

    5 *adj.* appropriate: *a just verdict*

K

5 **keen**
    5 *adj.* strongly felt: *he has a keen interest in his work*
    5 *adj.* desirous: *I am keen that she should go*
    6 *adj.* acute: *he's got a keen intelligence*
    7 *adj.* sharp: *that knife has a keen edge*

1 **keep**
    1 *v.* remain: *keep quiet*
    1 *v.* cause to remain: *keep your hands in your pockets*
    2 *v.* continue to hold: *keep these for me*
    3 *v.* cause to continue: *keep the fire going*
    3 *v.* stock: *do you keep ball bearings?*
    4 *v.* detain: *what kept you so long?*
    4 *v.* manage: *she keeps house for him*
    4 *v.* guard: *he keeps goal for Leeds United*
    5 *v.* maintain: *you can't keep a family on that salary*
    6 *n.* (food needed for) support: *she earns her keep*

5 **keep at** *v.* (cause to) persist at
4 **keep back**
    4 *v.* (cause to) stay at a distance
    5 *v.* withhold (information)
5 **keep down** *v.* repress, not raise, control
3 **keep in** *v.* detain indoors, restrain
4 **keep off**
    4 *v.* (cause to) stay away from
    5 *v.* (cause to) not to eat or drink something
3 **keep on**
    3 *v.* continue
    5 *v.* retain in employment
4 **keep up** *v.* maintain (standards)
5 **keep up with** *v.* progress at same rate as
4 **keeper** *n.*
4 **kettle** *n.*

2 **key**
    2 *n.* object to fit locks
    4 *n.* explanation: *the key to his success*
    6 *n.* music: *the key of C*
    7 *n.* finger pieces: *keys of a typewriter/piano*

2 **kick**
    2 *v.* strike with foot
    2 *n.* blow with foot: *he gave the ball a good kick*
    7 *n.* recoil: *the kick of a gun*
    7 *n.(pl.)* (colloq.) thrill: *he did it for kicks*

5 **kid**
    5 *n.* (colloq.) child
    6 *n.* young goat
    7 *adj.* leather made from goatskin
    7 *v.* tease by deceiving

2 **kill**
    2 *v.* put to death
    6 *v.* destroy: *that killed his chances*
    6 *n.* death of hunted animal
    7 *v.* neutralise: *the red carpet kills your curtains*

2 **kilo** *n.*
2 **kilometre** *n.*

1 **kind**
    1 *adj.* quality: *a kind person, act*
    1 *adj.* behaviour: *he is kind to me*
    2 *adj.* charitable: *it was kind of you to do that*
    3 *n.* class, sort or variety: *what kind of car does he drive?*
    6 *adv.* (colloq.) more or less: *kind of stupid*
    7 *n.* inferior sort: *they gave us a kind of coffee*
    7 *n.* goods: *payment in kind*

4 **kind-hearted** *adj.*
4 **kindness** *n.*
1 **king**
    1 *n.* male monarch
    4 *n.* powerful figure: *oil king*
    6 *n.* piece in chess

5 **kingdom**
   5 *n.* country ruled by a king
   6 *adj.* material category: *the animal*
     kingdom
   7 *n.* non-material realm: *the kingdom*
     of thought
5 **kiosk** *n.*
2 **kiss**
   2 *v.* touch with the lips: *they kissed*
     goodnight
   5 *n.: the kiss of life*
5 **kit**
   5 *n.* set of equipment: *a plumber's kit*
   6 *n.* clothing: *sports kit*
1 **kitchen** *n.*
5 **kite**
   5 *n.* toy
   7 *n.* bird of hawk family
2 **knee** *n.*
4 **kneel** *v.*
5 **knickers** *n.(pl.)*
1 **knife** *n.*
5 **knit** *v.*
2 **knock**
   2 *v.* strike a resounding blow
   2 *n.* a blow
   3 *v.* strike hard blows: *knock in a nail*
   7 *v.* make roughly: *knock together*

2 **knock down** *v.* cause to fall
5 **knock out**
   5 *v.* eliminate (in competition)
   5 *v.* make unconscious
   6 *n.* victory in boxing: *a knock out*
     (K.O.)
5 **knot**
   5 *n.* fastening in string/rope
   5 *v.* make a fastening
   7 *n.* gathering: *a knot in wood; a knot*
     of people
   7 *n.* sea-mile per hour
1 **know**
   1 *v.* command mentally: *he knows*
     Turkish
   2 *v.* be acquainted with: *do you know*
     him?
   3 *v.* be aware of: *I didn't know he was*
     ill
   4 *v.* have experience of: *he knows*
     Finland
   5 *v.* able to recognise: *he knows a*
     good Burgundy when he tastes one
3 **knowledge**
   3 *n.* understanding: *his knowledge of*
     gardening
   5 *n.* information: *I have no knowledge*
     of his movements

L

5 **label** *n.*
4 **labour**
   4 *n.* work: *manual labour*
   6 *n.* task: *a labour of love*
   5 *n.* workers as a class: *labour versus*
     management
   7 *v.* work with effort
3 **lack**
   3 *n.* being without: *a lack of money*
   5 *v.* be without: *the room lacks colour*
5 **lad** *n.*
3 **ladder**

   3 *n.* for climbing
   5 *n.* in women's stockings
5 **ladies**
   5 *n.(pl.)* WC: *the ladies*
   5 *adj.* female: *a ladies' magazine*
2 **lady**
   2 *n.* (courteously) any woman
   5 *n.* title: *Lady Alice*
   5 *n.* (attrib.): *a lady doctor*
   6 *n.* woman of the upper classes: *a*
     lady would not do that
   7 *n.* the Virgin Mary: *Our Lady*

2 **lake** *n.*
5 **lamb**
    5 *n.* young sheep
    5 *n.* meat
5 **lame**
    5 *adj.* not able to walk normally
    7 *adj.* weak: *a lame argument*
4 **lamp** *n.*
4 **lamp-post** *n.*
1 **land**
    1 *n.* opposite of sea: *by land and sea*
    2 *n.* natural territory: *my native land*
    2 *v.* touch down: *we landed at Heathrow*
    2 *v.* dock: *we landed at Dover*
    3 *n.* agricultural etc.: *plough land; good land*
    4 *n.* property: *he owns a lot of land*
4 **landing**
    4 *n.* platform at the top of the stairs
    5 *v.* act of coming to land
5 **landlady** *n.*
4 **landlord** *n.*
2 **language**
    2 *n.* particular form: *the French language*
    3 *n.* in general: *language is more than mere sound*
    4 *n.* context of use: *the language of diplomacy*
    5 *n.* non-verbal: *computer language*
    6 *n.* full of oaths, violent: *bad/strong language*
5 **lap**
    5 *n.* part of body
    6 *v.* drink with tongue
    7 *n.* circuit in a race
1 **large**
    1 *adj.* physically extensive: *a large field; a large sheet of paper*
    2 *adj.* numerous: *large numbers of people*
    4 *adj.* on a considerable scale: *a large business*
    6 *adj.* extensive in the abstract: *large powers*

1 **last**
    1 *adj.* latest in order, final: *the last day of the month*
    1 *adv.* latest in order: *he came last of all*
    3 *adv.* most recently: *when did you last see him?*
    4 *v.* go on: *how long will the rain last?*
1 **late**
    1 *adj.* after the usual times: *you are late for school*
    2 *adv.* after the usual time: *go to bed late*
    3 *adv.* far on in time: *help came too late*
    6 *adj.* towards end of period: *they keep late hours*
    6 *adv.* recently: *as late as last month*
    7 *adj.* recent (and now not living): *the late headmaster*
3 **lately** *adv.*
2 **later** *adj./adv.*
5 **latter** *adj.*
2 **laugh**
    2 *v.* show enjoyment
    3 *v.* ridicule: *they're laughing at him*
    3 *n.* sign of enjoyment
4 **laughter** *n.*
5 **launderette** *n.*
4 **laundry**
    4 *n.* place: *take these clothes to the laundry*
    5 *n.* clothes for washing: *the laundry has come back*
4 **lavatory** *n.*
3 **law**
    3 *n.* a body of laws: *common law*
    3 *n.* a particular legislation: *divorce law*
    5 *n.* general laws: *the laws of God/nature*
    6 *n.* scientific law: *Boyle's Law*
    6 *n.* social control: *law and order*
4 **lawyer** *n.*
3 **lay** *v.*
5 **lay by** *v.* save
5 **lay-by** *n.*
3 **lay out** *v.* arrange neatly

5 **layer** *n.* thickness of material:
layer of soil
2 **lazy** *adj.*
2 **lead**
  2 *v.* to guide: *they led me through the forest*
  3 *v.* to be in front: *the yellow car is leading*
  4 *v.* go to: *this road leads to Norwich*
  4 *v.* command, direct by example: *lead an army*
  5 *n.* metal
  5 *n.* strap: *keep your dog on a lead*
2 **leader**
  2 *n.* commander: *the leader of an army*
  6 *n.* principal player: *the leader of an orchestra*
  7 *n.* article: *a 'Times' leader*
4 **leadership** *n.*
1 **leaf**
  1 *n.* part of plant: *leaf of a tree*
  4 *n.* thin sheet: *leaf of a book*
  6 *v.* turn pages
  7 *n.* part of a table
5 **leaflet** *n.*
5 **leafy** *adj.*
4 **leak**
  4 *n.* hole or crack: *there's a leak in the roof*
  4 *v.* let water in or out: *the ship was leaking badly*
  6 *v.* cause to become known to the press
  6 *n.* item of secrecy transmitted to the press
4 **lean**
  4 *v.* incline, rest weight on
  5 *adj.* not fat: *lean meat*
  6 *v.* rely on
  7 *adj.* involving shortages: *lean times*
1 **learn**
  1 *v.* acquire skill, knowledge
  5 *v.* ascertain a fact: *I learn from your letter that . . .*
5 **learned** *adj.*
5 **learning** *n.*

2 **least**
  2 *adj.* smallest: *the least amount*
  3 *adv.* opposite of the most: *she spoke least*
2 **leather** *n.*
1 **leave**
  1 *v.* depart from: *leave the station*
  3 *v.* allow to remain: *leave the glass on the table*
  3 *v.* let something stay undone: *leave it alone*
  4 *v.* entrust: *leave it with me*
  5 *v.* pass on property at death: *he left her £1000 in his will*
  6 *n.* holiday in public service
  7 *n.* permission to do something
3 **leave in** *v.* allow to remain
3 **leave on** *v.* continue to use (light)
4 **leave out** *v.* omit
4 **lecture** *n.*
1 **left**
  1 *adj.* opposite of right
  6 *n.* political grouping: *the left*
4 **left-handed** *adj.*
1 **leg**
  1 *n.* part of body
  5 *n.* part of a chair/table
  6 *n.* section of journey: *the first leg of our trip to Japan*
4 **legal** *adj.*
4 **leisure** *n.* spare time
2 **lend**
  2 *v.* allow to borrow
  6 *v.* provide support: *this evidence lends credence to his theory*
3 **length**
  3 *n.* measurement from end to end: *the length of that car*
  5 *n.* distance: *300 yards in length*
  6 *n.* stretch of time: *he spoke at length on the matter*
  6 *n.* unit of measurement: *Cambridge won by 6 lengths in the boat-race last year*
  7 *n.* point of time: *they came at length to the main issue*
5 **lens**
  5 *n.* part of spectacles/telescope
  7 *n.* part of the eye

2 **less**
  2 *adj.* smaller in amount: *the noise became less*
  3 *adv.* not so much: *less noisy*
  5 *adv.* subtract: *6 less 2 = 4*
5 **lessen**
  5 *v.* make less: *lessen the costs*
  6 *v.* become less: *the sound lessened as we went away*
1 **lesson**
  1 *n.* period of instruction: *go to your music lesson*
  2 *n.* education in general: *Tom is fond of his lessons*
  6 *n.* punishing experience: *let that be a lesson to you all*
  7 *n.* passage from the Bible
2 **let**
  2 *v.* allow: *I let him do it*
  3 *v.* proposal: *let's go to the cinema*
  4 *v.* ensure: *let him know that*
  4 *v.* hire out: *let a house*
  4 *v.* leave: *let me alone*
  6 *v.* still less: *let alone . . .*
3 **let down**
  3 *v.* lower
  5 *v.* disappoint
3 **let in** *v.* allow to enter
5 **let off**
  4 *v.* allow to explode
  5 *v.* release (from duty, punishment)
3 **let out** *v.* release (from confinement)
3 **let through** *v.* allow to pass
1 **letter**
  1 *n.* written message
  2 *n.* character representing a sound
  7 *n.* precise meaning: *the letter of the law*
3 **level**
  3 *n.* height or depth: *water finds its own level*
  4 *adj.* even: *a level surface*
  5 *v.* make even
  7 *n.* instrument: *a spirit level*
5 **liar** *n.*
4 **liberty**
  4 *n.* state of being free
  7 *n.(pl.)* improper behaviour: *take liberties*

4 **librarian** *n.*
2 **library** *n.*
5 **licence**
  5 *n.* written or printed permission
  7 *n.* wrong use of freedom
5 **lick**
  5 *v.* pass the tongue over or under
  7 *v.* touch lightly: *the flames licked up the chimney*
4 **lid** *n.*
1 **lie**
  1 *v.* be laid flat or stretched out: *the book is lying on the table*
  2 *v.* become recumbent: *lie down*
  3 *n.* an untruth: *he told lies*
  3 *v.* tell an untruth: *he is lying*
  5 *v.* face: *the journey lying before you*
  5 *v.* is to be found: *the remedy lies in education*
3 **life**
  3 *n.* period from birth to death: *he spent his whole life in Wales*
  4 *n.* human being: *there were 70 lives lost in the accident*
  4 *n.* biography: *a life of Nelson*
  5 *n.* career: *that was the life for him!*
  5 *n.* condition of being alive: *how did life begin?*
  5 *n.* state of existence: *life is sweet*
  6 *n.* interest, liveliness: *there's not much life in that town on a Sunday afternoon*
  6 *n.* living model: *a picture drawn from life*
2 **lift**
  2 *v.* raise: *lift the lid*
  4 *v.* go up: *at last the fog lifted*
  4 *n.* elevator
  5 *n.* free trip in a car
  7 *v.* become airborne: *the rocket lifted off*
1 **light**
  1 *n.* brightness: *sunlight; electric light*
  2 *n.* lamp: *an electric light*
  2 *v.* kindle, switch on: *light the fire*
  3 *v.* illuminate: *lit by electricity*
  3 *adj.* not heavy: *aluminium is light*
  4 *adj.* not dense: *a light cake*

5 *adj.* not serious or weighty: *a light punishment; light music*
5 *adj.* not dark in colour: *light blue*
6 *n.* aspect: *look at it in a different light*
5 **lighten** *v.*
3 **lightning** *n.*
1 **like**
  1 *v.* be fond of: *I like hot toast*
  3 *adv.* in the manner of: *I wish I could write like that*
  3 *adv.* resembling: *it looks like a bird*
  4 *v.* wish: *I should like to go to Switzerland*
3 **likely**
  3 *adv.* probable: *it is not likely to happen*
  4 *adj.* reasonable, suitable: *this is a likely place for a picnic*
4 **limb**
  4 *n.* leg or arm
  7 *n.* bough of a tree
3 **limit**
  3 *n.* boundary: *up to a limit of £100*
  5 *v.* restrain: *limit yourself to one a day*
5 **limp**
  5 *v.* walk lamely
  5 *n.* lame walk
  7 *adj.* not stiff
2 **line**
  2 *n.* string or wire: *clothes line; telegraph line*
  3 *n.* mark: *a pencil line*
  4 *n.* printed matter: *a line of print*
  5 *n.* showing direction/tendency/type: *line of business*
  5 *n.* branch of network: *the Northern Line*
  6 *n.* military front/thrust: *the front line; line of attack*
  6 *n.* limit: *draw a line somewhere*
  6 *v.* provide inside layer: *line a coat*
  7 *v.* furrow: *his face was heavily lined*
5 **linen** *n.*
4 **liner**
  4 *n.* ship or aircraft of a company
  6 *n.* for make-up: *eye-liner*

4 **link**
  4 *v.* connect: *they linked him with the crime*
  5 *n.* one ring in a chain
  5 *n.* (fig.) person who connects others
  6 *n.* in place of buttons: *cuff links*
3 **lion** *n.*
3 **lip**
  3 *n.* edge of mouth
  4 *n.* (fig.) edge of cup etc.
5 **lipstick** *n.*
3 **liquid**
  3 *n.* fluid
  5 *n.* substance
  7 *adj.* smooth in texture: *liquid eyes; the liquid notes of the blackbird*
2 **list**
  2 *n.* series: *a shopping list*
  5 *v.* record in series: *list the applicants*
  7 *v.* tilt: *the ship listed in the wind*
1 **listen** *v.*
2 **listener** *n.*
4 **literary** *adj.*
5 **literature**
  5 *n.* all the writings of a country or period: *French literature; the literature of the nineteenth century*
  6 *n.* printed matter: *get the company to send you all their literature*
  7 *n.* area of study
2 **litre** *n.*
1 **little**
  1 *adj.* opposite of big: *a little child; my little one*
  2 *adj.* opposite of much/long: *in a little time; it's only a little way*
  4 *adj.* without 'a', opposite of much: *eat little meat*
  5 *n.* poor yield: *get little out of it*
  6 *adv.* only slightly: *little used; little known*
  7 *adv.* doesn't: *he little knows what lies in store for him*
1 **live**
  1 *v.* reside: *he lives in London*
  3 *v.* manner of life: *live in hope; live well*

4 *v.* subsist on: *live on fruit and vegetables*

5 *v.* have life: *live seventy years*

6 *adj.* alive: *live fish*

3 **live on**

   3 *v.* survive

   3 *v.* support oneself by means of

3 **live through** *v.* undergo period of strain

5 **live up to** *v.* reach expected standard

4 **lively**

   4 *adj.* full of life: *she's as lively as a kitten*

   4 *adj.* lifelike: *a lively description*

   6 *adj.* bright: *lively colours*

5 **living**

   5 *adj.* alive or now existent: *living languages; within living memory*

   7 *n.* earning one's livelihood: *he made a living selling coins*

2 **living-room** *n.*

3 **load**

   3 *v.* put goods on: *load a lorry*

   4 *n.* measure: *a lorry load*

   5 *v.* charge a weapon: *they loaded their rifles*

   7 *n.* charge in mechanics/electricity: *the load on this generator*

2 **loaf**

   2 *n.* bread

   7 *v.* waste time: *he loafed about the whole summer*

4 **loan** *n.*

5 **lobby**

   5 *n.* part of a building: *we met in the lobby of the theatre*

   7 *v.* bring influence to bear on politicians

3 **local**

   3 *adj.* special to a district: *the local doctor; local government*

   6 *adj.* affecting the part, not the whole: *local anaesthetic*

   7 *n.* person from neighbourhood: *he's a local*

2 **lock**

   2 *v.* fasten: *lock the car door*

   3 *n.* fastening: *put a new lock on that door*

6 *n.* catch on gun

6 *v.* become fixed: *locked in argument*

7 *n.:* *lock on a canal*

4 **lodge**

   4 *v.* stay with, host

   5 *n.* small house at entrance to large property

   6 *v.* become fixed: *the bullet lodged in his brain*

   7 *v.* place officially: *he lodged a protest*

4 **lodger** *n.*

4 **lodging** *n.*

4 **lodgings** *n.(pl.)*

5 **log**

   5 *n.* length of tree trunk or branch: *a log fire*

   6 *n.* logarithm

   7 *n.* record: *keep the log on a voyage*

5 **loneliness** *n.*

3 **lonely**

   3 *adj.* alone, sad: *feeling lonely; a lonely traveller*

   5 *adj.* uninhabited: *lonely moorland*

1 **long**

   1 *adj.* extended in space: *this line is 3 inches long*

   2 *adj.* extended in time: *a long life*

   4 *conj.:* *as long as*

   5 *n.* period of time: *not for long*

   5 *adv.* much time: *long before*

   6 *v.* desire: *long for someone*

5 **longing** *n.*

1 **look**

   1 *v.* observe: *look at me*

   2 *n.* act of looking: *take a look*

   4 *n.* facial expression: *a sad look*

   5 *v.* appear: *he looks like a banker*

   5 *n.(pl.):* *his good looks and charm made him popular*

   6 *v.* suggests: *it looks like rain*

3 **look after** *v.* care for

2 **look at** *v.* examine, consider

2 **look for** *v.* try to find

5 **look in** *v.* visit

5 **look into** *v.* investigate

3 **look on** *v.* be a spectator

3 **look out** *v.* take care

4 **look over** *v.* inspect, survey

4 **look through** *v*. scan
3 **look up** *v*. try to find information
5 **look up to** *v*. respect
5 **look-out** *n*.
3 **loose**
  3 *adj*. not bound: *let them loose*
  5 *adj*. not compact: *loose stones; loose earth; a loose attack*
  5 *v*. free: *loose the anchor*
  6 *adj*. not precise: *loose thinking*
5 **loosen**
  5 *v*. make slack: *loosen the rope*
  6 *v*. disengage: *the rain has loosened the stones*
  7 *v*. (fig.) make free: *wine loosens the tongue*
1 **lorry** *n*.
1 **lose**
  1 *v*. mislay: *I've lost my spectacles*
  2 *v*. be deprived of: *we shall lose our jobs*
  3 *v*. fail to retain control: *lose my way; lose my temper*
  3 *v*. fail to win: *Newcastle lost to Sunderland*
4 **loss**
  4 *n*. deprivation: *loss of life*
  5 *n*. trading setback: *losses in the business*
  7 *n*. death: *our losses were heavy in that battle*
1 **lot**
  1 *n*. much: *a lot of rice*
  2 *n*. many, much: *lots of people/water*
  5 *n*. all: *you can have the lot*
  7 *n*. site: *vacant lot*
5 **lottery** *n*. competition
2 **loud**
  2 *adj*. not quiet
  7 *adj*. of person's behaviour; colours
5 **loudspeaker** *n*.
5 **lounge**
  5 *n*. room: *tea is in the lounge*
  7 *v*. sprawl: *they were lounging in deck-chairs*
1 **love**
  1 *v*. like greatly
  2 *n*. strong attraction
  3 *v*. enjoy doing: *I love reading*

7 *n*. dear: *more pudding, love?*
3 **lovely**
  3 *adj*. beautiful, attractive: *a lovely woman*
  5 *adj*. enjoyable: *we had a lovely holiday*
4 **lover**
  4 *n*. one who enjoys: *a lover of food and drink*
  5 *n*. relationship: *they were lovers*
1 **low**
  1 *adj*. not high vertically: *a low building; low land*
  2 *adj*. not high in a scale: *low temperature/price/rank/note*
  3 *adv*. weakly: *the lamp burned low; speak low*
  6 *adj*. lacking standards: *low behaviour*
  7 *n*. a patch or period lacking in fullness: *she hit a low that year*
3 **lower**
  3 *adj*. not so high: *a lower class/note*
  4 *v*. make less high: *lower the roof/rents/pressure/one's voice*
  5 *v*. cause to descend: *lower the sails*
4 **loyal** *adj*.
5 **loyalty** *n*.
3 **luck**
  3 *n*. fortune (good or bad): *have good/bad/no luck*
  4 *n*. good fortune: *I had the luck to find him in*
3 **lucky** *adj*.
3 **luggage** *n*.
3 **lump**
  3 *n*. a piece: *a lump of clay/sugar*
  6 *n*. a protuberance: *a lump on the head*
  7 *v*. (fig.) form into groups: *lump together*
1 **lunch** *n*. meal
5 **lung** *n*. organ of body
4 **luxury**
  4 *n*. wealthy style: *live in luxury*
  6 *adj*. with every comfort: *a luxury liner*
  7 *n*. inessentials: *mangoes are a luxury*

M

2 machine
  2 *n.* appliance
  6 *n.* political or administrative instrument: *the Nazi war machine*
4 machinery
  4 *n.* moving parts of a machine
  7 *n.* systems of government
3 mad
  3 *adj.* insane: *go mad*
  6 *adj.* angry: *I'm mad at him*
  7 *adj.* enthusiastic: *mad on dancing*
  7 *adj.* wild in behaviour: *he's nice but a bit mad*
5 madam *n.* polite form of address
5 madman *n.*
5 madness *n.*
3 magazine
  3 *n.* a periodical
  7 *n.* chamber of a gun/store for holding arms
3 magic
  3 *n.* use of supernatural forces: *black magic*
  5 *n.* trickery: *the conjurer used magic*
  6 *n.* (fig.): *the magic of Shakespeare's verse*
5 magnet
  5 *n.* metal that attracts iron
  6 *n.* (fig.): *she's like a magnet to the men*
5 magnetic *adj.*
4 magnificent *adj.*
4 maid *n.* woman servant
3 mail
  3 *n.* correspondence: *has my mail come yet?*
  5 *n.* postal system: *send it by mail*
3 main
  3 *adj.* chief, most important: *main road*
  6 *n.(pl.)* central supply channel (water, electricity): *turn water off at the mains*
5 mainland *n.*

4 maintain
  4 *v.* keep in working order: *maintain the car*
  5 *v.* keep up: *maintain friendly relations*
  6 *v.* support: *maintain a son at university*
4 maintenance *n.*
4 major
  4 *adj.* relatively greater: *a major road*
  6 *n.* army rank
  7 *v.* take a degree principally in: *major in English*
  7 *adj.* in music: *in C major*
4 majority *n.* the greater number
1 make
  1 *v.* construct, produce: *she made coffee for us*
  1 *v.* cause to appear: *he made a hole in the ground*
  2 *v.* cause to be: *the news made her happy*
  3 *v.* earn: *he makes £6000 a year*
  3 *v.* amount to: *5 and 7 make 12*
  4 *n.* brand: *what make is your car?*
  4 *v.* force, compel: *they made me tell them everything*
  4 *v.* turn into: *she made a good doctor*
  4 *v.* appoint: *he was made Director last year*
  5 *v.* estimate: *what time do you make it?*
3 make for *v.* move towards (place)
4 make out
  4 *v.* write out (bill, report)
  5 *v.* manage to see
5 make out of *v.* interpret (statement, situation)
4 make up
  4 *v.* compose, complete
  4 *v.* invent
  5 *v.* restore (looks, friendship)
  5 *n.* cosmetics
3 maker
  3 *n.* someone who creates something
  7 *n.* God: *the Maker of all things*

5 **male** *adj./n.*

1 **man/men**
  1 *n.* adult: *not a man but a boy*
  1 *n.* male: *man and wife*
  2 *n.* person: *any man would welcome it*
  3 *n.* human: *the brain of Man*
  6 *n.* soldier: *the officer led his men . . .*
  6 *v.* supply manpower: *who's manning this machine today?*

3 **manage**
  3 *v.* run a business
  4 *v.* succeed in: *I just managed to get there*
  6 *v.* control a living thing: *manage a horse*

4 **management**
  4 *n.* administration: *under new management*
  4 *n.* control staff: *management and workers*
  6 *n.* handling: *that matter calls for careful management*

4 **manager**
  4 *n.* controller of a business, hotel, etc.
  6 *n.* organiser: *my wife is a good manager*

5 **manhood**
  5 *n.* manly qualities: *he was proud of his manhood*
  7 *n.* men in a group: *the manhood of Scotland*

5 **mankind** *n.* the human species

5 **manly** *adj.*

3 **manner**
  3 *n.* way: *they eat in a different manner*
  5 *n.(pl.): good/bad manners*
  6 *n.* style of expression: *in the manner of Raphael*

3 **manufacture**
  3 *v.* make using machinery: *manufacture shoes*
  6 *n.* activity of making: *the manufacture of shoes*
  7 *v.* artificially invent: *manufacture an excuse*

1 **many**
  1 *adj.* numerous: *many people; many things; many years*
  3 *adj.* a proportion: *many of the people*
  6 *adj.* a considerable number: *many a time*

2 **map**
  2 *n.* in atlas: *a map of England*
  6 *v.* make a plan: *map out our actions*

1 **March** *n.* month

2 **march**
  2 *v.* walk like soldiers
  3 *n.* a distance: *a long march*
  5 *v.* walk decisively: *he marched into my office*

4 **margin**
  4 *n.* blank space at edge of paper
  5 *n.* edge: *margin of a lake*
  6 *n.* spare amount: *a safety margin*

2 **mark**
  2 *n.* indication of process/state: *a mark on her forehead; post mark*
  3 *n.* identification: *trade mark; boundary mark*
  4 *n.* valuation: *marks for homework*
  4 *v.* correct: *mark those essays*
  4 *v.* provide identification: *mark out the tennis court*
  5 *v.* notice: *have you marked any differences in him recently?*

1 **market**
  1 *n.* public place for buying and selling
  5 *n.* for sale: *what's on the market?*
  6 *v.* launch for sale: *market a product*
  7 *n.* the state of trade: *the tin market*
  7 *n.* international grouping: *the Common Market*

3 **marriage**
  3 *n.* ceremony: *I went to their marriage*
  5 *n.* state: *the marriage lasted nine years*

3 **married** *adj.*

2 **marry**
  2 *v.* join another in wedlock: *will you marry me?*

4 *v.* cause others to marry: *he married his daughter to a rich man; the priest married them*
5 **marvellous** *adj.*
5 **Marxist** *n. /adj.*
3 **mass**
  3 *n.* a large amount: *the garden is a mass of flowers*
  4 *n.* large numbers: *masses of people came*
  6 *n.* undifferentiated bulk: *a solid mass of rock*
  6 *v.* gather
  7 *n.* religious ceremony
2 **master**
  2 *n.* superior: *master and servant*
  3 *n.* teacher: *masters and boys*
  4 *n.* controller: *he's the master of the house*
  5 *v.* gain control over: *she mastered the flute*
  5 *n.* form of address: *Master John Smith*
  6 *n.* possessor of great skill: *he's a master at card tricks*
  7 *n.* title: *Master of a College /hounds etc.*
5 **masterpiece** *n.*
3 **mat** *n.* a small carpet
1 **match**
  1 *n.* light: *a box of matches*
  3 *n.* contest: *a football match*
  4 *v.* harmonise: *this scarf matches my coat*
  6 *n.* equal: *meet one's match*
4 **mate**
  4 *v.* unite sexually: *the rabbits mated*
  6 *n.* partner: *mate in marriage*
  7 *n.* end: *check mate*
2 **material**
  2 *n.* substance: *raw material; writing materials*
  6 *n.* data: *gather material for a life of de Gaulle*
  7 *adj.* not spiritual: *the material needs of man*
  7 *adj.* substantial: *material evidence*
4 **mathematics** *n.*

4 **maths** *n.*
1 **matter**
  1 *v.* signify: *it doesn't matter*
  2 *n.* trouble: *what's the matter?*
  4 *n.* affair: *business matters*
  6 *n.* substance: *dead matter; printed matter*
4 **mature**
  4 *adj.* fully developed: *this cheese is mature*
  5 *v.* come to full development
  6 *adj.* well-considered: *after mature deliberation*
4 **maximum** *n. /adj.*
1 **May** *n.* month
2 **may /might**
  2 *modal* possibility: *that may be true after all*
  3 *modal* possibility: *that might be true, I suppose*
  3 *modal* permission: *you may go now*
  4 *modal* request for permission: *might I perhaps explain*
  4 *modal* suggestion: *you might try the corner shop*
  5 *modal* no reason against: *we may as well stay*
  6 *modal* wish: *may you enjoy your holiday*
  7 *modal* purpose: *act now so that everything may be arranged in time*
2 **maybe** *adv.*
4 **mayor** *n.*
1 **me** *pron.*
5 **meadow** *n.*
1 **meal**
  1 *n.* occasion of eating
  1 *n.* the food that is eaten
  7 *n.* ground corn
2 **mean**
  2 *v.* signify: *what does this mean?*
  3 *v.* intend: *this is meant for you*
  5 *adj.* stingy: *he is mean with his money*
  6 *n.* average: *the mean is 13*
  7 *adj.* weak: *clear to the meanest intelligence*
3 **meaning** *n.*

4 **means**
4 *n.(pl.)* instruments: *ends and means;*
by all means
4 *prep.: by means of*
6 *n.(pl.)* income/value of possessions:
he lives beyond his means
4 **meantime** *n./adv.*
3 **meanwhile** *adv./n.*
5 **measles** *n.*
2 **measure**
2 *v.* determine: *the tailor measured*
me for a suit
5 *n.* instrument to determine
dimensions etc.: *a tape measure*
5 *n.* extent: *beyond measure*
6 *n.* act: *Parliamentary measures*
3 **measurement** *n.*
1 **meat** *n.* animal flesh for eating
5 **mechanic** *n.*
4 **mechanical**
4 *adj.* of machines
5 *adj.* unvarying, mindless: *her*
mechanical actions
6 *adj.* not electrical: *mechanical*
engineering
5 **media** *n.* system(s) for broadcasting
information: *it's been on the media*
3 **medical**
3 *adj.* of the art of medicine: *a*
medical examination
4 *adj.* not surgical: *a medical ward*
2 **medicine**
2 *n.* substance: *a bottle of medicine*
3 *n.* subject: *a doctor of medicine*
2 **Mediterranean** *n./adj.*
4 **medium**
4 *adj.* average: *medium height/income*
4 *n.* middle quality: *the happy medium*
5 *n.* bearer: *air is the medium of*
sound
5 *adj.* intermediate: *medium wave*
transmission
6 *n.* substance: *oil paint is a medium*
of creation
2 **meet**
2 *v.* encounter by chance: *I met him*
in the street
3 *v.* encounter by design: *we met to*
discuss this yesterday

4 *v.* join: *two rivers meet there*
5 *v.* hold a gathering: *Parliament*
meets next week
6 *v.* match: *meet your demands*
2 **meeting** *n.*
3 **melt**
3 *v.* lose shape in heat: *the iron*
melted
4 *v.* (cause to) lose shape in heat: *she*
melted the sugar in hot water
6 *v.* overcome resistance: *melt his*
heart
7 *v.* disappear: *the crowds melted*
away
3 **member**
3 *n.* one of a group: *Member of*
Parliament
7 *n.* limb
4 **membership**
4 *n.* state of being a member:
membership is for one year only
5 *n.* the total number of members
3 **memory**
3 *n.* mental power: *I have a good*
memory
4 *n.* things remembered: *happy*
memories
5 *n.* span of things remembered:
within living memory
6 *n.* commemoration: *in memory*
of . . .
2 **mend**
2 *v.* restore to good condition: *mend*
shoes
6 *n.* recovery: *the patient is on the*
mend
7 *v.* improve: *mend your ways*
4 **mental** *adj.*
3 **mention**
3 *v.* refer: *he mentioned it*
5 *n.* reference: *no mention of it*
7 *v.* commend: *he was mentioned in*
despatches
4 **menu** *n.*
3 **merchant**
3 *n.* trader
4 *n.* shopkeeper: *a wine merchant*
4 *adj.* engaged in (overseas) trade: *a*
merchant ship

5 **merciful** *adj.*
5 **merciless** *adj.*
5 **mercy** *n.* (capacity for) clemency: *he showed mercy*
4 **mere** *adj.* not more than: *she's a mere child*
4 **merely** *adv.*
3 **merry** *adj.* jolly, mirthful: *a merry gathering*
5 **mess**
  5 *n.* confusion: *don't make a mess in the living room*
  6 *v.* make dirty or disorderly
  7 *n.* place for eating together: *the officers' mess*
2 **message**
  2 *n.* piece of news
  6 *n.* significance: *the message in this book*
5 **messenger** *n.*
2 **metal** *n./adj.*
3 **method**
  3 *n.* way: *modern methods of teaching*
  6 *n.* system: *there's method in his madness*
2 **metre**
  2 *n.* unit of length
  7 *n.* verse rhythm
4 **microphone** *n.*
5 **microscope** *n.*
1 **midday** *n.*
1 **middle**
  1 *n.* central place: *in the middle of the room*
  3 *adj.* central, in between: *the middle arch; my middle name; middle-class*
  6 *n.* waist: *I was measured round my middle*
4 **middle-aged** *adj.*
5 **Middle Ages, the** *n.(pl.)*
3 **Middle East, the** *n.*
1 **midnight** *n.*
2 **might** *modal*
3 **mild**
  3 *adj.* not cold or stormy: *mild weather; mild winter*
  4 *adj.* not excited: *mild interest*
  5 *adj.* not severe: *mild discipline*
  6 *adj.* not strong tasting: *mild tobacco*

2 **mile** *n.*
5 **mileage**
  5 *n.* distance run: *what's the mileage on your car?*
  7 *n.* headway: *you won't get much mileage out of the boss*
  7 *n.* rate of reimbursement: *charge the mileage for your trip*
4 **military** *adj.*
1 **milk**
  1 *n.* liquid
  2 *v.* obtain milk (from cow) by hand or machine
  5 *n.* milk-like liquids: *coconut milk*
2 **milkman** *n.*
4 **milky** *adj.*
3 **mill**
  3 *n.* machine to grind corn
  5 *v.* grind
  6 *n.* factory building
  7 *n.* building for grinding corn
2 **million** *n.*
2 **mind**
  2 *n.* thoughts: *his mind was filled with sad thoughts*
  3 *n.* memory: *call to mind*
  4 *n.* reason, judgement: *a cultivated mind*
  4 *v.* look after: *mind the baby*
  5 *n.* decision: *an open mind*
  5 *v.* consider, be careful: *don't mind me; mind the step*
  5 *v.* object to, care about: *do you mind if I smoke?*
  6 *n.* mood, temperament: *peace of mind; state of mind*
2 **mine**
  2 *pron.* my: *this house is mine*
  5 *n.* pit: *a coal mine*
  5 *v.* dig: *mine coal*
  7 *n.* explosive: *they laid mines in the harbour approaches*
5 **miner** *n.*
5 **mineral** *n.*
5 **minibus** *n.*
4 **minimum** *n.*
3 **minister**
  3 *n.* Government member: *the Minister of Health*

5 *n.* clergyman
7 *v.* give help or service
4 **minor**
  4 *adj.* relatively smaller: *a minor road*
  5 *adj.* relatively less significant: *minor poets*
  7 *n.* below legal age: *she's still a minor*
  7 *adj.* in music: *it's in B minor*
5 **minority** *n.* the smaller number
1 **minute**
  1 *n.* unit of time: *sixty minutes*
  3 *n.* a short space of time: *wait a minute*
  5 *adv.* immediately: *I'll do it this minute*
  5 *conj.* as soon as: *the minute I see him*
  6 *n.* note: *the Director's minute of the 28th says . . .*
  6 *n.* unit of space: *latitude 66° 30' N*
  7 *n.* record: *the minutes of a meeting*
  7 *adj.* very small or detailed: *minute particles; minute description*
2 **mirror**
  2 *n.* a looking glass
  6 *v.* reflect: *Pepys's Diary mirrors the times*
3 **miserable**
  3 *adj.* sad: *he felt miserable in her absence*
  5 *adj.* wretched: *miserable slums*
  6 *adj.* contemptible: *a miserable coward*
5 **misery**
  5 *n.* painful discomfort: *suffering misery from toothache*
  6 *n.* sorrows: *all the miseries of humanity*
5 **misfortune** *n.*
5 **mislead** *v.*
2 **miss**
  2 *n.* title for young girl or unmarried woman
  3 *v.* not hit: *miss a shot*
  3 *v.* not meet: *sorry I missed you at the station*
  4 *v.* omit: *he missed his breakfast*
  6 *v.* feel loss: *we miss her terribly*

5 **miss out** *v.* fail to take part
4 **missing** *adj.* being lost: *there's a pound missing; missing persons*
5 **mission**
  5 *n.* sending of people on a special journey: *trade mission*
  6 *n.* set of buildings: *the Catholic Mission at Kisubi*
  7 *n.* main purpose: *his mission in life was . . .*
5 **mist**
  5 *n.* vapour
  6 *v.* grow watery or unclear: *his eyes misted over*
2 **mistake**
  2 *n.* error: *correct your mistakes*
  3 *v.* make an error: *I mistook the time*
  4 *v.* recognise wrongly: *mistake Mr A for Mr B*
  5 *v.* misunderstand: *I mistook your meaning*
4 **mistress**
  4 *n.* female companion of man
  5 *n.* woman in authority (esp. teacher)
  6 *n.* person highly skilled: *she is a mistress of needlework*
4 **misunderstand** *v.*
2 **mix**
  2 *v.* cause to mingle: *mix flour and water*
  3 *v.* commingle: *oil and water don't mix*
  5 *v.* confuse: *they mix up Swiss and Swedish*
  6 *v.* become involved: *they're mixed up in that scheme*
5 **mixed**
  5 *adj.* from two groups: *mixed bathing*
  5 *adj.* heterogeneous: *a mixed population; mixed motives*
5 **mixer**
  5 *n.* instrument: *a mixer for the kitchen*
  6 *n.* sociability: *he's a good mixer*
4 **mixture**
  4 *n.* composite: *a mixture of fact and fiction*
  7 *n.* medicine: *take the mixture 3 times a day*

3 **model**
   3 *n*. design: *this is the latest model*
   4 *n*. person to be imitated: *let him be your model*
   4 *n*. solid representation: *a model train*
   5 *n*. person to be drawn or photographed: *a fashion model*
   5 *v*. pose: *she models for them*

4 **moderate**
   4 *adj*. average: *of moderate size*
   5 *adj*. not extreme: *he has moderate opinions*
   6 *n*. person without extreme views: *he's a moderate*
   7 *v*. reduce volume: *please moderate your voice*

5 **moderately** *adv*.

2 **modern**
   2 *adj*. up to date: *modern weapons*
   4 *adj*. recent: *modern history*

4 **modest**
   4 *adj*. decent: *modest in her dress*
   5 *adj*. unobtrusive: *his modest manner was reassuring*
   6 *adj*. humble: *pensioners have only modest means*

5 **modesty** *n*.

5 **moist** *adj*.

2 **moment**
   2 *n*. very brief period of time: *just a moment*
   4 *conj*. as soon as: *I started the moment your letter arrived*
   7 *n*. importance: *of little moment*

1 **Monday** *n*.

1 **money** *n*.

2 **monkey** *n*. animal

5 **monster**
   5 *n*. abnormally misshapen animal
   7 *n*. person remarkable for bad quality: *a monster of injustice*

1 **month** *n*.

2 **monthly** *adj./adv*.

4 **mood**
   4 *n*. state of mind: *a good mood*
   7 *n*. grammatical term: *in the subjunctive mood*

1 **moon**
   1 *n*. satellite of earth
   2 *n*. satellite of other planet
   7 *v*. move listlessly: *he's mooning about, as usual*

5 **moonlight** *n*.

4 **moral**
   4 *adj*. concerning right and wrong: *moral goodness*
   5 *adj*. as opposed to legal: *a moral right*
   6 *n*. ethical content: *the moral of this tale*
   6 *n*. social behaviour: *his morals shocked the village*
   6 *adj*. as opposed to physical: *moral courage*
   7 *adj*. chaste: *a moral private life*

5 **morality**
   5 *n*. behaviour of society: *standards of morality are lower today*
   6 *n*. system of behaviour: *Christian morality*

2 **more**
   2 *det*. greater amount or number: *more money*
   2 *adv*. comparative (with adjectives): *more expensive*
   3 *adv*. in excess: *work more than before*
   3 *pron*. a greater amount: *I want to know more*
   3 *adv*. comparative (with adverbs): *more quickly*
   5 *conj*. in proportion: *the more he gets the more he wants*

4 **moreover** *conj*.

1 **morning**
   1 *n*. before noon or lunch-time: *this morning*
   2 *adj*.: *morning call*

5 **mosque** *n*.

5 **mosquito** *n*.

2 **most**
   2 *adj*. greatest in amount or number: *Tom had most money amongst us*
   2 *adv*. comparative (with adjectives): *this is the most difficult of all*

3 *pron.* greatest in amount or number: *most of these pupils*

4 *adv.* comparative (with adverbs): *he did it the most skilfully of all*

5 *adj./adv.* very: *that's most kind; she asked most politely*

6 *adj.* greater: *for the most part*

5 **motel** *n.*

1 **mother**
　1 *n.* parent
　2 *adj.* female: *a mother bird*
　6 *n.* head member of religious order: *Mother Teresa*
　7 *n.* title: *Mother Nature*

5 **motion**
　5 *n.* (manner of) moving: *set it in motion*
　6 *n.* gesture, movement of body: *all her motions were graceful*
　7 *n.* proposal: *the motion before this meeting*

3 **motor**
　3 *n.* device for producing power
　7 *adj.* powered: *motor cycle*
　7 *v.* travel: *motor from London to Brighton*

5 **motorist** *n.*

3 **motorway** *n.*

4 **mount**
　4 *v.* go up: *mount a hill*
　4 *v.* get onto: *to mount a horse*
　5 *n.* mountain (in names): *Mount Everest*
　6 *v.* increase: *our bills are mounting*
　7 *v.* assemble: *mount a gun*
　7 *v.* organise, produce: *to mount an offensive*

2 **mountain** *n.*

3 **mouse/mice** *n.*

3 **moustache** *n.*

1 **mouth**
　1 *n.* part of face: *open your mouth*
　4 *n.* outlet, inlet: *mouth of a cave; mouth of a river*
　6 *n.* persons: *too many mouths to feed*

5 **mouthful** *n.*

1 **move**
　1 *v.* change position: *move your hand*

1 *v.* change location: *move aside, please*

5 *v.* change domicile: *they moved to Paris last spring*

6 *n.* action: *it's time to make a move in this matter*

3 **movement**
　3 *n.* action of changing position/location: *I watched his movements*
　6 *n.* group with common aims: *a political movement*

1 **much**
　1 *adj.* amount: *how much is there in the box?*
　1 *adj.* price: *how much is that pen?*
　1 *adv.* greatly: *very much*
　3 *adj.* a lot of: *I couldn't eat much breakfast*
　4 *n.* a great part of: *much of our success was due to . . .*
　4 *adv.* greatly (in comparison): *much bigger*
　6 *adv.* more or less: *much the same; he thinks much as I do*
　5 *n.* that amount: *as much again; you shouldn't pay that much*

4 **mud** *n.*

4 **muddy** *adj.*

5 **multiplication**
　5 *n.* in mathematics: *the multiplication tables*
　7 *n.* increase: *that will mean a multiplication of effort*

3 **multiply**
　3 *v.* in mathematics: *multiply 17 by 5*
　6 *v.* increase: *the population has multiplied*

4 **mum**
　4 *n.* (colloq.) mother
　7 *adj.* quiet: *keep mum*

4 **mummy**
　4 *n.* (colloq.) mother
　6 *n.* embalmed body

5 **mumps** *n.*

3 **murder**
　3 *n.* act of killing intentionally: *fifty murders a year*

3 *v.* kill intentionally: *he murdered his partner*
5 *n.* cruel slaughter: *the bombing of the peasants was murder*
7 *v.* distort badly: *to murder a piece of music*
5 **murderer** *n.*
4 **muscle** *n.*
3 **museum** *n.*
1 **music** *n.*
3 **musical**
  3 *adj.* to do with music: *a musical evening*
  5 *adj.* talented at music: *a musical disposition*
  6 *n.* performance: *a musical in the West End*
4 **musician** *n.*
5 **Muslim** *n./adj.*

1 **must**
  1 *modal* have to: *must go*
  5 *modal* most probably: *he must be there by now*
  7 *modal* can't help: *I must say, I'm rather surprised*
1 **my**
  1 *det.* (possessive): *this is my house*
  1 *det.* (relatedness): *my father; my request*
  4 *det.* term in address: *My Lord; My dear Richard*
  5 *int.* (surprise): *My!*
2 **myself** *pron.*
4 **mysterious** *adj.*
4 **mystery**
  4 *n.* strange occurrence: *the murder remained a mystery*
  7 *n.* ceremony: *the Greek Mysteries*

N

3 **nail**
  3 *n.* hard covering at end of fingers: *cut your nails*
  4 *n.* metal spike
  5 *v.* close with nails: *nail that lid down*
  7 *v.* detain: *he nailed me in the hall*
4 **naked**
  4 *adj.* unclothed
  6 *adj.* unprotected: *a naked light*
  7 *adj.* undisguised: *the naked truth*
1 **name**
  1 *n.* for person/place/thing: *his name is Stewart*
  3 *v.* provide with a name: *they named her Elaine*
  4 *v.* list by name: *name all the plants in the garden*
  6 *n.* authority: *in the name of the King*
  7 *v.* state clearly: *name the day; name your price*

5 **napkin** *n.*
1 **narrow**
  1 *adj.* not wide: *a narrow path*
  4 *adj.* close: *narrow escape*
  6 *adj.* restricted: *a narrow outlook*
3 **nasty**
  3 *adj.* dirty, unpleasant: *a nasty smell*
  5 *adj.* morally dirty: *a nasty mind*
  6 *adj.* dangerous: *a nasty corner*
  7 *adj.* easy to rouse: *a nasty temper*
3 **nation** *n.*
3 **national**
  3 *adj.* of a nation: *the national situation*
  6 *n.* member of a nation: *British nationals in Spain*
3 **nationality** *n.*
5 **native**
  5 *n.* person born in: *a native of Wales*
  6 *adj.* indigenous: *native customs*
  7 *adj.* natural to character: *native ability*

3 **natural**
  3 *adj.* normal: *a natural reaction*
  4 *adj.* simple, not affected: *natural behaviour*
  5 *adj.* concerned with/produced by nature: *natural gas; natural environment*
  6 *adj.* innate: *he's a natural orator*
  7 *n.* person perfectly suited: *he's a natural for the job*
2 **nature**
  2 *n.* essential qualities: *the nature of the substance*
  4 *n.* as opposed to the works of man: *a lover of nature*
  5 *n.* controlling power: *Laws of Nature*
  6 *n.* character (of person): *a generous nature; human nature*
3 **navy** *n.*
1 **near**
  1 *prep.* in vicinity: *the house is near the river*
  2 *adv.* close: *she came near*
  2 *adj.* physically close: *the nearest bus stop*
  5 *adj.* close in relation: *a near relative*
  6 *adj.* on the kerb side: *a puncture in the near-side front wheel*
  7 *adj.* narrow: *a near escape*
2 **nearly**
  2 *adv.* almost: *it's nearly two o'clock*
  5 *adv.* closely: *we're nearly related*
  5 *adv.* (with 'not') far from: *it's not nearly enough*
3 **neat**
  3 *adj.* tidy: *a neat garden; neat handwriting*
  5 *adj.* elegant: *a neat dress*
2 **necessary** *adj.*
4 **necessity**
  4 *n.* essential: *food is a necessity of life*
  5 *n.* need: *the necessity of providing more houses*
2 **neck**
  2 *n.* part of human body
  6 *n.* narrow section: *a neck of land*
5 **necklace** *n.*

1 **need**
  1 *v.* want, require: *I need food; this car needs oil*
  3 *v.* be compelled: *you needn't go yet*
  4 *n.* compulsion: *there's no need to go*
  5 *v.* lack of necessity (in past): *you needn't have written after all*
  5 *n.* want, requirement: *the need for food in Bihar*
4 **needless** *adj.*
3 **needle**
  3 *n.* instrument for sewing
  5 *n.* part of head on record player
  6 *n.* instrument for injecting
4 **negative**
  4 *adj.* opposite of affirmative: *a negative answer*
  5 *n.* film before printing
  7 *n.* in electricity: *connect the negative here*
  7 *adj.* opposite of positive: *negative criticism*
3 **neglect**
  3 *v.* leave unattended to: *neglect one's studies*
  4 *v.* omit or fail to do: *he neglected to write*
5 **negro** *n.*
3 **neighbour** *n.*
4 **neighbourhood** *n.*
2 **neither**
  2 *adj./pron.* not one (or the other): *neither of them; neither one*
  3 *adv./conj.: neither do I*
3 **nephew** *n.*
5 **nerve**
  5 *n.* of the body: *deaden the nerve*
  5 *n.(pl.)* irritability: *suffering from nerves*
  6 *n.* boldness: *plenty of nerve*
  6 *n.* cheek: *what a nerve!*
4 **nervous**
  4 *adj.* anxious: *are you nervous in the dark?*
  5 *adj.* of the mind: *a nervous breakdown*
  6 *adj.* of the body: *the nervous system*
3 **nest**
  3 *n.* bird's home

4 *v.* make home (birds): *some swallows are nesting in the barn*

3 **net**
  3 *n.* knotted material: *fishing net; hair net*
  6 *v.* catch: *net something*
  7 *adj.* clear: *net profit*

5 **network**
  5 *n.* linked system in broadcasting: *the BBC network*
  6 *n.* any complex connected system: *a railway network*

1 **never**
  1 *adv.* at no time: *she never goes to the cinema*
  6 *adv.* emphatic not: *this will never do!*
  7 *adv.* surprise: *well I never did!*
  7 *adv.* don't: *never mind*

1 **new**
  1 *adj.* not known or existing before: *a new play*
  3 *adj.* another: *a new start*
  4 *adj.* fresh: *new potatoes*
  5 *adj.* newly arrived: *I am new here*

2 **news** *n.*

4 **newsagent** *n.*

2 **newspaper** *n.*

5 **New Year's Day** *n.*

4 **New Zealand** *n.*

5 **New Zealander** *n.*

1 **next**
  1 *adj.* nearest in space/order: *the next house*
  2 *adv.* nearest in space/order: *next to him; the next best thing*
  3 *adv.* future: *next Monday*
  4 *adv.* on the first occasion: *when I next see him*

1 **nice**
  1 *adj.* pleasant: *nice weather; nice to the taste*
  3 *adv.* pleasantly (with 'and'): *nice and hot*
  6 *adj.* exact: *a nice point of law*
  7 *adj.* unpleasant: *a nice mess*
  7 *adj.* scrupulous: *he's not so nice in his business methods*

3 **niece** *n.*

1 **night**
  1 *n.* one period of darkness: *two days and nights*
  3 *n.* the state of darkness: *it was night when I awoke*
  6 *n.* activity during darkness: *a night out*

4 **nightfall** *n.*

1 **nine** *n./adj.*

1 **nineteen** *n./adj.*

1 **ninety** *n./adj.*

2 **ninth** *adj.*

1 **no**
  1 *int.* opposite of yes: *no, it isn't*
  2 *adj.* not one/any: *she had no umbrella*
  2 *adj.* (elliptical constructions): *no smoking*
  6 *adj.* definitely not a: *he's no friend of mine*

3 **noble**
  3 *n.* worthy of respect or admiration: *a noble deed*
  5 *n.* rank in society: *the nobles*
  7 *adj.* formal element in title: *the noble lord*

2 **nobody**
  2 *n.* no-one: *we saw nobody we knew*
  7 *n.* of no significance: *he's a nobody*

3 **nod**
  3 *v.* move head in agreement
  3 *n.* motion of the head: *he gave me a nod*
  5 *v.* move head in greeting
  7 *v.* be falling asleep: *sit nodding by the fire*

1 **noise** *n.*

4 **noisy** *adj.*

1 **none**
  1 *det.* not any: *have you any? No, I've none*
  2 *det.* not one: *none of my friends*
  6 *adj.* in no way: *none the better*

3 **nonsense** *n./int.*

2 **noon** *n.*

2 **no-one** *pron.*

2 **nor**
  2 *conj.* (with 'not' or 'neither'): *neither up nor down*

3 *conj.* and . . . not: *I don't like it, nor does he*
3 **normal** *adj.*
1 **north** *n./adj.*
5 **northeast** *n./adj.*
4 **northern** *adj.*
5 **northward/s** *adv.*
5 **northwest** *n./adj.*
3 **North Sea** *n.*
1 **nose**
  1 *n.* part of body
  4 *n.* leading end of moving object: *nose of an aeroplane*
1 **not/n't**
  1 + *adj.*: *it's not hot*
  1 *aux.* +: *he hasn't done it yet*
  1 + any: *there aren't any more*
  2 + *adj.* + 'enough': *it's not hot enough yet*
  4 + to + *v.*: *I told him not to come late*
  5 *v.* (hope etc.) +: *I hope not*
  6 understatement: *not a few*
2 **not only. . . but also** *conj.*: *not only did it rain, but it also hailed*
2 **note**
  2 *n.* written memorandum, jotting, letter
  3 *n.* money: *a pound note*
  4 *v.* write memo etc.: *note it down*
  5 *n.* footnote
  5 *n.* music: *the notes on the piano; the note of a bird*
  7 *n.* mark, sign: *a note of terror*
  7 *n.* significance: *a person of note*
2 **notebook** *n.*
1 **nothing**
  1 *n.* absence: *nothing in the cupboard*
  3 *n.* zero: *he asked for nothing*
  4 *adv.* in no way: *nothing like/near*
2 **notice**
  2 *n.* printed/written information: *a notice on a wall*
  3 *v.* observe: *notice signs of spring*
  4 *n.* attention: *sit up and take notice*

5 *n.* warning: *give him a month's notice*
7 *n.* short particulars of a new book
3 **noticeable** *adj.*
4 **novel**
  4 *n.* a story in prose
  6 *adj.* strange and new
1 **November** *n.*
1 **now**
  1 *adv.* at this moment: *he is here now*
  3 *int.*: *now, sit down here and tell me. . .*
  5 warning: *now, now!*
  6 *adv.* at that juncture (past tense): *the war was now almost ended*
  6 *conj.* since: *now that he knows, there'll be action*
3 **nowadays** *adv.*
2 **nowhere** *adv.*
5 **nuclear** *adj.*
3 **nuisance** *n.*
1 **number**
  1 *n.* figures: *3 and 33 are numbers*
  2 *n.* amount: *a large number of people*
  3 *n.* telephone number: *give me your number*
  4 *n.* turn: *she'll call your number, then you can go in*
  5 *v.* enumerate: *let's number them*
  6 *v.* amount to: *they numbered over 100*
3 **nurse**
  3 *n.* hospital staff: *two nurses to each ward*
  3 *v.* look after: *nurse a patient*
  6 *v.* breast-feed: *nurse a child*
5 **nursery** *n.*
3 **nut**
  3 *n.* fruit of trees
  6 *n.* fitting to bolt
3 **nylon**
  3 *n.* synthetic fibre
  5 *n.(pl.)* stockings: *three pairs of nylons*

o

5 **oak** *n.* / *adj.*
3 **oar** *n.*
5 **obedience** *n.*
5 **obedient** *adj.*
3 **obey** *v.*
3 **object**
  3 *n.* thing: *a distant object*
  5 *v.* do not accept: *I object to that*
  6 *n.* purpose: *my object is to*
5 **objection** *n.*
5 **objective**
  5 *n.* goal
  7 *adj.* opposite of subjective: *objective truth*
4 **oblige** *v.*
5 **observation**
  5 *n.* steady attention: *keep him under observation*
  6 *n.* remark
  7 *n.* finding: *has he published his observations?*
5 **observe**
  5 *v.* watch: *observe the flight of birds*
  6 *v.* remark
  7 *v.* obey: *observe the Sabbath*
4 **obtain** *v.* get
5 **obvious** *adj.* clear
3 **occasion**
  3 *n.* juncture: *on this occasion*
  6 *n.* reason: *we've had no occasion to visit them*
5 **occasional**
  5 *adj.* irregular: *occasional showers*
  7 *adj.* for an event: *occasional tables*
4 **occasionally** *adv.* now and then
5 **occupation**
  3 *n.* job
  6 *n.* act of occupying (a country)
5 **occupy**
  3 *v.* occupy a house
  6 *v.* occupy a country
5 **ocean** *n.*
1 **o'clock** *adv.*
1 **October** *n.*
4 **odd**
  4 *adj.* not even: *odd numbers*
  5 *adj.* one of a set: *odd volumes; an odd shoe*
  6 *adj.* miscellaneous: *odd jobs*
  6 *adj.* strange: *he's odd*
  7 *adj.* with a little extra: *500 odd visitors*
1 **of**
  1 *prep.* connection: *the first of June; the cause of the accident*
  1 *prep.* measure: *a pint of milk*
  1 *prep.* origin: *the works of Shakespeare*
  1 *prep.* separation in space: *to the north of London*
  2 *prep.* substance: *it's made of steel*
  3 *prep.* description: *a girl of ten; the city of Durham*
  3 *prep.* cause: *they died of hunger*
  3 *prep.* subject of action: *the love of a mother for her child*
  4 *prep.* object of action: *the love of study; the building of that house*
  4 *prep.* deprivation, liberation: *that cured him of smoking*
  5 *prep.* from among: *one of my friends; a friend of mine*
  5 *prep.* on the part of: *how kind of you to come*
1 **off**
  1 *prep.* away from: *fall off a ladder*
  3 *adv.* distant: *it's three miles off*
  3 *adv.* disconnected: *the water's off*
  4 *adv.* departed: *he's off to London*
  4 *adv.* cancelled: *the marriage is off*
  4 *adv.* free: *she's taken the day off*
  5 *prep.* near: *they have a shop off Piccadilly*
  6 *prep.* not taking: *she's off drugs now*
  6 *adj.* rotten: *the fish is off*
3 **off duty**
5 **offence**
  5 *n.* minor crime: *commit an offence*
  6 *n.* displeasure: *give offence*
4 **offend** *v.* hurt, displease, annoy

2 offer
  2 *v.* show readiness to give: *I offered her a cigarette*
  3 *n.* proposal: *make an offer for the car*
  6 *v.* occur: *take the first occasion that offers*
  7 *v.* sacrifice: *offer up to God*

1 office
  1 *n.* administration room
  1 *n.* building
  4 *n.* public department: *Foreign Office*
  5 *n.* public post: *he' held office for 7 years*
  6 *n.* duty: *the office of host*
  7 *n.* services: *through the good offices of . . .*

2 officer
  2 *n.* person in command
  6 *n.* person in a position of trust: *the Officers of the Debating Society*

3 official
  3 *n.* a person in authority: *government officials*
  4 *adj.* carrying authority: *the official version*
  5 *adj.* characteristic of authority: *written in the official style*

1 often *adv.* frequently

1 oh *int.*

2 oil
  2 *n.* liquid for fuel or lubrication
  4 *v.* lubricate: *oil your bike*
  6 *n.* paint: *an oil painting*

5 oil-producing *adj.*: *oil-producing country*

1 okay/OK *int.*

1 old
  1 *adj.* opposite of young: *an old man*
  2 *adj.* opposite of new: *old wine*
  4 *adj.* opposite of modern: *old writers*
  5 *adj.* opposite of recent: *his old way of thinking*
  6 *adj.* friendly familiarity: *old chap; old Peter*

5 omelette *n.*

5 omit
  5 *v.* fail: *he omitted to do it*
  6 *v.* leave out: *this chapter may be omitted*

1 on
  1 *prep.* contiguous: *a rug on the floor*
  1 *prep.* location: *he's on the train*
  1 *prep.* direction: *she hit him on the cheek*
  1 *prep.* occurrence: *he comes on Sundays*
  2 *prep.* proximity: *a house on the main road*
  2 *prep.* about: *a lecture on Tolstoy*
  2 *adv.* happening, showing: *what's on tonight?*
  3 *adv.* wearing: *he had nothing on*
  3 *adv.* connected: *the lights are all on*
  3 *prep.* basis: *act on his advice*
  3 *prep.* subsequence: *on his death, the house was sold*
  4 *prep.* membership: *he's on the committee*

4 on account of *prep.*: *the outing was cancelled on account of the bad weather*

5 on behalf of

2 on business

2 on duty

2 on fire

1 on foot

4 on the one hand

4 on the other hand

1 on holiday

1 on a journey

5 on purpose

3 on sale

3 on time

4 on the whole

1 once
  1 *adv.* a single time: *once a week*
  2 *adv.* at one time: *I met him once in Singapore*
  5 *conj.* as soon as: *once he knows, he'll tell you*

1 one
  1 *n./adj.* numeral: *one; one hundred*
  2 *adj./pron.* certain: *one day; one of them*
  3 *pron.* (to avoid repetition): *I must buy one*

3 *adj.* emphatic: *we are one people*
4 *pron.* impersonal: *one must do what one can*
5 *det.* each: *one another*
2 **oneself** *pron.*
5 **onion** *n.*
1 **only**
 1 *adv.* solely: *only boys; under tens only*
 2 *adv.* simply: *I did it only to please you*
 3 *adj.* sole: *the only person present; an only child*
 4 *adv.* merely: *not only but also*
 5 *conj.* but
4 **onto** *prep.*
1 **open**
 1 *adj.* not closed: *the door is open*
 1 *v.* unfasten: *open the box*
 2 *adj.* unfolded: *the letter lay open*
 3 *v.* begin: *open an account*
 3 *adj.* not enclosed: *open country*
 4 *adj.* not covered: *an open boat*
 5 *adj.* free access: *an open invitation*
3 **open out** *v.* broaden, unfold
4 **open up** *v.* unfasten
4 **opening**
 4 *n.* gap: *an opening in a hedge*
 4 *n.* beginning: *the opening of a play*
 6 *n.* opportunity: *there are openings in computer technology*
5 **opera** *n.*
4 **operate**
 4 *v.* cause to work
 5 *v.* act as surgeon
4 **operation**
 4 *n.* working: *the machine is in operation*
 5 *n.* surgical action
 6 *n.* series of actions: *a military operation*
5 **operator** *n.* person who works a machine
3 **opinion**
 3 *n.* view: *what's your opinion?*
 5 *n.* climate of thought: *public opinion*
5 **opponent** *n.*
3 **opportunity** *n.*
4 **oppose** *v.*

2 **opposite**
 2 *adj.* reverse: *in the opposite direction*
 2 *n.* contrary: *black is the opposite of white; they are opposites*
 3 *prep./adv.* facing: *the house is opposite the school; just opposite*
1 **or**
 1 *conj.* alternatively: *black or white*
 2 *conj.* in series: *one or two or three*
 5 *conj.* otherwise: *stop, or I'll fire*
4 **oral**
 4 *adj.* spoken: *oral examination*
 6 *adj.* of the mouth: *oral contraceptives*
1 **orange** *n./adj.*
4 **orchestra**
 4 *n.* for playing music
 7 *n.* part of theatre
2 **order**
 3 *n.* command: *the order to advance*
 3 *v.* give an order: *he ordered lunch*
 4 *n.* turn: *in alphabetical order*
 4 *conj.: in order to*
 5 *conj.: in order that*
 5 *n.* control: *order was restored by the police*
 6 *n.* arrangement, rank: *the lower orders; holy orders; an order of insects*
5 **orderly**
 5 *adj.* well arranged/behaved
 7 *n.* servant in army or hospital
3 **ordinary**
 3 *adj.* usual: *an ordinary day's work*
 6 *adj.* mediocre: *a very ordinary person*
5 **organ**
 5 *n.* musical instrument
 6 *n.* part of the body
 7 *n.* instrument in a system: *organ of the government*
3 **organisation**
 3 *n.* body: *a business organisation*
 4 *n.* system: *you need organisation to run a business*
3 **organise**
 3 *v.* put into working order

6 *v.* form an association of members
5 **oriental** *adj.*
4 **origin** *n.*
4 **original**
  4 *adj.* first or earliest: *the original inhabitants*
  5 *adj.* new: *a very original idea*
  5 *n.* the document first made: *the originals are in the safe*
5 **ornament** *n.*
5 **ornamental** *adj.*
1 **other**
  1 *adj.* different, alternative to: *not this one but the other*
  2 *adj.* second, additional: *I have other things to do*
  4 *adj.* recent: *the other day/week*
3 **otherwise**
  3 *conj.* if not: *I went early, otherwise I would have missed him*
  4 *adv.* in another way: *otherwise engaged*
  5 *adv.* in other respects: *cross-eyed but otherwise good-looking*
  7 *adj.* changed: *I would not wish it otherwise*
2 **ought**
  2 *modal* obligation: *you ought to do it*
  3 *modal* desirability: *there ought to be more buses*
  5 *modal* probability: *he ought to be there by now*
4 **ounce** *n.*
1 **our** *pron.*
2 **ours** *pron.*
2 **ourselves**
  2 *pron.* reflexively: *no use worrying ourselves about that*
  2 *pron.* emphatically: *we've often made that mistake ourselves*
1 **out**
  1 *adv.* not in: *he's gone out for a walk*
  2 *adv.* released: *the news is out*
  2 *adv.* extinction: *put that cigarette out*
  3 *adv.* distant: *he's out in Australia now*
  5 *adj.* mistaken: *you're not far out*

1 **out of**
  1 *prep.* place: *he's out of town this week*
  1 *prep.* movement: *she walked out of the room*
  2 *prep.* from amongst: *choose any one out of these ten*
  2 *prep.* from material: *she made it out of a few scraps*
  3 *prep.* origin: *copy it out of that book*
  5 *prep.* motive: *they helped us out of kindness*
5 **out of breath**
5 **out of control**
4 **out of danger**
3 **out of date**
3 **out of doors**
4 **out of order**
3 **out of place**
5 **out of practice**
5 **out of the question**
4 **out of reach**
4 **out of sight**
3 **out of stock**
4 **out of turn**
3 **out of work**
5 **outbreak** *n.*
5 **outcome** *n.*
5 **outcry**
  5 *n.* loud shout
  6 *n.* public protest
3 **outdoor/s** *adj./adv.*
4 **outer** *adj.*
5 **outlet**
  5 *n.* way out (for water etc.)
  6 *n.* release for feelings
4 **outline**
  4 *n.* drawing, contour
  5 *v.* describe main features
4 **outlook**
  4 *n.* view: *outlook over the valley*
  6 *n.* prospect: *the outlook for foreign trade*
  7 *n.* attitude: *I don't like his outlook*
4 **output**
  4 *n.* quantity produced
  6 *n.* power, energy, information from a computer

2 **outside**
   2 *adv.* not within: *the car is waiting outside*
   3 *n.* exterior: *the outside of the house*
   4 *adj.* external: *outside help; the outside world*
   5 *n./adj.* extreme: *at the very outside; an outside estimate*
5 **outskirts** *n.(pl.)*
5 **outstanding** *adj.*
5 **outward/s**
   5 *adv.* movement to the exterior: *they moved outwards from the centre*
   6 *adj.* external: *the outward appearance of things*
   7 *adj.* opposite of return: *the outward journey*
4 **oven** *n.*
1 **over**
   1 *prep.* above physically: *over my head*
   2 *prep.* across all parts: *put this cloth over the cups*
   3 *adv.* across: *come over and see us*
   3 *adv.* more than: *she's over two hours late*
   4 *adv.* finished: *your troubles will soon be over*
   4 *prep.* ranked superior: *rule over; preference over*
   5 *adv.* at a distance: *over in America*
   5 *prep.* at (during): *a long time over dinner*
5 **overall/s**
   5 *adj.* extreme: *the overall measurements*
   6 *n.* garment: *he wore his overalls*
5 **overboard** *adv.*
4 **overcoat** *n.*
4 **overcome** *v.* conquer: *overcome the enemy*

5 **overflow** *v.*
5 **overhang**
   5 *v.* be directly above: *the cliffs overhang the stream*
   7 *v.* continue to threaten: *these dangers still overhang us*
5 **overlook**
   5 *v.* give on to from above: *my study overlooks the bay*
   6 *v.* fail to notice: *his services were overlooked*
   6 *v.* pass over without punishing: *I cannot overlook a fault*
   7 *v.* superintend
4 **overnight**
   4 *adj.* during the night: *stay overnight with a friend*
   6 *adv.* on the night before: *make preparations overnight*
5 **overseas** *adj./adv.*
5 **overtake**
   5 *v.* pass by going faster: *he overtook the car*
   6 *v.* possess (passive): *he was overtaken by fear*
5 **overtime** *adj./adv.*
3 **owe**
   3 *v.* be in debt: *owe money*
   6 *v.* be indebted for: *we owe this fact to the research of . . .*
5 **owing to** *prep.*: *owing to the rain, we stayed in all day*
2 **own**
   2 *adj.* personal: *I cooked my own dinner*
   3 *v.* possess: *he owns a lot of land*
   7 *v.* admit: *own that; own up to*
3 **owner** *n.*
5 **ownership** *n.*
5 **ox** *n.*
3 **oxygen** *n.*

P

2 **Pacific** *n./adj.*
2 **pack**
  2 *v.* place in container: *pack my bag*
  4 *n.* packet: *pack of cigarettes*
  4 *n.* a set of cards: *you need two packs for that game*
  5 *v.* fill with people: *the room was packed*
  6 *n.* a group of animals: *hunting pack*
  7 *n.* bundle
4 **package** *n.*
2 **packet** *n.* small bundle or parcel
5 **pad**
  5 *n.* container filled with soft material: *put a pad on that wound*
  5 *n.* wad (of paper etc.)
  6 *n.* ink cushion
  6 *n.* launching ground
  7 *n.* underfoot of dog
  7 *v.* move softly about
1 **page**
  1 *n.* leaf in a book
  7 *v.* call (in hotel etc.): *paging Mr Johnson*
2 **pain** *n.* suffering: *be in pain; a pain in the knee*
2 **painful** *adj.*
5 **pains** *n.(pl.)* care
2 **paint**
  2 *n.* substance
  2 *v.* cover surface with paint: *paint a wall*
  3 *v.* create a picture in colour
3 **painter** *n.*
3 **painting** *n.*
2 **pair**
  2 *n.* two: *a pair of shoes*
  6 *n.* man and woman: *they make a nice pair*
3 **palace**
  3 *n.* residence of royalty
  7 *n.* the court: *the palace*
3 **pale** *adj.* having little colour
5 **paleness** *n.*
3 **pan** *n.* cooking utensil
5 **pants** *n.(pl.)*

1 **paper**
  1 *n.* a sheet
  2 *n.* a newspaper
  4 *n.* examination: *the biology paper was difficult*
  5 *n.(pl.)* documents
  5 *v.* cover with paper: *let's paper this wall*
  7 *n.* lecture: *he read a paper*
5 **parade**
  5 *n.* marching ceremony
  6 *v.* march in parade
  7 *n.* thoroughfare (partly) for walking
4 **paragraph**
  4 *n.* section in a continuous piece of writing
  7 *n.* small newspaper article
3 **parallel**
  3 *n.* line in geometry and in latitude
  4 *n.* comparison: *draw a parallel between*
  6 *v.* be closely similar: *his experiences parallel mine*
  6 *n.* equal: *a career without parallel*
2 **parcel**
  2 *n.* package for posting
  5 *v.* wrap up
3 **pardon**
  3 *n.* excuse me: *I beg your pardon*
  5 *n.* forgiveness: *ask pardon for an offence*
  7 *v.* exonerate: *he was pardoned by the king*
2 **parent** *n.*
2 **park**
  2 *n.* area of land for recreation
  3 *v.* station (a car etc.): *park here*
2 **part**
  2 *n.* a piece: *a part of the garden*
  4 *v.* separate: *the lovers parted*
  4 *n.* share in an activity: *take part in a debate*
  6 *v.* separate oneself from: *part with*
  6 *v.* snap: *the rope parted*
  7 *n.* side: *for my part*
3 **partly** *adv.*

5 **partial**
  5 *adj.* not entire: *a partial eclipse*
  6 *adj.* disposed: *partial to /towards*
5 **particle**
  5 *n.* minute piece, speck: *a particle of dust*
  7 *n.* grammatical category
3 **particular**
  3 *adj.* not general or universal: *my particular opinion*
  4 *n.* detail: *take down the particulars*
  5 *adj.* especial: *my particular thanks are due to . . .*
  7 *adj.* fussy: *he's very particular*
4 **partner**
  4 *n.* colleague in business/crime etc.
  5 *n.* other person in paired dancing
4 **part-time** *adj.: part-time work*
1 **party**
  1 *n.* celebration: *birthday/dinner party*
  2 *n.* political grouping: *the Labour party*
  7 *n.* person/body in contract or dispute: *party in treaty*
2 **pass**
  2 *v.* move across: *I saw people passing*
  2 *v.* cause to pass: *pass the salt; pass on information*
  3 *v.* succeed in test: *pass an exam*
  4 *n.* permit: *you need a pass to get in there*
  5 *v.* cause to go through: *pass a law*
  5 *n.* narrow defile: *a mountain pass*
  6 *v.* happen: *come to pass*
5 **pass away** *v.* die
4 **pass off**
  4 *v.* recede (pain)
  5 *v.* take place (ceremony, occasion)
3 **pass out**
  3 *v.* distribute
  5 *v.* lose consciousness
3 **passage**
  3 *n.* narrow walkway
  4 *n.* section in a book
  6 *n.* journey: *a sea passage*
2 **passenger** *n.*
3 **passport** *n.*

2 **past**
  2 *prep.* beyond: *half past seven; past the border*
  3 *n.* what has happened: *in the past*
  3 *adj.* bygone: *past events*
5 **paste**
  5 *v.* glue, stick
  6 *n.* foodstuffs
4 **pastime** *n.*
4 **pat**
  4 *v.* tap gently: *a pat on the back*
  6 *n.* something formed by patting: *a pat of butter*
2 **path**
  2 *n.* a walkway
  4 *n.* line of movement: *the moon's path*
4 **patience**
  4 *n.* calmness in waiting: *a nurse must have patience*
  5 *n.* steadiness: *it needs care and patience*
3 **patient**
  3 *n.* sick person in hospital
  4 *adj.* uncomplaining: *be patient in suffering*
  4 *adj.* calm: *be patient with the child*
  5 *adj.* steady, unhurried: *patient work*
3 **pattern**
  3 *n.* ornamental design
  4 *n.* ways of behaving/moving: *new patterns in family life*
  5 *n.* a model drawing for a designer
  6 *v.* model something/oneself upon
3 **pause**
  3 *v.* cease temporarily: *the speaker paused for a moment*
  4 *n.* hiatus: *a pause in the conversation*
4 **paw**
  4 *n.* foot of dogs, cats etc.
  7 *v.* handle roughly
2 **pay**
  2 *v.* give money for goods or services
  4 *n.* wages: *I earn my pay*
5 **pay back** *v.* punish (in retribution)
3 **pay in** *v.* put money into a bank account

4 **pay off**
4 *v.* settle (debts)
5 *v.* give final wages to
5 **pay out** *v.* disburse
5 **pay up** *v.* hand over the final amount
due
4 **payment**
4 *n.* action of paying: *a cash
payment*
6 *n.* instalment: *10 monthly payments*
7 *n.* reward, punishment
5 **pea** *n.*
3 **peace**
3 *n.* absence of war or civil disorder
5 *n.* calm and quietness
4 **peaceful**
4 *adj.* loving peace: *peaceful nations*
5 *adj.* calm and quiet: *a peaceful
evening*
5 **pear** *n.*
5 **pearl**
5 *n.* precious stone: *a pearl necklace*
7 *n.* person of great value: *she's a
pearl*
5 **peck** *v.* strike with beak: *the hens peck
at the corn*
4 **peculiar**
4 *adj.* odd: *a peculiar fellow*
6 *adj.* special: *of peculiar interest*
7 *adj.* individual: *every nation has its
own peculiar character*
5 **pedestrian**
5 *n.* person walking in streets
5 *adj.* connected with walking
7 *adj.* ordinary and dull
1 **pen**
1 *n.* writing instrument
5 *n.* enclosure: *a cattle/play pen*
7 *n.* writing as a profession: *make a
living by one's pen*
3 **pence** *n.* coins; also **p.**
1 **pencil**
1 *n.* drawing instrument
6 *n.* narrow shape: *a pencil of light*
3 **penny** *n.* coin; also **p.**: *one penny*
5 **pension**
5 *n.* retirement allowance
6 *v.* retire: *he's been pensioned off*
7 *n.* boarding house

1 **people**
1 *n.* a number of persons: *room
crowded with people*
3 *n.* the mass: *common people*
5 *n.* all persons in a nation: *the people
of France*
7 *n.* family: *you must come and meet
my people*
7 *v.* cause to inhabit: *Iceland was
peopled from Norway*
5 **pepper**
5 *n.* seasoning
7 *v.* shoot at: *pepper with questions*
5 **per**
5 *prep.* for each: *per annum*
7 *prep.* by means of: *per post*
3 **per cent**
3 *adv.* rate or number per hundred
4 *n.* proportion
3 **perfect**
3 *adj.* complete, without fault: *a
perfect circle*
4 *adj.* grammatical term: *the perfect
tense*
6 *v.* gain mastery over skill: *perfect
oneself*
7 *adj.* utter: *a perfect fool*
5 **perfection** *n.* faultless completion: *the
perfection of detail in this miniature*
3 **perform**
3 *v.* carry out: *perform one's tasks*
5 *v.* act: *perform in a play*
6 *v.* behave: *how is your car
performing?*
4 **performance**
4 *n.* carrying out of duties
5 *n.* show: *a theatrical performance*
6 *n.* functioning: *performance of a
car etc.*
5 **performer** *n.*
5 **perfume** *n./v.*
5 **perhaps** *adv.*
3 **period**
3 *n.* stretch of time: *the period of the
French Revolution*
4 *n.* lesson: *she teaches 20 periods a
week*
6 *n.* full stop
7 *n.* menstruation

4 **permanent** *adj.*
5 **permission** *n.*
3 **permit**
  3 *v.* allow: *smoking is not permitted*
  5 *n.* document: *a permit to enter the building*
1 **person**
  1 *n.* human being: *any person trespassing will . . .*
  6 *n.* self: *in person*
3 **personal**
  3 *adj.* private: *my personal affairs*
  4 *adj.* individual: *a personal interview*
  5 *adj.* of the body: *personal cleanliness*
  7 *adj.* of the nature of a human being: *a personal God*
3 **persuade** *v.* convince: *persuade somebody of something*
5 **persuasion**
  5 *n.* power of convincing
  7 *n.* belief
3 **pet**
  3 *n.* animal
  4 *v.* fondle: *pet a child*
  6 *n.* favourite: *teacher's pet*
  6 *adj.* favourite: *a pet aversion*
2 **petrol** *n.*
4 **phase**
  4 *n.* stage of development: *a phase of history*
  5 *v.* change gradually: *phase in/out*
  7 *n.* period in moon's visibility
4 **philosophy** *n.*
2 **phone**
  2 *v.* call by telephone
  2 *n.* telephone
2 **photo** *n.* photograph
2 **photograph** *n.*
3 **photographer** *n.*
5 **photographic** *adj.*
4 **photography** *n.*
4 **phrase**
  4 *n.* group of words with syntactic coherence
  6 *n.* series of notes in music
  7 *v.* express: *he phrased his request skilfully*

4 **physical**
  4 *adj.* material: *the physical world*
  5 *adj.* of the body: *physical exercises*
  5 *adj.* of the world: *physical geography*
  7 *adj.* of the laws of nature: *it's a physical impossibility*
5 **physics** *n.*
3 **piano** *n.* musical instrument
2 **pick**
  2 *v.* take up: *pick flowers; pick up a pin*
  4 *v.* select: *pick and choose; pick one's way*
  5 *v.* obtain: *pick up a message*
  5 *v.* take on board: *the bus picked up a few passengers*
  6 *n.* instrument: *they were using picks to dig up the road*
  6 *v.* steal: *pick pockets*
5 **pick-up** *adj.*: *pick-up van*
2 **picnic**
  2 *n.* meal out of doors: *picnic in the country*
  3 *v.* take a meal out of doors
  7 *n.* easy matter to accomplish: *life's no picnic*
1 **picture**
  1 *n.* painting, photograph
  3 *n.* a film: *the picture on TV tonight*
  5 *n.* beautiful scene
  6 *n.* broad features of situation: *put someone in the picture*
  7 *v.* imagine: *picture it to oneself*
  7 *n.* model: *a picture of health*
5 **pie** *n.* food
1 **piece**
  1 *n.* portion: *a piece of land/cake*
  2 *n.* bit, bits: *break to pieces*
  3 *n.* specimen: *a nice piece of furniture*
  6 *n.* coin: *10p. piece*
  5 *v.* fit: *piece together*
3 **pig**
  3 *n.* domestic animal
  5 *n.* dirty/greedy/selfish person
5 **pigeon** *n.*
3 **pile**
  3 *n.* heap: *a pile of books*

5 *v.* heap together: *pile those branches over here*

7 *n.* multiple crash: *a pile-up*

5 **pill**
    5 *n.* medicine
    5 *n.* oral contraceptive

5 **pillar**
    5 *n.* upright column
    7 *n.* abstract support: *a pillar of the establishment*

3 **pillow** *n.*

3 **pilot**
    3 *v.* control aircraft in flight
    3 *n.* controller of aircraft
    6 *n.* controller of large ship at harbour mouth

3 **pin**
    3 *n.* object to fasten things together
    4 *v.* fasten: *pin up this hem*

5 **pinch**
    5 *v.* squeeze: *he pinched my arm*
    5 *n.* compression: *give him a pinch*
    6 *v.* steal
    6 *n.* small portion: *a pinch of salt*

3 **pink**
    3 *n./adj.* colour
    7 *adj.* (political) left-wing

3 **pint** *n.*

2 **pipe**
    2 *n.* tube
    3 *n.* for tobacco
    6 *n.* musical instrument

3 **pity**
    3 *v.* feel compassion for
    4 *n.* disappointment: *it's a great pity it's raining*

1 **place**
    1 *n.* part of space: *which place is it in?*
    1 *n.* city, town, village
    1 *v.* put
    2 *n.* area: *a sore place on my neck*
    2 *n.* passage, point: *I've lost my place in the text*
    3 *n.* position: *he took third place in the race*
    3 *n.* step in argument: *in the first place*

3 *v.* appoint: *she was placed in command*

4 *n.* office, employment: *he found a place in the Civil Service*

4 *n.* invest: *place £500 in National Savings*

4 *v.* order: *place an order for books*

5 *n.* dwelling: *they have a place in Wiltshire*

6 *n.* rank, station: *Victorian servants knew their place*

6 *v.* identify: *it's a difficult melody to place*

3 **plain**
    3 *adj.* clear and simple: *plain words; it's plain to me*
    4 *n.* a flat area: *the plains of India*
    5 *adj.* dull (of food and clothing): *plain fare*
    6 *adj.* unprepossessing
    6 *adj.* forthright: *to be plain with you*

3 **plan**
    3 *n.* outline drawing or diagram
    4 *n.* arrangement for doing something
    5 *v.* make such arrangements

1 **plane**
    1 *n.* aeroplane
    3 *n.* flat surface
    6 *n.* tree
    7 *v.* glide
    7 *v.* smoothe a piece of wood

5 **planet** *n.*

1 **plant**
    1 *n.* something growing in the ground
    2 *v.* place in the ground
    5 *n.* industrial works
    6 *v.* cause to take root (abstract): *to plant an idea*
    7 *n.* action or object to incriminate

5 **plaster**
    5 *n.* covering for walls or ceiling
    5 *v.* render a surface
    5 *n.* cloth etc. placed over wound
    7 *v.* spread liberally: *plaster hair with oil*

2 **plastic**
    2 *n./adj.* substance: *made of plastic*
    6 *adj.* shaping: *plastic surgery; the plastic arts*

1 **plate**
  1 *n.* shallow dish: *a plate of chips*
  5 *n.* notice: *name plate*
  6 *n.* covering: *dental plate; gold plate*
  7 *v.* cover: *plate with chromium*
4 **platform**
  4 *n.* raised dais: *railway platform*
  7 *n.* set of views: *political platform*
1 **play**
  1 *v.* have fun, amuse oneself
  2 *n.* recreation: *all children need play*
  3 *n.* theatrical piece: *a play by Shakespeare*
  4 *v.* perform musically: *play the violin*
  4 *v.* perform theatrically: *she played Cleopatra*
  5 *v.* make move in a game: *it's you to play*
  6 *n.* pun: *a play on words*
  7 *n.* movement: *play in a joint*
5 **play away** *v.* have match away from home
2 **play back** *v.* replay a tape
4 **playground** *n.*
3 **player**
  3 *n.* person engaged in sports/game
  5 *n.* actor, musician
3 **pleasant** *adj.*
1 **please**
  1 *int.* requests: *come in, please*
  3 *v.* make happy: *this will please you*
  5 *v.* like, decide: *I shall do as I please*
  6 *v.* in prayer: *please God*
2 **pleasure**
  2 *n.* feelings: *pleasure and pain; show pleasure*
  5 *n.* source of happiness: *it's a pleasure*
  6 *n.* sensual satisfaction: *live only for pleasure*
4 **plentiful** *adj.*
2 **plenty** *n.*
3 **plot**
  3 *n.* secret plan (good or bad)
  4 *n.* make a plan
  5 *n.* area: *a plot of land*
  5 *v.* mark out: *plot the position*
  6 *n.* action sequence in fiction: *plot of a novel*

3 **plough**
  3 *n.* implement for farming
  3 *v.* turn the soil
  6 *n.* constellation: *the Plough*
5 **plug**
  5 *v.* stop up: *plug a leak*
  5 *n.* stopper (esp. in a washbasin)
  6 *n.* device for making an electrical connection
5 **plunge** *v.* dive, immerse
4 **plural** *adj.* more than one
4 **plus** *conj.*
1 **pocket**
  1 *n.* holder in garment: *coat pocket*
  6 *v.* appropriate: *he pocketed the profit*
  7 *n.* referring to money: *an empty pocket*
  6 *n.* depression, cavity etc.: *a pocket of air*
3 **poem** *n.*
3 **poet** *n.*
3 **poetry**
  3 *n.* the practice of a poet: *reading poetry demands concentration*
  3 *n.* poems: *the poetry of Byron*
  6 *n.* rhythmic elegance: *the poetry of motion*
1 **point**
  1 *n.* sharp extremity: *point of a needle/land*
  1 *v.* indicate: *point at*
  2 *n.* exact place: *draw a line through a point*
  4 *n.* angle, aspect: *point of view*
  4 *prep.* close to: *on the point of going*
  5 *n.* item in exposition or argument
  5 *n.* critical level/phase: *boiling point*
  5 *n.* items in a score: *points in a game*
3 **poison**
  3 *n.* substance
  4 *v.* administer poison
3 **poisonous** *adj.*
3 **pole**
  3 *n.* length of wood
  5 *n.* focus of forces: *magnetic pole*
5 **Pole Star, the** *n.*

2 **police**
  2 *n.* constabulary
  5 *v.* patrol: *the UN policed the area*
1 **policeman** *n.*
3 **polish**
  3 *v.* cause to shine: *polish your shoes*
  4 *n.* substance: *a tin of shoe polish*
  6 *v.* improve to higher level: *polish a piece of writing*
  7 *v.* bring to completion: *polish it off*
2 **polite**
  2 *adj.* showing good manners
  7 *adj.* educated: *polite society*
5 **politeness** *n.*
3 **political** *adj.*
4 **politician** *n.*
3 **politics**
  3 *n.* statecraft
  5 *n.* strategic considerations: *the politics behind that meeting*
  6 *n.* political views/colouring: *what are your politics?*
5 **pollution** *n.*
4 **pond** *n.*
2 **pool**
  2 *n.* shallow stretch of water
  3 *n.* swimming bath
  6 *n.* money staked: *a pool in gambling/business*
  5 *n.* staff/stock with common purposes: *typing pool*
  5 *v.* put together: *they pooled the remaining resources*
1 **poor**
  1 *adj.* having little money: *rich and poor*
  2 *adj.* showing pity: *poor boy*
  4 *adj.* lacking, inferior: *poor in minerals*
5 **pop**
  5 *adj.* (abbrev.) popular: *pop music*
  6 *n.* sound of light explosion
  7 *v.* move quickly, suddenly: *pop in/out/off*
3 **popular**
  3 *adj.* well-liked by many
  4 *adj.* appealing to people in general: *popular science*

5 **popularity** *n.*
3 **population** *n.*
2 **port**
  2 *n.* harbour
  4 *n./adj.* left side of ship or aircraft
  6 *n.* wine of Portugal
4 **porter** *n.*
4 **Portugal** *n.*
4 **Portuguese** *n./adj.*
3 **position**
  3 *n.* location: *find the position of the ship*
  4 *n.* posture of the body: *an uncomfortable position*
  5 *n.* job, post: *a good position as headmaster*
  5 *n.* state of affairs: *the present position*
  6 *n.* view in a matter: *I have changed position over the years*
  7 *v.* place: *the general positioned his army*
5 **positive**
  5 *adj.* definite: *positive orders*
  6 *adj.* helpful: *positive criticism*
  7 *n.* print in photography
  7 *adj.* complete: *a positive fool*
3 **possess** *v.* own: *possess a house*
3 **possession**
  3 *n.* things owned: *my private possessions*
  4 *n.* ownership: *in possession of this property*
  7 *n.* territories: *Britain's earlier overseas possessions*
4 **possibility**
  4 *n.* state of being possible: *is there any possibility that . . .*
  5 *n.* something that is possible: *I see great possibilities in the scheme*
2 **possible**
  2 *adj.* that can be done: *come as quickly as possible*
  4 *adj.* reasonable: *a possible answer is . . .*
2 **post**
  2 *v.* place in pillar box: *post a letter*
  2 *n.* service: *catch the post*
  4 *n.* winning post

5 *n.* position: *the post of headmaster*
5 *n.* place: *trading post*
5 *v.* display: *post up a notice*
4 **postage** *n.*
5 **postal** *adj.*
2 **postcard** *n.*
2 **postman** *n.*
3 **postpone** *v.*
1 **pot**
  1 *n.* vessel: *tea pot*
  4 *v.* place in pots: *pot plants*
  6 *n.(pl.)* lots: *pots of money*
  7 *n.* (colloq.) marijuana
1 **potato** *n.*
2 **pound**
  2 *n.* unit of money/weight
  6 *v.* strike heavily: *he pounded on the door*
  6 *v.* crush: *pound the garlic*
  6 *v.* move heavily: *he pounded along the road*
2 **pour**
  2 *v.* cause to flow: *pour water into a glass*
  4 *v.* flow: *they poured out of the hall*
5 **poverty** *n.*
3 **powder**
  3 *n.* substance in fine particles: *talcum powder*
  4 *v.* apply powder
  6 *n.* medicine
3 **power**
  3 *n.* legal or political control and influence: *power to arrest; the party in power*
  4 *n.* physical or mental ability: *do all that is within my power*
  5 *n.* mechanical power: *the power of the engine*
  6 *n.* instrumental strength: *the power of a lens*
3 **powerful** *adj.*
3 **practical**
  3 *adj.* not theoretical: *practical agriculture*
  4 *adj.* useful in practice: *practical shoes for the country*
  6 *adj.* experienced in the practice: *a practical man*

2 **practice**
  2 *n.* repeated action: *practice makes perfect*
  5 *n.* action not theory: *the practice of medicine*
  7 *n.* area of medical activity: *a doctor's practice*
3 **practise**
  2 *v.* learn through exercises: *she practises the piano*
  3 *v.* do: *practise what you preach*
  5 *v.* exercise a profession: *practise law*
3 **praise**
  3 *v.* laud: *praise a man for his courage*
  5 *n.* honour: *Praise be to God*
  7 *n.* act of praising
2 **pray** *v.* commune with, thank: *pray to God for help*
3 **prayer**
  3 *n.* act of praying: *kneel down in prayer*
  3 *n.* form of worship: *morning prayers*
  4 *n.* form of words: *the Lord's Prayer*
3 **precious**
  3 *adj.* valuable: *gold is a precious metal*
  5 *adj.* cherished: *precious memories*
3 **prefer** *v.* like better: *I prefer tea*
4 **preferable** *adj.*
5 **preference**
  5 *n.* act of preferring: *a preference for tea*
  6 *n.* special consideration (esp. in business): *giving preference to*
5 **pregnant** *adj.* with child (or young): *she's been pregnant for 3 months*
4 **prejudice**
  4 *n.* preformed opinion
  7 *n.* injury to someone's rights
4 **preparation**
  4 *n.* act of making ready: *the treaty is in preparation*
  7 *n.* specially prepared material: *pharmaceutical preparation*
3 **prepare**
  3 *v.* make a thing ready: *prepare the ground for planting*

3 *v.* make: *prepare a meal*

5 **prescription** *n.*

5 **presence**
   5 *n.* being there: *in the presence of his friends*
   7 *n.* alertness for swift reaction: *presence of mind*

1 **present**
   1 *adj.* not absent: *I was present at the meeting*
   3 *n.* the time now: *for the present*
   3 *adj.* current: *the present headmaster; present time*
   4 *n.* gift: *a Christmas present*
   5 *v.* give on special occasion: *present a clock*
   6 *v.* cause to be present, show: *present oneself for examination*

5 **preservation**
   5 *n.* act of keeping from decay: *the preservation of food*
   6 *n.* condition: *in a good state of preservation*

4 **preserve**
   4 *v.* keep intact: *preserve from danger*
   5 *v.* conserve from decay: *preserve food*
   6 *v.* maintain: *preserve one's looks; preserve discipline*

3 **president** *n.* actual or ceremonial head of country/society etc.

3 **press**
   3 *v.* push: *press the button*
   4 *n.* printing and newspaper: *the press*
   4 *v.* flatten surface: *press a suit*
   6 *v.* put emphasis on: *press the point*
   6 *n.* machine: *a sugar press*
   6 *v.* (idea of urgency): *time presses*

4 **pressure**
   4 *n.* pressing: *air pressure in a car tyre*
   5 *n.* intensity: *pressure of business*
   6 *n.* strong influence: *do it under pressure*

3 **pretend** *v.* make believe: *boys pretend they are pirates*

3 **pretty**
   3 *adj.* good-looking: *a pretty child*
   5 *adv.* quite, fairly: *I'm pretty sure*

7 *adj.* (ironic): *a pretty pass*

3 **prevent** *v.*

5 **prevention** *n.*

4 **previous**
   4 *adj.* earlier: *on a previous occasion*
   6 *prep.* before: *previous to*

2 **price**
   2 *n.* cost: *the price of potatoes*
   5 *n.* value, worth: *pearls of great price*
   6 *v.* mark the cost: *all our goods are clearly priced*
   7 *v.* set values: *price oneself out of the market*

5 **prick**
   5 *v.* pierce lightly: *I've pricked my finger*
   5 *n.* marks: *pricks made by a pin*

3 **pride**
   3 *n.* satisfaction: *look with pride at one's garden*
   5 *n.* self respect: *his pride was wounded*
   6 *n.* arrogance: *pride comes before a fall*
   7 *n.* object of satisfaction: *she's her mother's pride and joy*
   7 *v.* feel proud about: *pride oneself upon something*

4 **priest** *n.*

4 **primary**
   4 *adj.* leading in time or order: *a primary school*
   6 *adj.* basic in development: *primary colours*

4 **prince** *n.*

4 **princess** *n.*

4 **principal**
   4 *adj.* most important: *the principal rivers of Europe*
   5 *n.* head: *Principal of a College or other organisation*
   7 *n.* money lent for purposes of building/finance/business*

4 **principle**
   4 *n.* basic truth: *the principles of geometry*
   5 *n.* guiding rules: *moral principles*

7 *n.* lines: *these machines work on the same principles*

3 **print**
  3 *n.* typeset published material: *in large print*
  3 *v.* produce in typeset form
  4 *v.* write in capitals: *print your name*
  4 *v.* develop: *print a photograph*
  6 *n.* fabric: *a cotton print*

3 **printer** *n.*

3 **prison** *n.*

3 **prisoner** *n.*

3 **private**
  3 *adj.* to which the public are not admitted: *private grounds*
  4 *adj.* not official: *private persons*
  6 *adj.* secret: *keep this private*
  7 *n.* soldier without rank

3 **prize**
  3 *n.* reward: *a prize in a competition*
  4 *v.* value: *she prized his gifts to her*
  7 *n.* use force to open
  7 *n.* captured ship

3 **probable** *adj.*

2 **problem** *n.*

5 **procedure** *n.*

5 **proceed**
  5 *v.* continue: *let us proceed*
  7 *n.(pl.)* takings: *the proceeds from the bazaar*

4 **process**
  4 *n.* action sequence: *the process of digestion*
  5 *v.* submit something to a procedure: *process a film/piece of information*

3 **procession** *n.*

3 **produce**
  3 *v.* make: *the South of France produces wine*
  4 *v.* show, cause to be seen: *produce a play*
  6 *n.* yield: *agricultural produce*

5 **producer**
  5 *n.* creator or recreator of a play/film
  6 *n.* opposite of consumer

4 **product**
  4 *n.* something produced by nature or man
  7 *n.* outcome of mathematical process

3 **production**
  3 *n.* process of making: *the production of textiles*
  4 *n.* output: *production has increased*
  6 *n.* thing produced: *an epic production*

3 **profession**
  3 *n.* occupation
  7 *n.* a body of skilled men: *the profession*
  7 *n.* declaration: *a profession of faith*

3 **professional**
  3 *adj.* of a skill: *professional skill; professional man*
  4 *n./adj.* opposite of amateur (usually sport and music)
  6 *adj.* competent, good: *a professional piece of work*

3 **professor** *n.* academic title

5 **proficiency** *n.*

3 **profit**
  3 *n.* money gained
  5 *n.* advantage gained
  6 *v.* gain advantage: *profit from/by*

3 **programme**
  3 *n.* series of performances/events: *TV programme*
  6 *n.* agenda: *what's the programme for tomorrow?*
  7 *n.* action sequence: *a computer program(me)*

3 **progress**
  3 *n.* forward movement/development
  5 *v.* move forward, develop: *the work is progressing*

5 **project**
  5 *n.* a scheme: *an agricultural development project in Mali*
  6 *v.* throw forward: *project a film*
  7 *v.* publicise, depict: *project the British way of life*
  7 *v.* jut out: *the balcony projects over the street*

2 **promise**
  2 *v.* undertake to do: *I promised him £5*
  2 *n.* undertaking: *keep a promise*
  6 *v.* entail: *this promises trouble for the future*

6 *n.* potential: *he shows great promise*
5 **promotion**
  5 *n.* advancement in career: *win promotion*
  7 *n.* publicity: *promotion of a product*
5 **prompt**
  5 *adj.* without delay
  6 *v.* urge: *I felt prompted to ask . . .*
  7 *v.* whisper next words (in the theatre)
2 **pronounce**
  2 *v.* utter clearly: *pronounce this word*
  6 *v.* announce formally: *I pronounce you man and wife*
4 **pronunciation**
  4 *n.* way in which a word is pronounced: *which of these pronunciations do you prefer?*
  5 *n.* way in which language is spoken
  5 *n.* person's way of speaking
3 **proof**
  3 *n.* evidence in general
  6 *n.* trial copy
  7 *adj.* safe: *proof against inflation*
2 **proper**
  2 *adj.* as it ought to be, right: *the proper time/place/dress*
  3 *adj.* polite, good mannered: *proper behaviour*
  7 *adj.* naming an individual person or thing: *a proper noun*
  7 *pron.* itself: *the agreement proper*
  7 *adj.* real, complete: *a proper gentleman*
3 **property**
  3 *n.* possessions: *that case isn't your property*
  4 *n.* land, buildings: *he has property up in Scotland*
  7 *n.* characteristics: *the properties of a chemical*
4 **proportion**
  4 *n.* relation: *the proportion of imports to exports*
  5 *n.* share: *your proportion of the hand-out*
  5 *n.* balance: *a room of good proportions*
  6 *n.* size: *of majestic proportions*

4 **proposal**
  4 *n.* a plan or scheme
  5 *n.* offer of marriage
3 **propose**
  3 *v.* put forward an idea/scheme for consideration
  4 *v.* offer marriage
  6 *v.* offer as candidate: *propose somebody for a post*
3 **protect** *v.*
3 **protection**
  3 *n.* safekeeping: *the protection of the police*
  6 *n.* defensive measure: *as a protection to the steel industry*
4 **protest**
  4 *v.* (against) raise an objection: *the Liberals protested*
  4 *n.* objection: *protests came from many quarters*
5 **Protestant** *n./adj.*
3 **proud**
  3 *adj.* showing proper pride: *proud of their success*
  3 *adj.* arrogant: *she's too proud for my liking*
  5 *adj.* arousing proper pride: *it's a proud day for the school*
3 **prove**
  3 *v.* supply proof: *they proved his guilt*
  4 *v.* show genuineness: *prove a will/a man's worth*
  6 *v.* turn out to be: *it proved to be different*
  7 *v.* establish own ability: *prove oneself*
3 **provide**
  3 *v.* furnish: *provide a meal*
  4 *v.* use foresight, insure: *provide for one's children*
5 **provided** *conj.* so long as: *provided we go now we will . . .*
5 **province**
  5 *n.* administrative division
  6 *n.* region(s) at some distance from the capital
  7 *n.* area of action, learning: *that's outside my province*

4 **provision**
  4 *n.* supply: *provision of water and gas*
  5 *n.* allowance: *make provision for breakdowns*
  6 *n.* condition of agreement: *he agreed to come with the provision that . . .*
  7 *n.* supplies: *provisions of food*
4 **psychological**
  4 *adj.* of (the study of) the mind
  7 *adj.* critical: *the psychological moment*
5 **pub** *n.*
2 **public**
  2 *adj.* relating to people in general: *public holiday / opinion*
  3 *adj.* opposite of private: *make it public*
  3 *n.* people in general: *the general public*
  5 *adj.* relating to the state: *public ownership / education*
5 **publication**
  5 *n.* something published (book, report, etc.)
  6 *n.* act of publishing: *publication is tomorrow*
4 **publish**
  4 *v.* bring out in print
  7 *v.* make information known
5 **pudding** *n.*
1 **pull**
  1 *v.* opposite of push: *pulling a heavy cart up the hill*
  1 *n.* act of pulling: *just give this handle a pull*
  5 *v.* strain: *he's pulled a muscle in his back*
  6 *v.* row: *the oarsmen weren't pulling together*
  7 *n.* influence: *he has a lot of pull with the manager*
  7 *v.* draw in smoke: *he was pulling at his pipe*
4 **pull down** *v.* demolish
4 **pull in** *v.* draw to a halt (train, car)
4 **pull off**
  4 *v.* remove
  5 *v.* succeed against odds

4 **pull on** *v.* put on clothing
4 **pull out**
  4 *v.* extract
  4 *v.* begin to move (train, ship, car into traffic)
4 **pull up** *v.* slow down and stop (bus, car, bike)
5 **pullover** *n.*
3 **pump**
  3 *n.* machine, instrument: *a petrol pump*
  3 *v.* use such a machine
  6 *v.* force against resistance: *pump facts into their heads*
3 **punctual** *adj.*
3 **punish**
  3 *v.* chastise: *punish for wrongdoing*
  7 *v.* treat roughly: *he punished his opponent in the match*
4 **punishment** *n.*
1 **pupil**
  1 *n.* learner
  6 *n.* part of the eye
4 **purchase**
  4 *v.* buy: *she purchased a mink coat*
  4 *n.* things bought: *she put her purchases in the car*
3 **pure**
  3 *adj.* unmixed: *pure water*
  5 *adj.* not applied: *pure maths*
  5 *adj.* innocent: *my heart is pure*
  7 *adj.* complete: *pure invention / nonsense*
5 **purity** *n.*
4 **purple** *adj. / n.*
3 **purpose**
  3 *n.* aim: *for what purpose?*
  4 *n.* intention: *she did it on purpose*
  7 *n.* resolution: *he lacks purpose*
  7 *n.* need: *purpose-built*
2 **purse**
  2 *n.* small bag for money
  6 *n.* government funds: *the public purse*
  7 *v.* compress: *purse one's lips*
4 **pursue**
  4 *v.* go after
  5 *v.* continue with: *pursue one's studies*

1 push
1 *v.* opposite of pull: *push the table nearer the wall*
1 *n.* act of pushing: *can you give my car a push*
5 *v.* urge: *she'll push him on in his career*
6 *v.* promote: *what's that advert pushing?*
1 put
1 *v.* move: *he put the book down*
1 *v.* place: *put a new handle on this knife*
4 *v.* bring, cause: *put him to shame/great expense*
6 *v.* submit: *I put it to him that . . .*
4 put aside *v.* reserve
3 put away *v.* return to proper place for keeping
4 put back
4 *v.* change time on clock
5 *v.* defer
3 put down *v.* write down
5 put in for *v.* apply for

4 put off
4 *v.* postpone
5 *v.* discourage
5 *v.* distract
2 put on
2 *v.* get dressed in
2 *v.* switch on (light)
3 *v.* increase (in weight)
2 put out
2 *v.* extinguish
4 *v.* issue (information)
2 put through *v.* connect (by telephone)
3 put up
3 *v.* raise (price)
5 *v.* provide lodging
5 put up with *v.* tolerate
4 puzzle
4 *n.* difficult question or problem: *a crossword puzzle*
5 *v.* confuse: *I'm puzzled about this*
6 *v.* seek to resolve: *puzzle over something*
3 pyjamas *n.(pl.)*

Q

5 qualification
5 *n.* degree, diploma etc.
7 *n.* act of modifying/limiting
4 qualify
4 *v.* complete training: *he qualified as a teacher in 1958*
6 *v.* make less inclusive or general: *that remark needs to be qualified*
3 quality
3 *n.* standard: *poor quality goods*
4 *n.* characteristics: *he has many good qualities*
3 quantity
3 *n.* amount: *a small quantity*
7 *n.* factor: *an unknown quantity*
7 *n.* abundance: *we've had quantities of rain*

2 quarrel
2 *v.* argue, disagree: *they're quarrelling about money*
2 *n.* angry argument
1 quarter
1 *n.* fourth part: *quarter of a pound/hour*
5 *n.* area: *the Italian quarter*
5 *n.* part of year
6 *n.* point of the compass/directions: *from all quarters*
6 *n.* US coin: *a dollar and a quarter*
7 *n.(pl.)* residence: *my quarters*
1 queen
1 *n.* ruler of a country, wife of a king
2 *n.* supreme person: *beauty queen*
7 *n.* piece in chess

5 **queer**
  5 *adj.* strange, unwell
  7 *adj.* distort: *to queer someone's pitch*
  7 *n.* (colloq.) homosexual
1 **question**
  1 *n.* enquiry: *ask a question; question mark*
  3 *n.* subject under discussion
  6 *v.* doubt, reconsider: *I question your right to act*
3 **queue**
  3 *n.* line of people/cars waiting
  4 *v.* line up: *queue up for a bus*
1 **quick**
  1 *adj.* rapid: *a quick walk/movement/word*
  3 *adv.* rapidly: *do it quick*
  5 *adj.* lively: *quick temper/eye*
1 **quiet**
  1 *adj.* not noisy: *be quiet; keep quiet; as quiet as a . . .*
  3 *adj.* not active: *the stock market was quiet*
  3 *adj.* undisturbed: *a quiet smoke/mind etc.*
  4 *n.* restfulness: *peace and quiet*
  6 *adj.* secret: *keep it quiet*
5 **quietness** *n.*
2 **quite**
  2 *adv.* entirely: *quite certain; I can't quite believe it*
  5 *adv.* rather: *quite pretty*
  6 *adv.* entirely so, I agree

R

3 **rabbit** *n.*
3 **race**
  3 *v.* rush: *the children raced towards me*
  3 *v.* compete in speed: *X is racing in the 100 yards*
  3 *n.* competition: *a horse race*
  5 *n.* species: *the human race*
  5 *n.* variety: *the Mongolian race*
  6 *n.* nation: *the German race*
4 **racket**
  4 *n.* noise: *the drunks made a racket*
  5 *n.* bat for tennis (also **racquet**)
  6 *n.* dishonest trade, dealing
5 **radar** *n.*
1 **radio**
  1 *n.* instrument/set for listening
  2 *n.* communication system: *the police were in touch by radio*
  5 *v.* communicate: *they radioed for help*
5 **rag** *n.* bit of cloth
3 **rail**
  3 *n.* travelling system: *go by rail*
  5 *n.* length of metal: *the coach left the rails*
  7 *n.* bar: *a stair rail for the carpet*
5 **railing** *n.*
5 **railroad** *n.*
2 **railway** *n.*
1 **rain**
  1 *n.* water from clouds
  1 *v.* precipitate in weather: *it's raining*
  7 *n.* tropical season: *the rains*
5 **rainbow** *n.*
4 **raincoat** *n.*
5 **rainfall** *n.*
4 **rainy** *adj.*
2 **raise**
  2 *v.* lift, cause to come or go up: *raise a flag*
  3 *v.* cause to increase: *raise prices/the temperature*
  5 *v.* cause to grow up: *raise a family; raise horses*
  6 *v.* provoke: *raise a rebellion/question*
  6 *n.* salary increase (US): *I need a raise*

7 *v*. cause to project or erect: *raise a monument*

7 *v*. gather: *raise an army/money/taxes*

7 *v*. elevate in rank or position

5 **raisin** *n*.

5 **rake**

  5 *n*. implement: *a garden rake*

  5 *v*. gather: *rake up the leaves*

  7 *v*. search: *rake through the files in search of a letter*

4 **range**

  4 *n*. scale or variety: *a range of goods/choices*

  4 *n*. line of mountains

  5 *n*. distance in space/time: *long range; range of vision*

  6 *v*. browse, ponder: *he let his mind range over the events*

  6 *v*. search: *they ranged far and wide*

  7 *v*. draw up for action: *the general ranged his troops*

  7 *v*. reach: *this gun ranges over 6 miles*

3 **rank**

  3 *n*. level in hierarchy: *the rank of Colonel*

  4 *n*. line: *a taxi rank; the front ranks*

  5 *v*. assess: *he ranks that scheme amongst the failures*

3 **rapid**

  3 *adj*. speedy

  6 *n.(pl.)* disturbed stretch of water in river: *the rapids*

4 **rare**

  4 *adj*. infrequent: *a rare event*

  6 *adj*. thinly distributed: *rare air*

  7 *adj*. lightly grilled/roasted: *rare steak*

5 **rat**

  5 *n*. animal

  7 *n*. traitor

3 **rate**

  3 *n*. standard of reckoning: *rate of exchange; bank rate*

  3 *n*. quality: *first rate; second rate*

  4 *n*. manner of proceeding: *at this/that/any/rate*

  5 *n*. ratio: *the birth/death rate*

6 *n.(pl.)* municipal taxes: *water rates*

6 *v*. assess: *how do you rate this?*

2 **rather**

  2 *adv*. more: *it's a jacket rather than a shirt*

  3 *adv*. to some extent: *I rather think; rather earlier than usual*

  4 *adv*. in preference: *I would rather not go*

5 **rattle**

  5 *v*. make short sharp sound repeatedly, often irregularly

  5 *n*. short sharp sound

  6 *n*. toy: *a child's rattle*

  6 *v*. accomplish fast: *to rattle something off*

  7 *v*. irritate, disconcert: *to rattle someone*

3 **raw**

  3 *adj*. uncooked: *raw meat*

  4 *adj*. unprocessed: *raw material*

  6 *adj*. sensitive: *a raw place on my shoulder*

  7 *adj*. harsh: *a raw deal*

3 **razor** *n*.

2 **reach**

  2 *v*. attain: *we reached London at 6.00*

  3 *v*. stretch out: *reach out your hand*

  4 *n*. capacity to do: *beyond my reach*

5 **react**

  5 *v*. respond

  6 *v*. oppose: *the people reacted against the government*

  7 *v*. affect chemically: *how do acids react on metals?*

4 **reaction**

  4 *n*. response: *a healthy reaction*

  6 *n*. conservatism: *the forces of reaction*

  6 *n*. (science): *a nuclear reaction*

1 **read**

  1 *v*. understand writing

  2 *v*. understand language: *can you read Chinese?*

  2 *v*. reproduce writing vocally: *read me that letter*

  5 *v*. interpret: *read thoughts*

  6 *v*. show (measure): *what does the thermometer read?*

7 *v.* study: *he's reading for a degree*
2 **reader**
  2 *n.* one who understands writing
  3 *n.* person with reading habits: *the readers of a magazine*
  5 *n.* a textbook
  6 *n.* academic title
2 **ready**
  2 *adj.* prepared: *dinner is ready*
  5 *adj.* willing: *I am ready to trust you*
  7 *adj.* quick to respond: *a ready tongue/pen/wit*
  7 *adj.* available for quick use: *ready money/reckoner*
3 **real**
  3 *adj.* existing: *in the real world*
  3 *adj.* natural, pure: *real silk*
5 **realisation** *n.*
3 **realise**
  3 *v.* understand as a reality: *too young to realise*
  6 *v.* make real: *realise one's ideals*
4 **reality** *n.* actuality: *the reality is different*
1 **really**
  1 *adv.* genuinely: *it's really old*
  2 *adv.* intensive: *it's really a pity*
  5 *int.* astonishment: *well, really!*
  7 *int.* showing lack of interest: *she's very nice – Really?*
5 **rear**
  5 *adj.* posterior: *the rear lamps*
  5 *n.* back: *the rear of the house*
  6 *v.* raise: *rear cattle*
  7 *v.* lift/rise suddenly: *the animal reared its head*
2 **reason**
  2 *n.* logical cause or motive: *for what reason did he go?*
  4 *v.* argue: *reason it out with him*
  5 *n.* faculty: *the voice of reason*
  6 *n.* sensible limits: *anything within reason*
3 **reasonable**
  3 *adj.* sensible: *a reasonable man/decision*
  4 *adj.* not excessive: *reasonable price*

4 **receipt**
  4 *n.* proof of payment: *give me a receipt*
  7 *n.* income: *business receipts*
  7 *n.* act of receiving: *the receipt of your letter*
2 **receive**
  2 *v.* be given, obtain: *receive a letter/present*
  3 *v.* take in: *we received the news*
  4 *v.* (of abstract things): *receive attention/power*
  7 *v.* accept a visit from: *the King received the Ambassador*
5 **receiver** *n.* part of telephone
3 **recent** *adj.*
4 **reception**
  4 *n.* receiving of visitors: *a reception room*
  5 *n.* taking in message: *radio reception*
  6 *n.* public response: *his book had a favourable reception*
5 **recipe** *n.*
2 **recognise**
  2 *v.* know again, identify: *I didn't recognise her*
  4 *v.* admit as true: *recognise the fact*
  6 *v.* admit as legal or valid: *recognise a government/claim*
5 **recognition**
  5 *n.* act of recognising
  6 *n.* acceptance (in law)
3 **recommend**
  3 *v.* speak favourably of: *I can recommend this soap*
  4 *v.* advise: *recommend him to try*
4 **recommendation**
  4 *n.* suggestion: *on the recommendation of a friend*
  5 *n.* proposal: *a list of recommendations*
2 **record**
  2 *n.* disc: *gramophone record*
  4 *n.* account: *records of the past*
  4 *v.* note down, remember or make recording
  6 *n.* best performance: *break the record*
  7 *n.* career: *military record*

4 record-player *n.*
3 recover
3 *v.* get better from illness/weakness
5 *v.* get back what was lost
6 *v.* regain control
7 *v.* cover again: *we'll recover these chairs*
5 recreation *n.*
1 red
1 *n./adj.* colour
6 *n./adj.* Russian, Soviet, left-wing
7 *n.* debt: *get in the red*
5 reddish *adj.*
3 reduce
3 *v.* make less: *reduce one's expenses*
6 *v.* bring to different condition: *reduce to order*
7 *v.* lose weight: *she's been reducing all summer*
4 reduction *n.* diminution: *reduction in numbers*
3 refer
3 *v.* turn to for information: *he referred to the dictionary*
4 *v.* allude to: *referring to your letter*
5 *v.* hand over: *the affair was referred to the UN*
7 *v.* credit: *he referred his success to good teaching*
4 reference
4 *n.* allusion: *here's a reference to . . .*
5 *n.* information store: *reference book/library*
7 *n.(pl.)* testimonials: *he has good references*
7 *n.* specification: *terms of reference*
4 reflect
4 *v.* throw back: *a mirror reflects light*
5 *v.* indicate: *the newspaper reflects public opinion*
6 *v.* credit, discredit: *your conduct reflects well/badly*
7 *v.* ponder: *let me reflect on that*
5 reflection
5 *n.* image: *my reflection in a mirror*
7 *n.* consideration: *after careful reflection*

5 refresh
5 *v.* restore: *refresh oneself with a cup of tea*
6 *v.* recall: *refresh one's memory*
5 refreshment(s)
5 *n.(pl.)* food and/or drink: *light refreshment*
6 *n.* restoration: *feel refreshment of mind and body*
4 refrigerator *n.*
5 refusal
5 *n.* saying no: *the refusal of an invitation*
7 *n.* opportunity to say no: *give me first refusal*
2 refuse
2 *v.* not to accept: *refuse help*
7 *n.* garbage: *a refuse dump*
3 regard
3 *n.* reference: *with regard to your letter*
5 *n.* consideration: *without any regard to cost*
5 *v.* consider: *regard it as an insult*
6 *n.* esteem: *high or low regard*
5 regardless *adj.*
4 regards
4 *n.(pl.)* greetings: *with kind regards*
5 *prep.:* *as regards*
4 region *n.*
4 register
4 *v.* record officially: *register a birth*
4 *n.* official record
5 *v.* show: *the thermometer registered 35°C*
7 *v.* pay special rate to ensure delivery: *register a letter*
3 regret
3 *v.* be sorry (polite formula): *I regret to inform you . . .*
5 *n.* sadness at loss: *they have no regrets*
5 *v.* feel sorry for: *I regret my mistake*
2 regular
2 *adj.* at steady intervals: *regular meals/lessons*
4 *adj.* uniform, symmetrical: *regular teeth/features*

6 *adj.* conforming to rule: *regular in his habits; a regular verb*
5 **regularity** *n.*
4 **regulation**
    4 *n.* rules: *the current regulations*
    6 *n.* putting into perfect working condition: *the regulation of a clock*
    7 *adj.* prescribed: *regulation size*
5 **rejoice** *v.* feel happy, cheer: *they rejoiced when they heard the news*
4 **relate**
    4 *v.* be linked through family: *he's related to me by marriage*
    5 *v.* tell: *relate a story*
    6 *v.* feel in communion: *I find it difficult to relate to them*
    6 *v.* link: *I can't relate the cause to the effect*
3 **relation**
    3 *n.* linking of people: *friendly relations between two organisations*
    4 *n.* linking of things: *relation of height to weight*
    5 *n.* kin: *near relations*
4 **relationship**
    4 *n.* link, connection: *a relationship between those facts*
    5 *n.* friendship: *a lasting relationship with someone*
4 **relative**
    4 *n.* member of family: *a relative of mine lives in Brussels*
    6 *adj.* other things: *relative position*
    6 *adj.* connecting in grammar: *relative pronoun*
4 **relax** *v.* loosen: *relax discipline*
5 **release**
    5 *v.* allow to go free: *release a man from prison*
    6 *v.* publish, distribute: *release news; release a film*
    7 *n.* item of news: *a release by the Mauritanian government*
5 **reliable** *adj.*
4 **relief**
    4 *n.* easing: *relief from pain*
    6 *adj.* standing out in profile: *a relief map*

7 *n.* rescue from danger: *relief of a town*
5 **relieve**
    5 *v.* ease: *relieve anxiety/pain*
    7 *v.* supplant: *relieve the guard*
3 **religion**
    3 *n.* belief in God
    6 *n.* obsessional concern: *she makes a religion of work*
5 **rely** *v.*
2 **remain**
    2 *v.* stay: *I shall remain here another 3 years*
    3 *v.* continue to exist: *little remains of the town*
3 **remark**
    3 *n.* comment: *he made some remarks about the plan*
    3 *v.* comment: *he remarked on the proposals*
    6 *v.* notice: *she remarked the change in his tone*
4 **remedy**
    4 *n.* means of putting right: *a remedy for an illness*
    5 *v.* put right, cure: *remedy an evil*
1 **remember**
    1 *v.* keep in memory
    5 *v.* pass greeting: *remember somebody to somebody*
    7 *v.* make a present to: *please remember the waiter*
3 **remind** *v.*
4 **removal** *n.*
2 **remove**
    2 *v.* take off or away: *remove my hat*
    3 *v.* get rid of: *remove a stain*
    5 *v.* shift furniture and belongings: *remove a household*
3 **rent**
    3 *v.* hire: *rent a cottage*
    3 *n.* payment: *the rent here is £25 a week*
    6 *n.* tear: *the rent in the curtain*
2 **repair**
    2 *n.* mending: *house repairs*
    3 *v.* mend: *repair shoes*
    6 *n.* state: *in good repair*
    7 *v.* make up for: *repair the wrong*

2 **repeat**
  2 *v.* say again, say from memory:
    repeat that three times
  5 *v.* do again: *repeat a success*
  5 *n.* another of the same: *a repeat
    performance*
4 **replace**
  4 *v.* substitute: *can you replace me in
    the team?*
  5 *v.* put back: *replace it on the shelf*
2 **reply**
  2 *v.* answer: *reply to a letter*
  3 *n.* response: *they could make no
    reply*
2 **report**
  2 *n.* account, assessment: *make a
    report*
  2 *v.* bring or send news
  4 *n.* rumour: *do not believe the report
    that . . .*
  6 *v.* give in a name: *report on
    arrival*
  7 *n.* sound of explosion: *report of a
    gun*
4 **reporter** *n.*
4 **represent**
  4 *v.* show: *this diagram represents our
    1977 sales*
  5 *v.* symbolise: *the circle represents
    the sun*
  6 *v.* act in place of: *Mr X represented
    the Ambassador*
5 **representative**
  5 *n.* person acting for: *a
    representative of the people*
  6 *adj.* typical: *it's not a representative
    example*
5 **reproduce**
  5 *v.* copy a photograph
  5 *v.* play recording
  6 *v.* bring forth young: *rabbits
    reproduce quickly*
5 **reproduction**
  5 *n.* act of copying photograph/record
  6 *n.* process of reproducing
5 **republic** *n.* system of government
5 **reputation** *n.*
3 **request**
  3 *n.* asking: *grant a request*

4 *v.* ask: *request you to send*
4 **require**
  4 *v.* need: *we require extra help*
  6 *v.* order: *students are required
    to . . .*
3 **rescue** *v./n.*
4 **research**
  4 *n.* investigation in depth
  6 *v.* carry out research: *they
    researched into the effects of
    cigarette smoking for years*
5 **reservation**
  5 *n.* grounds for hesitation: *I have my
    reservations*
  6 *n.* booking: *a reservation (on a
    train)*
3 **reserve**
  3 *n.* spare stock: *reserves of food*
  4 *v.* hold back, store: *reserve
    money/food*
  6 *n.* coolness, control: *he spoke with
    reserve*
4 **resident**
  4 *n.* as opposed to visitors, tourists: *a
    resident of Hull*
  5 *adj.* living in: *a resident nurse*
5 **resign**
  5 *v.* give up position/membership: *the
    chairman has resigned*
  7 *v.* be ready to accept: *resign oneself
    to one's fate*
5 **resignation**
  5 *n.* act of resigning: *give in one's
    resignation*
  7 *n.* uncomplaining acceptance: *accept
    something with resignation*
5 **resist**
  5 *v.* stand up to: *resist an enemy*
  6 *v.* keep away from: *I must resist
    chocolate*
4 **resistance**
  4 *n.* struggle: *he made no resistance*
  4 *n.* strength to repel: *resistance to
    pressure/disease*
  6 *n.* electrical part
4 **resource/s**
  4 *n.* wealth, potential: *natural
    resources*
  7 *n.* ingenuity: *a man of resource*

3 **respect**
3 *v.* show reverence/consideration: *respect our elders/oneself*
4 *v.* act in accordance with: *we must respect his needs*
6 *n.* acknowledgement, greeting: *pay our respects to*
7 *prep.* in relation to: *in respect of*

5 **respectful** *adj.*

5 **response**
5 *n.* answer: *my letter brought no response*
6 *n.* reaction: *little response to the new medicine*

3 **responsibility**
3 *n.* authority: *on one's own responsibility*
4 *n.* duties: *the Prime Minister's responsibilities*

3 **responsible**
3 *adj.* liable: *responsible to/for*
4 *adj.* dependable: *a responsible person*
6 *adj.* with significant authority: *responsible position*

1 **rest**
1 *n.* recuperation: *a night's rest*
2 *v.* recuperate: *I advise you to rest*
3 *n.* remainder: *the rest of them*
4 *v.* place: *rest it on the table*

2 **restaurant** *n.*

5 **restless** *adj.*

5 **restore**
5 *v.* give back: *restore to its rightful owner*
6 *v.* bring back: *restore order*
7 *v.* return to original condition: *restore a building/a picture*

2 **result**
2 *n.* outcome: *the results of the exam*
6 *v.* produce: *his journey resulted in a great discovery*

3 **retire**
3 *v.* give up work: *he will retire on a pension next year*
6 *v.* retreat: *the army retired*
7 *v.* withdraw: *retire to one's bed*

5 **retirement**
5 *n.* state of having retired: *live in retirement*
7 *n.* act of retiring: *there have been several retirements*

1 **return**
1 *v.* go back: *return home*
1 *v.* come back: *we will return to this subject later*
2 *n.* act of coming back: *his return home*
3 *v.* take/send back: *return books to the library*
5 *n.* repayment, reward: *no return for his labours*
6 *v.* revert: *return to the old customs*

5 **revenge**
5 *n.* satisfaction for an offence: *in revenge for the suffering undergone*
6 *v.* act to obtain satisfaction for offence: *revenge an insult/an injustice*

5 **reverse**
5 *n.* opposite: *he always does the reverse*
5 *v.* cause to go backwards: *reverse the car into the garage*
6 *n.* other side of object/matter: *the reverse of a coin*
7 *n.* misfortune in scheme/affairs: *suffer a reverse*

4 **revise**
4 *v.* prepare: *revise for an exam*
5 *v.* correct, update: *a revised edition*
6 *v.* reconsider: *revise one's opinion*

3 **revolution**
3 *n.* fundamental change in system: *the French Revolution*
5 *n.* full turns/cycles: *four thousand revolutions a minute*

3 **reward**
3 *n.* recompense: *a high reward for finding the criminal*
4 *v.* recognise service(s) by making gift: *he was rewarded for his bravery*

4 **rhythm** *n.*

3 **ribbon**
3 *n.* band of cloth: *silk ribbons*

6 *n.* (fig.) strip: *ribbon development in urban planning*
1 **rice** *n.*
1 **rich**
  1 *adj.* wealthy: *a rich man/country*
  3 *adj.* productive: *rich soil*
  4 *n.* people: *the rich*
  5 *adj.* ample: *a rich supply of*
  5 *adj.* sumptuous: *a rich dress*
  6 *adj.* oily: *rich food*
  6 *adj.* intense: *rich colour*
5 **rid**
  5 *adj.* clear, free: *get rid of this rubbish*
  7 *v.* make free: *he wanted to rid himself of debt*
1 **ride**
  1 *v.* travel: *ride (on) a horse/(in) a bus*
  3 *n.* a short distance travelled
  7 *v.* stay as it is: *let something ride*
4 **rider**
  4 *n.* horseman, cyclist
  7 *n.* connected observation
5 **ridiculous** *adj.*
5 **rifle**
  5 *n.* gun
  7 *v.* search thoroughly
1 **right**
  1 *adj.* correct: *what's the right time?*
  1 *adj.* suitable: *he's the right man for the job*
  1 *adj.* not left: *your right foot*
  2 *adj.* sound: *she feels all right now*
  2 *adv.* correctly: *if I remember right*
  3 *adv.* directly: *go right there*
  3 *adv.* completely: *he slipped right to the bottom*
  4 *adj.* ethically correct: *do what is right*
  4 *n.* claim: *she has a right to know*
  6 *v.* restore to proper condition: *the fault will right itself*
1 **ring**
  1 *n.* circle: *dance in a ring*
  1 *n.* ornament: *ring on my finger*
  2 *v.* cause to sound: *ring a bell*
  4 *n.* telephone call: *give him a ring*
  7 *n.* arena: *the (boxing) ring*
2 **ring back** *v.* telephone again

2 **ring off** *v.* end telephone conversation
2 **ring up** *v.* telephone
3 **ripe**
  3 *adj.* ready to harvest or eat
  6 *adj.* well considered: *ripe judgement*
  7 *adj.* ready for process to begin: *ripe for development*
  7 *adj.* matured: *ripe cheese*
5 **ripen** *v.*
2 **rise**
  2 *v.* go upwards: *the sun rises*
  3 *v.* stand up, get up: *he rose at 7.00 a.m.*
  4 *v.* of a slope: *the hill rises from the plain*
  4 *v.* increase: *his temperature rose*
  5 *n.* increase in money: *a rise in wages/in prices*
  6 *v.* rebel: *they rose against him*
  7 *n.* cause: *give rise to*
4 **risk**
  4 *v.* endanger: *to risk one's life*
  4 *n.* acts to endanger: *don't take risks on that road*
  6 *n.* uncertain quantity: *he's a risk*
5 **risky** *adj.*
5 **rival** *n.*
1 **river**
  1 *n.* natural stream of water
  5 *n.* a great flow: *a river of lava*
1 **road**
  1 *n.* way: *the roads of Scotland*
  5 *n.* (fig.): *the road to ruin*
3 **roar**
  3 *v.* make frightening/loud sound: *he roared with anger*
  3 *n.* loud sound: *the roar of traffic*
5 **roast**
  5 *v.* cook
  5 *n.* joint of meat: *a roast for Sunday lunch*
  7 *v.* warm oneself: *he was roasting in the sun*
4 **rob**
  4 *v.* steal
  6 *v.* deprive: *he was robbed of the rewards of his labours*
5 **robber** *n.*

5 **robbery** *n.*
2 **rock**
  2 *n.* stone: *a house built on a rock*
  3 *v.* sway: *rock a baby*
  5 *n.* style of music
5 **rod**
  5 *n.* stick: *fishing rod*
  6 *n.* stick for punishment
  7 *n.* shaft: *piston rods*
4 **role**
  4 *n.* actor's part in play
  5 *n.* function in transaction
2 **roll**
  2 *v.* move cyclically: *roll over and over; roll one's eyes*
  3 *v.* form by rolling: *roll into a ball; roll a cigarette*
  5 *n.* cylindrical bundle: *roll of paper*
  5 *v.* sway: *the ship was rolling heavily*
  6 *v.* go with smooth movement: *roll along in a car*
  6 *v.* flatten with a roller: *roll the lawn*
  7 *n.* list: *call the roll*
5 **roller** *n.* implement: *garden roller*
5 **Roman Empire, the** *n.*
2 **roof**
  2 *n.* covering of a building
  4 *v.* cover building: *roof it with straw*
  7 *n.* house: *living under the same roof*
1 **room**
  1 *n.* space in house etc.: *sitting room*
  2 *n.* space in general: *take up less room; make room*
  5 *n.* opportunity: *room for improvement*
  6 *n.(pl.)* lodgings: *let rooms*
3 **root**
  3 *n.* part of a tree/hair/tooth
  5 *n.* main cause: *the root of the trouble*
  5 *n.* origins: *one's roots*
  6 *n.* mathematical function: *square root*
  7 *v.* extirpate: *root out*
  7 *adj.* farm product: *root crops*
2 **rose** *n.* flower
5 **rot**
  5 *v.* decay: *plants rot in the rain*
  7 *n.* decay: *there's rot in that wood*

7 *n.* nonsense: *he talks rot*
5 **rotten** *adj.* decayed
3 **rough**
  3 *adj.* not smooth: *rough cloth/skin*
  4 *adj.* approximate: *a rough estimate/idea*
  5 *adj.* boisterous: *rough play/weather*
  6 *adj.* untrained, uncultured: *rough manners*
  7 *v.* draft: *rough out a plan*
1 **round**
  1 *adj.* shaped like a circle or a ball
  1 *prep.* circular movement: *the earth moves round the sun*
  1 *prep.* circular position: *sitting round the table*
  4 *v.* negotiate a curve: *the bus rounded the corner*
  5 *n.* stage: *in the tenth round of the fight*
  5 *v.* make round: *round the lips*
  6 *adj.* broad: *in round terms*
  6 *n.* set: *a round of drinks*
  7 *n.* song in overlapping parts
5 **roundabout**
  5 *n.* circular road junction
  6 *adj.* circuitous: *go by a roundabout route*
  7 *n.* attraction at fun fair
4 **route** *n.* way from one place to another
5 **routine** *n.*
3 **row**
  3 *n.* line: *a row of houses*
  5 *v.* propel with oars: *row a boat*
  6 *n.* quarrel: *have a row*
3 **royal** *adj.*
4 **rub**
  4 *v.* cause friction: *he rubbed his hands together*
  5 *v.* change by rubbing: *rub this oil in; rub the board clean*
3 **rub out** *v.* erase
3 **rubber**
  3 *n./adj.* substance: *rubber tyres*
  3 *n.* stationery article: *an India rubber*
3 **rubbish**
  3 *n.* waste material
  5 *n.* worthless nonsense: *this book is rubbish*

5 **rude**
  5 *adj.* impolite: *he's very rude*
  6 *adj.* startling: *a rude awakening*
  7 *adj.* primitive: *rude beginnings*
5 **rug**
  5 *n.* carpet
  6 *n.* blanket
4 **ruin**
  4 *v.* destroy, spoil utterly: *you've ruined my evening*
  5 *n.* complete destruction: *the ruin of our hopes*
  5 *n.* broken-down building: *a beautiful ruin*
  6 *n.* cause of collapse: *drink was his ruin*
  7 *v.* go bankrupt: *I'm ruined*
5 **ruins** *n.(pl.)*
2 **rule**
  2 *v.* govern: *he rules the country wisely*
  2 *n.* regulation: *make/break a rule*
  3 *n.* government: *British rule in India*
  4 *n.* laws: *the rules of grammar/mathematics*
  5 *v.* draw: *rule a line*
  5 *n.* general practice: *as a rule*
  6 *v.* decide: *the court ruled that*
2 **ruler**
  2 *n.* person who rules a country
  4 *n.* instrument for ruling lines
1 **run**
  1 *v.* move faster than walking
  2 *v.* flee
  3 *v.* manage: *she runs the business for him now*
  4 *v.* move smoothly: *the trains run on rubber wheels*
  4 *v.* leave: *trains run every 10 minutes*
  5 *v.* work (machines): *the engine is running rough*
  5 *v.* convey: *I'll run you to town*

5 *n.* journey: *it's a four-hour run to Paris from here*
  6 *v.* extend: *shelves running round the walls*
  6 *n.* unit of scoring: *he made 82 runs yesterday*
  7 *n.* series of performances: *a two-year run in the West End*
4 **run away with** *v.* take and remove contrary to law
3 **run down**
  3 *v.* knock down (on road)
  5 *v.* lose power
5 **run into** *v.* collide with, meet by chance
5 **run off** *v.* duplicate
4 **run out of** *v.* exhaust stocks
4 **run over**
  4 *v.* drive across
  5 *v.* scan, summarise
2 **runner**
  2 *n.* person/animal that runs
  6 *n.* messenger
  7 *n.* contact edges: *runners on a sledge*
  7 *n.* strip of cloth: *a runner on a sideboard*
2 **rush**
  2 *v.* go in haste: *they rushed down the street*
  3 *n.* swift flow: *they came in a rush*
  4 *v.* cause to move hastily: *they rushed him out of the room*
  5 *adj.* with heavy traffic: *the rush hour*
2 **Russian** *n./adj.*
5 **rust**
  5 *n.* deposit on iron
  6 *v.* develop rust: *the iron is rusting*
5 **rusty**
  5 *adj.* covered with rust
  6 *adj.* lacking in practice: *my German is a bit rusty*

S

4 **sack**
  4 *n.* large bag: *a sack of potatoes*
  5 *v.* dismiss: *he was sacked*
  5 *n.* dismissal: *he got the sack*
  7 *v.* plunder: *the invaders sacked the city*
  7 *n.* type of dress
5 **sacred**
  5 *adj.* connected with religion: *sacred writings*
  5 *adj.* solemn: *a sacred promise*
  6 *adj.* be treated with respect: *nothing is sacred*
5 **sacrifice**
  5 *n.* offering to God
  5 *n.* giving up something of value: *parents make sacrifices for their children's education*
  6 *n.* sale of something at less than its real value
  6 *v.* make a sacrifice (in all above meanings)
1 **sad**
  1 *adj.* unhappy
  6 *adj.* (of colours) dull
  7 *adj.* shameful, deplorable: *he cut a sad figure*
4 **saddle**
  4 *n.* seat on animal
  7 *v.* put a heavy burden on: *he was saddled with two men's tasks*
5 **sadness** *n.*
2 **safe**
  2 *adj.* free from danger
  3 *adj.* unhurt: *there's been an accident, but Jo is safe*
  4 *n.* box for keeping money and valuables
  6 *adj.* cautious: *a safe bet*
  7 *adj.* certain: *a safe seat for Labour in Parliament*
3 **safety** *n.*
2 **sail**
  2 *v.* move on water in boat or ship
  3 *n.* sheet of canvas

4 *v.* begin a voyage: *the ship sails for Canada today*
  5 *n.* pleasure trip on water: *let's go for a sail*
  7 *n.* set of boards on a windmill
  7 *v.* (fig.) move: *the moon sailed across the sky*
2 **sailor** *n.*
5 **sake** *n.* cause, behalf: *he gave up smoking for her sake*
5 **salad** *n.*
3 **salary** *n.*
3 **sale**
  3 *n.* act of selling: *the sale of his house*
  4 *n.* offering of goods at low prices: *summer sale*
  5 *n.* instance of selling something: *I haven't made a sale all week*
4 **salesman** *n.*
2 **salt**
  2 *n.* condiment
  6 *v.* preserve: *salt it down for the winter*
  7 *n.* (fig.) something that gives zest
1 **same**
  1 *adj.* identical: *the same thing*
  1 *pron.* not different: *it's the same*
  6 *adj.* very: *on that same day*
5 **sample**
  5 *n.* specimen
  6 *v.* test a part of/one of
1 **sand**
  1 *n.* covering of the shore
  7 *v.* smooth by rubbing
5 **sandbank** *n.*
2 **sandwich**
  2 *n.* snack
  5 *v.* squash: *she was sandwiched between two large men*
4 **sandy**
  4 *adj.* covered with sand
  5 *adj.* yellowish colour: *sandy hair*

4 satisfaction
4 *n.* state of being satisfied: *to my great satisfaction*
5 *n.* something that satisfies: *his success was a satisfaction to us all*
7 *n.* revenge or compensation: *he demanded satisfaction for the loss incurred*
4 satisfactory *adj.*
3 satisfy
3 *v.* make contented: *he is never satisfied*
4 *v.* be enough: *the meal satisfied his hunger*
6 *v.* convince: *he satisfied me that he could work well*
1 Saturday *n.*
5 sauce
5 *n.* liquid flavouring: *cheese sauce*
7 *n.* impudence: *that's enough sauce*
3 saucer *n.*
3 sausage *n.*
2 save
2 *v.* make safe, rescue: *she saved the boy*
3 *v.* keep for future purposes: *she saved £5*
5 *v.* make unnecessary: *a stitch in time saves nine*
6 *v.* (Christian) release from sin: *Jesus saves*
6 *n.* preventing a goal being scored: *what a save!*
7 *v.* make a reservation about something: *a saving clause*
7 *prep.* except: *all save Paul*
4 savings *n.(pl.)*
3 saw
3 *n.* tool
4 *v.* cut: *he sawed through the log*
6 *v.* capable of being sawn: *the wood saws easily*
1 say
1 *v.* utter, make a remark
4 *v.* suppose, give an opinion about: *I can't really say when they'll come*
6 *n.* expression of view: *let him have his say*

4 scale
4 *n.* series of marks for measuring
5 *n.(pl.)* balance for weighing: *put the meat on those scales*
5 *n.* proportions between the size of something and the map
5 *n.* (music) series of tones: *she was practising scales*
6 *n.* covering of fish or reptile
6 *n.* chalky deposit in kettle
7 *v.* climb up
5 scarce
5 *adj.* not available in sufficient quantity: *sugar is scarce in San Seriffe*
6 *adj.* rare: *rhinos are now very scarce in India*
5 scarcity *n.*
4 scare
4 *v.* frighten: *the gunfire scared her*
6 *n.* feeling of alarm: *we had a scare on the motorway in fog yesterday*
4 scatter
4 *v.* move in different directions: *the crowd scattered*
4 *v.* throw in various directions: *they scattered the seed*
3 scene
3 *n.* view: *a beautiful scene*
5 *n.* place of an actual or imagined event: *the scene of the battle*
5 *n.* section of an act in a play: *act II scene 4*
6 *n.* description of an incident: *scenes of clerical life*
6 *n.* emotional outburst: *she made a scene*
4 scenery
4 *n.* general landscape
6 *n.* backdrop in theatre
5 scent
5 *n.* special smell: *the scent of flowers*
5 *n.* perfume: *a bottle of scent*
6 *n.* smell left by animal: *the distinctive scent of zebra*
6 *n.* sense of smell: *they hunt by scent*
6 *v.* discern by smell: *scent a fox*
7 *v.* begin to suspect the presence of: *he scented trouble*

7 *v.* make fragrant: *roses scented the air*

4 **scheme**
  4 *n.* plan
  6 *n.* secret or dishonest plan
  6 *n.* arrangement: *a colour scheme*
  7 *v.* make (dishonest) plans: *he schemed for the collapse of the enterprise*

4 **scholarship**
  4 *n.* award to a scholar: *he gained a scholarship to study at Oxford*
  5 *n.* learning: *this book is supported by meticulous scholarship*

1 **school**
  1 *n.* place of instruction
  4 *n.* division of university: *School of Oriental and African Studies*

5 **schoolmaster** *n.*

5 **schoolmistress** *n.*

3 **science**
  3 *n.* knowledge arranged in an orderly manner
  4 *n.* branch of knowledge: *the science of chemistry*
  7 *n.* expert's skill: *science is more important than strength*

3 **scientific**
  3 *adj.* connected with science
  4 *adj.* using expert skill or knowledge

3 **scientist** *n.*

3 **scissors** *n.*

5 **scold**
  5 *v.* blame with angry words
  6 *v.* speak angrily or complainingly

5 **scooter**
  5 *n.* type of motor-bike
  6 *n.* child's toy

2 **score**
  2 *n.* points, goals, runs etc.: *the half-time score*
  3 *v.* make such points: *he scored 20*
  6 *n.* musical writing: *a detailed score*
  7 *v.* orchestrate: *the piece is scored for woodwind*
  7 *n.* twenty: *a score of people*
  7 *n.* reason, account: *no problems on that score*

5 **scorn**
  5 *n.* contempt

6 *v.* feel/show contempt for

5 **scornful** *adj.*

4 **Scotland** *n.*

4 **Scots** *n.*

5 **Scotsman** *n.*

4 **Scottish** *adj.*

3 **scout**
  3 *n.* member of boys' outdoor association
  5 *n.* person sent in advance to get information
  6 *v.* search

5 **scrape**
  5 *v.* remove covering/filling: *they scraped the saucepan*
  5 *v.* injure by scratching: *they scraped the paintwork*
  5 *n.* act/sound/result of scraping
  6 *v.* pass close to: *they scraped along the wall*
  7 *n.* awkward situations: *he is always getting into scrapes*

3 **scratch**
  3 *v.* make lines on the surface: *the cat scratched me*
  4 *n.* cut: *a nasty scratch*
  4 *v.* get scratched by accident: *he scratched his hands while cutting the roses*
  5 *v.* rub to relieve itching
  7 *v.* withdraw: *the horse was scratched from the race*

2 **scream** *v./n.*

5 **screen** *v./n.*

3 **screw**
  3 *n.* metal peg
  4 *n.* action of turning: *give it another screw*
  4 *v.* fasten or tighten with a screw: *she screwed on the lid*

1 **sea** *n.*

4 **seaman** *n.*

5 **seaport** *n.*

3 **search**
  3 *v.* look for
  5 *n.* enquiry, quest: *there'll be a body search at that airport*

2 **seaside** *n.*

2 **season**
  2 *n.* division of the year
  3 *n.* period for particular activity: *the football season*
  5 *v.* flavour: *she seasoned the meat*
  6 *v.* weather: *this wood has not been seasoned*
  7 *v.* soften, moderate: *justice seasoned with mercy*

1 **seat**
  1 *n.* place to sit
  3 *n.* part of chair where one sits: *the seat of the chair*
  4 *n.* part of body/garment where one sits: *the seat of his pants*
  5 *n.* location: *the seat of government*
  6 *v.* sit, cause to sit: *they seated the children in rows of ten*

5 **seatbelt** *n.*

1 **second**
  1 *adj.* next after first
  2 *n.* sixtieth part of a minute
  6 *n.* support: *his second sat in the corner*
  7 *v.* rise or speak formally in support: *she seconded the motion*

4 **secondary** *adj.*

4 **second-hand** *adj.: second-hand car*

5 **Second World War, the** *n.*

2 **secret**
  2 *adj.* to be kept from the knowledge of others
  2 *n.* something secret
  5 *n.* hidden clause: *what's the secret of his success?*

3 **secretary**
  3 *n.* short-hand typist
  5 *n.* official in charge of correspondence etc. of a society
  7 *n.* minister: *the Secretary of State*

4 **section** *n.*

4 **security**
  4 *n.* freedom from danger/anxiety
  7 *n.* something valuable given as pledge for repayment of a loan

1 **see**
  1 *v.* have/use the power of sight: *I can't see through that hole*
  2 *v.* understand: *he didn't see the joke*
  3 *v.* meet to talk: *have you seen the doctor about it?*
  4 *v.* learn from printed sources: *I see from that paper that . . .*
  5 *v.* attend to: *see that the windows are properly shut*
  6 *v.* experience: *I never saw such kindness as they showed us in Yazd*

5 **see about** *v.* organise, remedy

5 **see off** *v.* say goodbye to (at station, airport etc.)

3 **see through** *v.* discern truth behind falsehood

5 **see to** *v.* ensure action

4 **seed**
  4 *n.* part of plant
  6 *v.* produce seeds
  7 *n.* cause, origin: *the seeds of the dispute*

5 **seeing that** *conj.: seeing that it's so late, let's not bother*

2 **seem** *v.* give the appearance of

4 **seize**
  4 *v.* take hold of: *she seized his hand*
  6 *v.* take possession of by law: *they seized his property to pay his debts*

3 **seldom** *adv.*

4 **select**
  4 *v.* choose
  5 *adj.* carefully chosen: *selected passages*
  7 *adj.* for carefully chosen people: *a select club*

4 **selection**
  4 *n.* act/process of choosing
  4 *n.* collection of chosen things: *a selection of chocolates*

5 **self-control** *n.*

5 **self-governing** *adj.*

5 **self-interest** *n.*

5 **self-respect** *n.*

5 **self-service** *n./adj.*

4 **selfish** *adj.*

1 **sell**
  1 *v.* give in exchange for money
  3 *v.* keep stocks of, for sale: *do you sell needles?*
  5 *v.* find buyers: *his new novel is selling well*

2 **seller** *n.*

5 **senate** *n.*

1 **send**
  1 *v.* cause to go: *send a telegram*
  2 *v.* cause to carry: *I sent Joe with a message*
  4 *v.* cause to move: *the sudden jolt sent him flying*
  4 *v.* cause to become: *this music sends me crazy*

3 **send for** *v.* order to come (by post, messenger)

4 **send in** *v.* submit

4 **send off** *v.* dispatch

5 **send on** *v.* forward (letters)

3 **send out**
  3 *v.* make person leave room
  5 *v.* emit

5 **sensation**
  5 *n.* quick and excited reaction: *their marriage was a sensation*
  6 *n.* ability to feel: *he has no sensation in his legs*

3 **sense**
  3 *n.* one of the five senses: *the sense of touch*
  4 *n.* appreciation of value or worth: *a sense of humour*
  5 *n.* purpose, use: *there's no sense in doing that*
  5 *n.* power of judgement: *common sense*
  5 *n.* meaning: *a word with many senses*
  5 *v.* feel, realise: *he sensed something was wrong*
  7 *n.* general feeling or opinion: *he took the sense of the meeting*

5 **senseless**
  5 *adj.* foolish
  6 *adj.* unconscious

5 **sensible**
  3 *adj.* showing good sense
  7 *adj.* that can be perceived by the senses: *a sensible fall in the temperature*

5 **sensitive**
  5 *adj.* easily receiving impressions: *sensitive skin*

5 *adj.* easily hurt, offended: *sensitive to criticism*
6 *adj.* able to record small changes: *a sensitive barometer*

3 **sentence**
  3 *n.* grammatical unit
  6 *n.* punishment: *he got a 10-year sentence*
  6 *v.* decree punishment

2 **separate**
  2 *adj.* divided
  3 *v.* divide
  4 *v.* go in different ways

5 **separation** *n.*

1 **September** *n.*

4 **series** *n.*

2 **serious**
  2 *adj.* solemn, thoughtful
  3 *adj.* important because of possible danger: *a serious illness*
  5 *adj.* earnest, sincere: *a serious worker*

2 **servant** *n.*

3 **serve**
  3 *v.* be a servant, work for: *she served the family*
  4 *v.* attend to (e.g. customers in a shop): *have you been served?*
  5 *v.* perform duties for: *he served his country*
  6 *v.* be satisfactory for a need or purpose: *the cushion served as a seat*
  7 *v.* act towards: *they served him shamefully*
  7 *v.* pass the usual number of years: *he served 12 years in prison*

3 **service**
  3 *n.* system to supply public needs: *a train service*
  4 *n.* something done to help others: *a doctor's services*
  4 *n.* maintenance (car etc.)
  4 *v.* maintain (car etc.)
  5 *n.* department of public work: *the Civil Service*
  6 *n.* form of worship: *three services every Sunday*

7 *n.* set of crockery: *a dinner service given at their wedding*

2 **set**
2 *n.* number of things that go together: *a set of clothes*
3 *n.* action taken to shape hair
3 *v.* shape hair on head: *I set my hair this morning*
4 *n.* radio: *what set is that you've bought?*
4 *v.* go down (sun, moon)
5 *n.* group of persons with similar tastes
6 *n.* group of articles for stage production
6 *adj.* fixed: *she has a set attitude about entertainment*

5 **set back** *v.* hinder progress
5 **set down** *v.* record on paper
5 **set in** *v.* begin an extended period (weather, season)

3 **set off**
3 *v.* begin a journey
4 *v.* effect (reaction, explosion)

3 **set out**
3 *v.* begin a journey
3 *v.* begin work towards an objective
3 *v.* arrange items or points

4 **set up** *v.* establish, organise

4 **setting**
4 *n.* framework in which something is set: *the setting of a jewel*
5 *n.* descent of the sun

3 **settle**
3 *v.* make an agreement: *they settled the dispute*
4 *v.* become composed: *the weather has settled down after that storm*
5 *v.* pay: *he settled the bill*
6 *v.* make one's home in: *he settled in France*
6 *v.* come to rest: *the bird settled on the branch*

4 **settlement**
4 *n.* act of settling a dispute
6 *n.* process of settling people in a colony
6 *n.* group of persons engaged in welfare work

5 **settler** *n.*
1 **seven** *n. / adj.*
1 **seventeen** *n. / adj.*
2 **seventh** *adj.*
1 **seventy** *n. / adj.*

2 **several**
2 *adj.* three or more
7 *adj.* separate: *they went their several ways*

4 **severe**
4 *adj.* stern, strict
5 *adj.* vigorous: *a severe storm*
6 *adj.* making great demands on skill: *severe competition*
7 *adj.* (of style) simple, without ornament

3 **sew** *v.*

3 **sex**
3 *n.* being male or female: *what sex is it?*
4 *n.* differences between males and females: *sex appeal*
5 *n.* sexual activity: *a novel concerned with sex*
6 *n.* sexual intercourse: *have sex*

5 **sexual** *adj.*
5 **sexy** *adj.*

2 **shade**
2 *n.* comparative darkness: *he sat in the shade*
4 *n.* darker parts of a picture
4 *n.* degree or depth of colour
5 *n.* something that shuts out the light: *a lamp shade*
5 *v.* protect: *he shaded his eyes*
6 *v.* darken with pencil lines: *he shaded the picture*
7 *n.* degree of difference: *a word with many shades of meaning*

2 **shadow**
2 *n.* area of shade
4 *n.* partial darkness
6 *n.* slightest trace: *beyond a shadow of doubt*

5 **shadowy** *adj.*

5 **shady**
5 *adj.* giving shade
6 *adj.* (colloq.) of doubtful honesty: *a shady deal*

3 **shake**
  3 *v.* move
  3 *n.* shaking of the head
  4 *v.* shook: *she was badly shaken by the accident*
  5 *v.* tremble: *her voice shook with emotion*
  6 *n.* drink: *a milk-shake*
1 **shall** *modal*
3 **shallow** *adj.*
5 **shallowness** *n.*
3 **shame**
  3 *n.* distress, embarrassment: *he felt no shame*
  5 *n.* dishonour: *he brought shame on his family*
  5 *n.* pity: *what a shame!*
5 **shameful** *adj.*
1 **shape**
  1 *n.* form
  3 *v.* give shape to
  5 *n.* condition: *her affairs are in good shape*
  6 *n.* sort: *I have no proposals in any shape or form*
  6 *n.* indistinct form: *two shapes could be seen in the twilight*
5 **shapeless** *adj.*
3 **share**
  3 *v.* divide
  3 *n.* a division
  5 *n.* part taken or received in an action: *what share of the blame is his?*
  7 *n.* one part of a company: *she holds 5000 shares*
2 **sharp**
  2 *adj.* not blunt
  3 *adj.* well-defined: *a sharp outline*
  4 *adj.* changing direction quickly: *a sharp bend*
  5 *adj.* shrill: *a sharp cry*
  5 *adv.* punctuality: *at 5 o'clock sharp*
  6 *adj.* quickly aware of things: *a sharp mind*
  6 *adv.* suddenly: *turn sharp left*
  7 *adj.* unscrupulous
  7 *n.* (musical) not a flat
5 **sharpen** *v.*

3 **shave**
  3 *v.* cut hair with a razor
  4 *n.* shaving of the face
  6 *v.* pare off
  6 *v.* pass very close to, without touching: *the bus shaved the wall*
  7 *n.* close approach without touching: *a narrow/close shave*
1 **she** *pron.*
4 **shed**
  4 *n.* hut
  6 *v.* fall, come off: *the trees shed their leaves*
  6 *v.* throw off, discard: *people shed their winter clothes*
  7 *v.* spread: *a fire sheds warmth*
1 **sheep** *n.*
3 **sheet**
  3 *n.* piece of linen
  5 *n.* broad/flat piece of some material: *a sheet of paper/steel*
  7 *n.* wide expanse: *the rain came down in sheets*
3 **shelf** *n.* supported surface for carrying objects
3 **shell**
  3 *n.* brittle covering of egg/crustacean
  6 *n.* walls/outer structure of unfinished building
  6 *n.* metal case filled with explosive
  7 *v.* fire at: *the guns shelled the bridge*
3 **shelter**
  3 *n.* something that gives safety or protection
  5 *n.* condition of being kept safe: *provide shelter for lost children*
  5 *v.* give protection to
5 **shilling** *n.* coin now superseded by 5p piece
1 **shine**
  1 *v.* give or reflect light
  3 *v.* polish
  4 *n.* polish: *put a shine on your shoes*
  6 *v.* (fig.) excel: *he shone at maths*
1 **ship**
  1 *n.* vessel
  4 *v.* transport: *the goods were shipped from Mombasa*
5 **shipbuilding** *n.*

5 **shipwreck** *n.*

1 **shirt** *n.*

3 **shock**
  3 *n.* violent blow or shaking: *the shock of an earthquake*
  4 *n.* effect caused by electricity: *he got a shock when he touched the wire*
  4 *n.* sudden/violent disturbance of feelings
  5 *v.* cause shock to, fill with horror, disgust

1 **shoe**
  1 *n.* footwear
  6 *v.* fit with shoes
  7 *n.* part of a brake

5 **shoelace** *n.*

2 **shoot**
  2 *v.* fire a gun
  2 *v.* try to score a goal
  4 *v.* move quickly: *the flames shot up from the burning house*
  5 *n.* new growth on or of a plant
  6 *v.* traverse quickly: *shoot the rapids*

1 **shop**
  1 *n.* emporium
  3 *v.* go shopping

4 **shopkeeper** *n.*

5 **shoplifting** *n.*

2 **shopping** *n.*

2 **shore**
  2 *n.* stretch of land bordering the sea
  6 *v.* provide support for a structure: *shore up the wall*

1 **short**
  1 *adj.* not long
  6 *adj.* not reaching the usual: *he gave you short weight on those goods*
  6 *adj.* abrupt: *he was very short with me*

5 **shorten** *v.*

2 **shorts** *n.* garment

3 **shot**
  3 *n.* firing of a gun
  4 *n.* attempt to hit something: *good shot!*
  5 *n.* something that is fired from a gun
  5 *n.* photograph: *take a shot of John on the donkey*

6 *n.* person who shoots: *he's a good shot*

6 *n.* injection with a needle: *a shot of LSD*

2 **should** *modal*

3 **shoulder**
  3 *n.* part of the body
  6 *v.* take responsibility for: *shoulder this task*
  7 *v.* push: *he shouldered me aside*

2 **shout**
  2 *v.* say in a loud voice
  3 *n.* loud call or cry

1 **show**
  1 *v.* bring, produce to be seen: *show your ticket*
  2 *v.* indicate: *the diagram shows how it works*
  3 *v.* prove: *that shows he never really cared about it*
  3 *n.* display: *flower show*
  4 *n.* performance: *what shows are on tonight?*
  4 *v.* allow to be seen: *that suit doesn't show the dirt*
  5 *v.* be noticeable: *fear showed in his eyes*

3 **show in** *v.* guide someone in

5 **show off** *v.* display to impress

4 **show up**
  4 *v.* be noticeable
  5 *v.* arrive

3 **shower**
  3 *n.* brief fall of rain
  4 *n.* implement in bathroom
  5 *v.* wash under shower
  6 *n.* large number of things arriving together: *a shower of gifts*
  7 *v.* overwhelm somebody with something: *they showered us with gratitude*

5 **shrink**
  5 *v.* become smaller
  7 *v.* move away from, showing dislike

1 **shut**
  1 *v.* close: *he shut the window*
  4 *v.* become closed: *the door won't shut*

3 **shy**
  3 *adj.* self-conscious
  4 *adj.* (of animals) easily frightened
  6 *v.* (of horse) turn away from in alarm
  7 *v.* throw: *shying stones at bottles*
2 **sick** *adj.*
5 **sickness** *n.*
1 **side**
  1 *n.* surface: *this box has four sides; both sides of the paper*
  1 *n.* location: *come to the side of the house*
  2 *n.* slope: *the side of a mountain*
  2 *n.* half: *the right side of his body is paralysed*
  4 *n.* opposing group: *whose side are you on?*
  5 *v.* support: *who do you side with?*
5 **sideboard** *n.*
5 **sideways** *adv.*
4 **sigh** *v. /n.*
3 **sight**
  3 *n.* power of seeing: *eye-sight*
  4 *n.* seeing or being seen: *their first sight of land*
  4 *n.* range of seeing: *in sight; out of sight*
  6 *v.* get sight of (distant object)
  7 *n.* opinion: *all men are equal in the sight of God*
4 **sightseeing** *n.*
2 **sign**
  2 *n.* words on a board to give a warning etc.: *traffic signs*
  3 *n.* mark, object, symbol
  4 *v.* write one's name on document etc.
  5 *n.* something that gives evidence: *signs of life*
  6 *n.* movement of the head or hand: *the sign language of the deaf*
  6 *v.* make known an order by making signs: *the policeman signed for them to stop*
3 **signal**
  3 *n.* message
  4 *v.* send a message

  5 *n.* event which is the immediate cause of activity
  6 *n.* electronic impulse
4 **signature** *n.*
3 **silence**
  3 *n.* being silent
  5 *v.* make silent
3 **silent** *adj.*
3 **silk** *n.*
2 **silly** *adj.*
3 **silver**
  3 *n.* metal
  6 *v.* coat with silver
  7 *v.* become white or silver in colour
3 **similar** *adj.*
3 **simple**
  3 *adj.* plain: *simple food*
  4 *adj.* not highly developed: *a simple life*
  4 *adj.* easily done: *a simple exercise*
  5 *adj.* not complex: *a simple sentence*
  5 *adj.* innocent, straightforward: *behave in a simple manner*
5 **simplicity** *n.*
5 **sin**
  5 *n.* act of breaking of Divine Law
  6 *n.* offence against convention
  6 *v.* do wrong
2 **since**
  2 *prep.* after: *since her marriage*
  3 *conj.* after: *since I last saw you . . .*
  3 *conj.* because: *since we had no money . . .*
  4 *adv.* after an event in the past: *the town has since been rebuilt*
3 **sincere** *adj.*
5 **sincerity** *n.*
2 **sing**
  2 *v.* use voice musically
  5 *v.* make a humming/buzzing noise: *the kettle was singing*
2 **singer** *n.*
3 **single**
  3 *adj.* for the use of one person: *a single room*
  5 *adj.* one and only: *I've only been there a single time*
  4 *adj.* not married

3 **sink**
    4 *v.* go down
    3 *n.* basin
    6 *v.* make by digging: *sink a well*
5 **sip** *v.* / *n.*
2 **sir** *n.*
1 **sister** *n.*
1 **sit**
    1 *v.* be seated
    2 *v.* cause to sit: *he sat the baby in a chair*
    6 *v.* (of Parliament) be in session: *Parliament is not sitting*
    6 *v.* hang: *this dress sits badly*
5 **sit for** *v.* take (examination)
5 **sit up** *v.* not go to bed / sit straight
3 **situation**
    3 *n.* condition / state of affairs: *it's an embarrassing situation*
    4 *n.* position: *the situation of the town*
    5 *n.* work, employment: *situations vacant*
1 **six** *n.* / *adj.*
1 **sixteen** *n.* / *adj.*
2 **sixth** *adj.*
1 **sixty** *n.* / *adj.*
3 **size**
    3 *n.* degree of largeness: *what size was it?*
    3 *n.* largeness of item of clothing: *she wears size 10*
5 **sketch**
    5 *n.* quick rough drawing
    5 *v.* make such a drawing
    6 *n.* short account or description
    7 *n.* short humorous play or piece of writing
4 **skilful** *adj.*
3 **skill** *n.*
4 **skilled**
    4 *adj.* trained, experienced: *a skilled craftsman*
    5 *adj.* needing skill: *skilled work*
2 **skin**
    2 *n.* covering of the body
    4 *n.* animal hide
    5 *n.* outer covering of plant or fruit
    6 *n.* thin layer that forms on surface of boiled milk

    6 *v.* take the skin off: *he's skinned his knuckles*
1 **skirt**
    1 *n.* garment
    5 *n.* border, outskirts
    6 *v.* pass along: *the road skirts the forest*
1 **sky** *n.*
5 **slacks** *n.(pl.)* garment
5 **slang** *n.*
4 **slap** *v.* / *n.*
5 **slave**
    5 *n.* person who belongs to another: *the slave trade*
    5 *n.* person compelled to work hard for another: *he made a slave of his wife*
    6 *v.* work very hard
    7 *n.* person under the control of another force: *a slave of fashion*
1 **sleep**
    1 *v.* rest, repose
    2 *n.* rest: *have a good sleep*
4 **sleepy**
    4 *adj.* needing sleep
    5 *adj.* quiet, inactive: *a sleepy little village*
3 **sleeve**
    3 *n.* part of garment
    5 *n.* covering for record
5 **slice**
    5 *n.* flat piece: *a slice of bread*
    5 *v.* cut / make into such pieces
    6 *n.* part, share: *a slice of good fortune*
    6 *n.* utensil: *egg slice*
    7 *v.* hit tangentially: *don't slice the ball*
3 **slide**
    3 *n.* smooth slope where people can slide
    4 *n.* picture mounted in a frame
    4 *v.* move smoothly along
    5 *n.* act of sliding
    5 *n.* glass plate for use under a microscope
    6 *v.* move quickly: *he slid behind the curtains*

3 **slight**
  3 *adj.* insignificant: *a slight error*
  6 *adj.* slim
  7 *v.* fail to show respect
3 **slightly**
  3 *adv.* somewhat
  6 *adv.* slenderly: *she is too slightly built for lifting those weights*
3 **slip**
  3 *v.* lose balance, (nearly) fall
  4 *n.* false step, small error
  4 *v.* elude grasp: *the book slipped from his hand*
  5 *v.* move unnoticed: *she slipped in*
  6 *v.* detach itself from: *the ship slipped its moorings*
5 **slippery**
  5 *adj.* polished
  6 *adj.* (fig.) unreliable: *a slippery person*
4 **slope**
  4 *n.* area of rising or falling ground
  5 *n.* slanting line
  5 *v.* slant
1 **slow**
  1 *adj.* not quick
  3 *adj.* (of clocks) behind the correct time
  4 *v.* go at a slower speed: *the car slowed down*
  5 *adj.* not quick to learn: *a slow child*
  6 *adj.* not interesting: *the film was rather slow*
4 **smack**
  4 *n.* blow: *a smack on the cheek*
  4 *v.* hit: *she smacked the child for misbehaving*
  6 *v.* suggest: *that smacks of dishonesty*
  7 *n.* small fishing-boat
1 **small** *adj.*
5 **smash**
  5 *v.* break into small pieces: *he smashed the window*
  5 *v.* rush into violently: *the car smashed into the wall*

6 *v.* conquer: *he smashed the world record*
2 **smell**
  2 *n.* what is noticed by the nose
  3 *n.* odour
  4 *n.* one of the five senses
  4 *v.* be aware of through nose: *can you smell burning?*
  5 *v.* give out unpleasant smell
1 **smile** *n./v.*
2 **smoke**
  2 *n.* vapour
  2 *v.* action of tobacco smoking
  4 *v.* give out smoke: *that chimney's smoking*
3 **smooth**
  3 *adj.* free from roughness: *a smooth skin*
  4 *adj.* free from bumping: *a smooth ride*
  6 *adj.* free from harshness: *smooth words*
  7 *adj.* (of person) flattering, over-polite
5 **snack-bar** *n.*
3 **snake** *n.*
5 **sneeze** *v./n.*
2 **snow** *n./v.*
4 **snowstorm** *n.*
4 **snowy** *adj.*
1 **so**
  1 *conj.* therefore: *it was late, so I went home*
  2 *adv.* to such an extent: *it's so expensive; it's not so big as mine*
  3 *adv.* very: *I'm so happy*
  4 *adv.* in such a way: *is that so? I hope so . . . and so am I*
  4 *conj.* result (+that): *it was so cold that I started shivering*
4 **so as to** *conj.*: *she spoke that way so as to annoy him*
5 **so far as** *conj.*: *so far as I know nothing happened*
4 **so long as** *conj.*: *you may go out so long as you are back by 10*
4 **so that** *conj.*: *they chose a quiet spot so that they could relax*
5 **so-called** *adj.*

2 **soap**
  2 *n.* substance for washing
  4 *v.* cover with soap
4 **social** *adj.*
5 **socialism** *n.*
5 **socialist** *n./adj.*
3 **society**
  3 *n.* social communities: *modern industrial society*
  4 *n.* organisation: *Philosophical Society*
  5 *n.* company, companionship: *in the society of friends*
  6 *n.* people of fashion: *high society*
2 **sock** *n.* short stocking
1 **soft**
  1 adj. yielding: *a soft cushion*
  2 *adj.* smooth: *as soft as silk*
  3 *adj.* not loud: *soft music was playing*
  3 *adj.* mild: *a soft breeze*
  4 *adj.* non-alcoholic: *soft drinks*
  4 *adj.* gentle: *her soft words soothed him*
  5 *adj.* feeble: *his muscles have gone soft*
5 **soften** *v.*
5 **softness** *n.*
3 **soil**
  3 *n.* ground
  6 *v.* make dirty: *he wouldn't soil his hands*
  7 *v.* be soiled: *this material soils easily*
3 **soldier** *n.*
5 **solemn**
  5 *adj.* causing deep thought or respect
  6 *adj.* serious-looking
3 **solid**
  3 *adj.* not liquid: *solid fuel*
  3 *adj.* not hollow: *a solid sphere*
  5 *adj.* strong, dependable: *a solid man/argument*
  6 *adj.* continuous: *for ten solid hours*
  7 *adj.* unanimous: *the miners are solid on this point*
4 **solution**
  4 *n.* answer: *the solution to the problem*

6 *n.* process of dissolving a solid: *a solution of sugar*
3 **solve** *v.*
1 **some** *det.*
2 **somebody** *pron.*
4 **somehow** *adv.*
2 **someone** *pron.*
2 **something** *pron.*
2 **sometimes** *adv.*
2 **somewhere** *adv.*
1 **son** *n.*
2 **song**
  2 *n.* singing
  4 *n.* poem set to music
  5 *n.* poetry, verse
1 **soon**
  1 *adv.* in a short time
  3 *adv.* early: *how soon can you be ready?*
  3 *conj.* as soon as
4 **sore**
  4 *adj.* hurting
  6 *adj.* causing sorrow: *a sore point*
  7 *n.* place where skin is injured
5 **sorrow** *n.*
5 **sorrowful** *adj.*
2 **sorry**
  2 *adj.* feeling regret/sympathy/pity
  6 *adj.* pitiful: *in a sorry state*
3 **sort**
  3 *n.* type: *the same sort as before*
  5 *v.* arrange
5 **soul**
  5 *n.* non-material part of the human body
  5 *n.* emotional and intellectual energy
  6 *n.* person: *not a soul in sight*
  7 *n.* person personifying an ideal: *the soul of discretion*
2 **sound**
  2 *n.* something heard: *the sound of heavy rain*
  3 *v.* produce sound: *the trumpets sounded*
  3 *v.* give an impression when heard: *it sounds as if he's snoring*
  4 *adj.* thorough: *what you need is a sound sleep*

5 *v.* give a mental impression: *that idea sounds familiar*
5 *adj.* healthy: *his teeth are still sound*
5 *adj.* dependable: *that's sound advice*
7 *v.* test the depth of the sea: *when did they last sound the harbour entrance?*
7 *v.* investigate attitudes: *sound out his views about . . .*
1 **soup** *n.* liquid food
4 **sour**
    4 *adj.* having sharp taste: *a sour plum*
    4 *adj.* having a taste of fermentation: *sour milk*
    5 *v.* turn sour
    6 *adj.* bad-tempered
4 **source**
    4 *n.* starting point of a river
    5 *n.* place from which something is got
    6 *n.* original document
1 **south** *n.*
5 **southeast** *n.*
4 **southern** *adj.*
5 **southward/s** *adv.*
5 **southwest** *n.*
5 **souvenir** *n.*
4 **Soviet Union** *n.*
3 **sow** *v.*
2 **space**
    2 *n.* distance between two objects
    3 *n.* area or volume: *fill in the open spaces*
    3 *n.* place beyond the atmosphere
    4 *n.* room: *there isn't enough space*
    6 *n.* period of time: *in the space of five years*
2 **spade**
    2 *n.* tool for digging
    6 *n.* one of the suits of cards
1 **Spain** *n.*
3 **Spaniard** *n.*
2 **Spanish** *n./adj.*
3 **spare**
    3 *adj.* additional to what is needed: *spare money*
    4 *v.* afford to give: *he couldn't spare the time*
    6 *v.* refrain from hurting: *she spared his life*

7 *adj.* lean: *a spare body*
7 *adj.* small in quantity: *a spare diet*
1 **speak**
    1 *v.* utter language: *please speak more slowly*
    1 *v.* know/use a language: *he speaks German fluently*
    2 *v.* discuss: *I was speaking with them about the new plans*
    4 *v.* declare views: *you can speak openly here*
    4 *v.* address an audience: *she spoke for over an hour at the ceremony*
3 **speaker**
    3 *n.* person who speaks
    4 *n.* mechanical apparatus: *the speakers on that hi-fi*
2 **special**
    2 *adj.* of a particular sort: *special interests*
    3 *adj.* exceptional: *special treatment for star performers*
4 **specialist** *n.*
3 **speech**
    3 *n.* talk in public
    4 *n.* power of speaking
3 **speed**
    3 *n.* rate of motion: *at great speed*
    4 *n.* swiftness: *more haste, less speed*
    4 *v.* move along quickly
    6 *v.* cause to move quickly: *speed him on his way*
1 **spell**
    1 *v.* name or write letters of a word
    6 *n.* period of time: *a spell in hospital*
    6 *n.* words used as a charm: *I put a spell on you*
    7 *n.* attraction, fascination: *the spell of her beauty*
4 **spelling** *n.*
2 **spend**
    2 *v.* pay out money
    3 *v.* pass time
    5 *v.* use up, consume: *all energy spent*
4 **spill**
    4 *v.* (of liquids) run out: *she spilt the wine*
    6 *n.* a fall: *a nasty spill on the slope*

4 spin
  4 *v.* cause to go/move round and round
  5 *v.* form by twisting: *she spun the wool*
  6 *v.* produce: *he spun a story*
  6 *n.* turning motion: *the spin of the ball*
  6 *n.* short ride in a car: *we went for a spin*
  7 *n.* twisting movement of an aeroplane: *the plane went into a spin*
4 spirit
  4 *n.* soul
  5 *n.* quality of courage, vigour: *put a little more spirit into it*
  5 *n.(pl.)* alcoholic drinks (whisky, brandy, rum etc.)
  6 *n.* sprite
  7 *n.* industrial alcohol
5 spit
  5 *v.* send liquid out of the mouth
  5 *n.* liquid sent out of the mouth
  7 *n.* metal spike for roasting meat etc.
  7 *v.* (of rain, snow) fall lightly
3 spite
  3 *n.* ill-will, grudge
  6 *v.* injure or annoy because of spite: *she spited her half-sister*
4 splash
  4 *v.* (cause to) fly about in drops
  4 *n.* scattering of liquid
  6 *n.* patch of colour: *a splash of blue*
4 splendid
  4 *adj.* magnificent: *a splendid sunset*
  5 *adj.* very satisfactory: *John's coming. – Splendid!*
4 split
  4 *v.* break: *he split the wood*
  5 *v.* break into parts: *let's split the cost*
  5 *n.* crack or tear: *a split in his trousers*
3 spoil
  3 *v.* make unsatisfactory, harm: *she spoilt the occasion*
  5 *v.* pay too much attention to: *they spoil their son*

  7 *n.* plunder
5 sponge
  5 *n.* porous material
  6 *v.* wipe: *sponge out the washbasin*
  7 *v.* get money from: *he sponged on me*
1 spoon *n.* utensil
2 sport
  2 *n.* exercise
  5 *n.(pl.)* meeting for athletic contests: *school sports*
  6 *n.* fun: *say something in sport*
  6 *v.* play about, amuse oneself: *sporting in the water*
5 sportsman
  5 *n.* person fond of sport
  7 *n.* person who plays fairly
3 spot
  3 *n.* mark: *red spots*
  3 *n.* dirty mark: *a spot on his trousers*
  4 *n.* particular place or area: *a pretty spot*
  5 *v.* mark: *material that spots easily*
  6 *v.* pick out, recognise: *I spotted him in the crowd*
3 spread
  3 *v.* extend
  4 *n.* spreading: *the spread of disease*
  5 *n.* paste: *salmon spread*
  6 *n.* well-stocked table: *what a spread!*
1 spring
  1 *n.* season
  4 *v.* act of springing
  4 *n.* (act of) springing
  5 *n.* place where water comes from the ground
  5 *n.* twisted piece of wire: *bed springs*
  6 *n.* elastic quality: *these rubber bands have lost their spring*
4 springtime *n.*
1 square
  1 *n./adj.* shape
  3 *n.* open four-sided area in a town: *Trafalgar Square*
  5 *adj.* balanced, settled: *he got his accounts square*
  5 *v.* make square
  5 *v.* settle, balance

6 *v.* multiply a number by itself
5 **squat**
  5 *v.* sit on one's heels
  5 *v.* settle on land or in property
    without permission
  7 *adj.* dumpy
5 **squatter** *n.*
4 **squeeze**
  4 *v.* press, yield to pressure
  4 *n.* act of squeezing: *a hug and a*
    squeeze
  7 *n.* policy of high taxation, high
    interest rates etc.
4 **staff**
  4 *n.* group of workers
  6 *n.* stick
  5 *v.* provide with staff
  7 *n.* group of senior army officers
3 **stage**
  3 *n.* raised platform in a theatre
  5 *n.* point in time: *a stage in history*
  6 *n.* journey between two stopping
    places: *we made the journey in easy*
    stages
  7 *v.* put on the stage
4 **stain**
  4 *n.* mark
  4 *v.* change the colour of
  5 *v.* become discoloured
4 **staircase** *n.*
1 **stairs** *n.(pl.)*
4 **stale**
  4 *adj.* not fresh
  6 *adj.* not interesting because heard
    before
  7 *adj.* overworked, overpractised: *I*
    feel stale
4 **stall**
  4 *n.* open-fronted shop
  5 *v.* (of engines) fail to keep going
  6 *n.* compartment for animal
  7 *v.* avoid giving a clear answer: *he*
    stalled for time
1 **stamp**
  1 *n.* thing stuck to letters
  2 *n.* object which stamps
  3 *n.* design stamped on a surface
  5 *n.* act of stamping with the foot
  5 *v.* put one's foot down with force

1 **stand**
  1 *v.* keep upright: *stand still while I*
    take your photo
  2 *v.* rise to your feet: *we stood (up) to*
    see better
  3 *v.* have a position: *the house stands*
    on the hill
  4 *v.* remain unchanged: *the agreement*
    must stand
  5 *v.* endure: *she can't stand going to*
    the dentist
  5 *n.* structure for display: *a stand for*
    flowers in the market
3 **stand back** *v.* remain at a distance
  from
5 **stand by**
  5 *v.* observe passively
  5 *v.* support
5 **stand for** ˙
  5 *v.* represent
  5 *v.* tolerate
5 **stand in for** *v.* deputise for
5 **stand out** *v.* be noticeable
5 **stand up for** *v.* support when under
  attack
5 **stand up to** *v.* resist, endure
4 **standard**
  4 *n.* something used as a test: *the gold*
    standard
  4 *n.* level: *a high standard in the*
    examination
  6 *adj.* upright support: *a standard*
    lamp
  7 *n.* distinctive flag: *the Royal*
    Standard
5 **standardise** *v.*
4 **stand-up** *adj.: stand-up lunch*
1 **star**
  1 *n.* object in the sky
  3 *n.* famous persons in films etc.
  4 *v.* take a leading part in a film etc.
  6 *v.* mark or decorate with a star
4 **stare** *v.*
2 **start**
  2 *v.* begin
  2 *n.* beginning
  3 *v.* leave: *we started on our journey*
  4 *n.* sudden movement: *he awoke with*
    a start

5 *v.* jump: *he started up from his seat*
6 *v.* move suddenly: *tears started to her eyes*
4 **starve**
  4 *v.* die of hunger
  5 *v.* feel hungry
3 **state**
  3 *n.* condition
  4 *n.* organised political community
  5 *v.* express in words
  7 *n.* rank, dignity: *he lives beyond his state*
3 **statement**
  3 *n.* stating of facts/views/report: *a bank statement*
  5 *n.* expression: *clearness of statement*
2 **station**
  2 *n.* place of arrival/departure: *bus station*
  3 *n.* place where a service is organised: *fire station*
  6 *n.* social position: *he lives beyond his station*
  7 *v.* position: *he stationed the troops*
4 **stationery** *n.*
1 **stay**
  1 *v.* remain: *stay to dinner*
  2 *v.* be a guest: *she stayed with friends*
  3 *v.* continue in a certain state: *she stayed young*
  4 *n.* period of being a guest: *she thanked them for a pleasant stay*
3 **steady**
  3 *adj.* not varying: *a steady worker*
  5 *adj.* firmly fixed: *she held the ladder steady*
  6 *v.* make firm: *she steadied the table*
3 **steal**
  3 *v.* take
  6 *v.* obtain by surprise: *she stole a glance at him*
  6 *v.* move quietly: *she stole out of the room*
3 **steam**
  3 *n.* gas, vapour: *steam engine*
  5 *v.* give out vapour
  5 *v.* move under the power of steam

5 *v.* cook by steam
5 **steamer** *n.* ship
3 **steel**
  3 *n.* metal
  6 *v.* harden: *he steeled himself against defeat*
3 **steep**
  3 *adj.* rising or falling sharply: *a steep slope*
  4 *adj.* excessive: *a steep bill*
  6 *v.* soak in liquid: *steeped in vinegar*
  7 *v.* (fig.) pervade with: *steeped in mystery*
5 **steer**
  5 *v.* direct
  6 *n.* ox or bull
5 **steering wheel** *n.*
4 **stem**
  4 *n.* base of a plant
  6 *n.* (grammatical) root or main part of noun, verb etc.
  7 *v.* check, stop
2 **step**
  2 *n.* a place: *two steps*
  3 *n.* change in level of the ground: *mind the step*
  3 *n.* sound made by someone walking: *steps in the dark*
  4 *v.* move the foot: *she stepped into the room*
  6 *n.* action: *take steps; a false step*
5 **stereo** *n.*
4 **stewardess** *n.*
1 **stick**
  1 *n.* pole: *a walking stick*
  3 *n.* rod-shaped piece: *a stick of chalk*
  3 *v.* glue
  4 *v.* push something pointed into: *she stuck pins into the model*
  4 *v.* put: *she stuck her pens behind her ear*
  6 *v.* bear: *I can't stick it any more*
3 **stick out**
  3 *v.* (cause to) project
  5 *v.* endure
5 **stick to** *v.* not abandon (person, task)
2 **sticky**
  2 *adj.* something that sticks
  6 *adj.* tricky: *a sticky problem*

3 **stiff**
  3 *adj.* not flexible: *stiff legs*
  5 *adj.* formal: *stiff manners*
  6 *adj.* difficult: *a stiff test*
  7 *adj.* great: *a stiff price*
  7 *adv.* greatly: *scared stiff*
5 **stiffen** *v.*
1 **still**
  1 *adv.* even until now/then: *he is still here*
  3 *adj./adv.* quiet, motionless: *a still night; sit still*
  4 *adv.* to a greater degree: *still more*
  6 *adj.* (of wines) not sparkling
  7 *n.* deep silence: *the still of the night*
  7 *n.* photograph: *have you seen the stills?*
  7 *n.* apparatus for making liquor
5 **stillness** *n.*
3 **sting**
  3 *n.* sharp pain: *bee sting*
  3 *v.* cause sharp bodily pain: *stung by a wasp*
  5 *v.* cause mental pain to: *he was stung by the insults*
  7 *v.* charge excessively: *how much did they sting you for?*
3 **stir**
  3 *v.* move vigorously: *she stirred her tea*
  5 *v.* move: *nothing stirred*
  6 *v.* excite: *the story stirred him up*
  7 *v.* be roused: *pity stirred him*
  7 *n.* commotion: *the news caused a stir*
4 **stitch**
  4 *n.* unit of sewing/knitting
  4 *v.* to sew
  6 *n.* sharp pain: *I've got a stitch*
4 **stock**
  4 *v.* supply: *he stocked the shop*
  4 *n.* store: *a stock of goods*
  5 *adj.* commonly used: *a stock response*
  6 *n.* money lent: *stocks and shares*
  7 *n.* line of ancestry: *Irish stock*
  7 *n.* liquid for cooking: *chicken stock*
3 **stocking** *n.*

3 **stomach**
  3 *n.* part of the body
  6 *v.* put up with: *he couldn't stomach the film*
2 **stone**
  2 *n.* (piece of) solid mineral: *a stone wall*
  4 *n.* centre of fruit: *cherry stones*
  6 *v.* throw stones at
4 **stony**
  4 *adj.* having many stones: *a stony path*
  6 *adj.* hard, cold, unsympathetic: *a stony silence*
5 **stoop**
  5 *v.* bend body: *she stooped to pick up something she'd dropped*
  5 *n.* a bend in the body
  7 *v.* lower oneself to: *stoop to*
1 **stop**
  1 *v.* end movement: *he stopped the train; the train stopped*
  1 *v.* discontinue: *the rain has stopped, so we can leave*
  3 *v.* desist from activity: *they stopped all at once*
  3 *n.* halting place: *we reached the stop and got out*
  4 *v.* prevent: *you can't stop him from playing tennis*
  5 *v.* block: *entering the disco, I stopped my ears*
3 **stop behind** *v.* remain (while rest go on)
3 **stop in** *v.* stay indoors (school, house)
4 **stop off** *v.* break journey briefly
4 **stop over** *v.* break journey for one or two nights
5 **storage** *n./adj.*
2 **store**
  2 *v.* keep: *she stored the vegetables*
  3 *n.* shop: *a grocery store*
  4 *n.* supply: *a store of coal*
  5 *v.* put away for safe-keeping: *she stored her furniture*
4 **storey** *n.*
2 **storm**
  2 *n.* violent weather

4 *n.* violent outburst of feeling: *a storm of protests*

5 *v.* give violent expression to anger: *she stormed out of the room*

6 *v.* force a way into a building: *police stormed the airport*

4 **stormy**

  4 *adj.* marked by a strong wind

  6 *adj.* marked by strong feelings

1 **story**

  1 *n.* tale: *a short story*

  3 *n.* account of past events: *the story of Columbus*

3 **story-telling** *n.*

5 **stove** *n.*

2 **straight**

  2 *adj.* not curved: *a straight road*

  3 *adv.* directly: *come straight home*

  3 *adj.* level: *your skirt isn't straight*

  4 *adj.* (of person) upright: *a straight man*

  6 *n.* part of race-track: *the final straight*

5 **straighten** *v.*

3 **strain**

  3 *n.* something that tests one's powers: *the strain of sleepless nights*

  4 *n.* exhaustion: *mental strain*

  5 *n.* condition of being stretched: *the rope broke under the strain*

  5 *v.* sprain: *she strained her wrist*

  5 *v.* stretch tightly

  5 *v.* make a great effort: *she strained every nerve*

  6 *n.* manner of speaking or writing: *in a lofty strain*

  6 *n.* tendency in a person's character: *there is a strain of insanity in the family*

  6 *v.* pass liquid through a sieve

2 **strange** *adj.*

2 **stranger** *n.*

5 **strap** *v./n.*

4 **straw**

  4 *n.* stacks of wheat, barley, etc.

  5 *n.* tube for sucking liquid: *a straw for his lemonade*

3 **stream**

  3 *n.* brook

  4 *n.* steady flow: *a stream of people*

  5 *v.* flow freely: *sweat was streaming down his face*

  6 *v.* float or wave: *her hair streamed in the breeze*

  6 *n.* division of class of children according to ability: *the A stream*

  6 *v.* divide children in school according to ability

1 **street** *n.*

3 **strength**

  3 *n.* quality of being strong

  4 *n.* that which makes someone strong: *his friendship was a source of strength*

  6 *n.* large numbers: *the supporters were there in strength*

4 **stretch**

  4 *v.* pull: *she stretched the elastic*

  5 *v.* extend: *forests stretched for miles*

  6 *n.* extent: *a stretch of woodland/time*

  6 *v.* make a word include more than is right: *she stretched the meaning*

4 **strict**

  4 *adj.* stern: *a strict teacher*

  6 *adj.* clearly and exactly defined: *in the strict sense of the word*

4 **strike**

  4 *n.* stoppage at work

  4 *v.* hit

  4 *v.* refuse to work

  4 *v.* produce by friction: *she struck a match*

  5 *v.* come upon: *they struck oil*

  5 *v.* impress: *the idea struck me as sound*

  6 *v.* sound: *he struck a chord on the piano*

  7 *v.* produce by stamping: *they struck a medal*

3 **string**

  3 *n.* cord

  6 *v.* put strings on: *string a bow*

5 **strip**

  5 *v.* take off clothes, covering

  6 *n.* band: *a strip of plaster*

4 stripe
  4 *n*. band of colour: *a shirt with stripes*
  5 *n*. badge on a uniform: *3 stripes for a sergeant*
4 stroke
  4 *v*. caress: *she stroked the cat*
  4 *n*. blow: *one stroke of the sword*
  4 *n*. sound made by clock: *at the stroke of ten*
  5 *n*. single movement in games: *a good stroke*
  6 *n*. effort or occurrence: *a stroke of genius/good luck*
  6 *n*. mark made by a pen or brush: *fine strokes*
  6 *n*. cerebral haemorrhage
1 strong *adj*.
4 structure
  4 *n*. way something is put together/organised
  6 *n*. building: *the Parthenon is a magnificent structure*
  6 *v*. form: *structure one's argument*
3 struggle
  3 *v*. fight, wrestle
  3 *n*. fight, task requiring effort: *a struggle to replace that wheel*
1 student *n*.
1 study
  1 *v*. learn
  2 *v*. get knowledge
  3 *n*. something investigated: *social studies*
  4 *v*. examine carefully: *he studied the map*
  4 *n*. room used for learning
  6 *n*. sketch etc. for practice: *Chopin's Studies Opus 10*
4 stuff
  4 *n*. material, substance
  5 *v*. fill tightly with: *she stuffed the cushions*
  6 *v*. fill with flavoured food: *she stuffed the chicken*
  7 *v*. fill carcass to preserve: *a stuffed cat*

  7 *v*. overeat: *he didn't stop stuffing himself*
3 stupid *adj*.
5 stupidity *n*.
4 style
  4 *n*. manner: *in the Gothic style*
  4 *n*. fashion: *the latest style*
  4 *n*. general appearance, form: *this style*
  5 *n*. superior quality: *she does things in style*
  5 *v*. design
3 subject
  3 *n*. something to be discussed: *the subject for an essay*
  4 *n*. grammatical category: *the subject of this sentence*
  6 *n*. national of a state: *he's a French subject by birth*
  6 *v*. cause to undergo: *subject yourself to criticism*
  7 *adj*. not independent: *subject peoples*
  7 *adj*. conditional upon: *subject to your approval*
3 substance
  3 *n*. matter: *what sort of substance is it?*
  4 *n*. firmness, solidity: *this material has some substance*
  6 *n*. meaning, weight: *an argument of little substance*
  7 *n*. money, property: *a man of substance*
3 subtract *v*.
4 suburb *n*.
5 subway *n*.
3 succeed
  3 *v*. be successful
  6 *v*. come next: *who will succeed as Prime Minister?*
  7 *v*. inherit: *he succeeded to the property*
3 success *n*.
3 successful *adj*.
2 such
  2 *adv*. (+a) very: *it was such a long time ago*
  3 *adj*. of the same kind: *people such as these; no such thing*

6 *adj.* something referred to: *such was not my intention*
6 *pron.* in a given capacity: *I am the captain and as such insist . . .*
5 **such . . . that** *conj.: there was such a heavy downpour that the town centre was flooded*
3 **sudden** *adj.*
3 **suffer**
  3 *v.* be in pain
  4 *v.* undergo: *he suffered defeat*
  6 *v.* tolerate: *how can you suffer that noise?*
4 **sufficient** *adj.*
1 **sugar**
  1 *n.* sweet substance
  5 *v.* put sugar in: *did you sugar my tea?*
3 **suggest**
  3 *v.* propose
  5 *v.* bring/come into the mind: *his white face suggested fear*
1 **suit**
  1 *n.* clothing: *the brown suit or the green*
  3 *v.* be convenient: *that day suits me*
  4 *v.* look good on: *red suits you*
  6 *n.* any of the four sets of cards
  7 *n.* (formal) request: *he granted his suit*
  7 *n.* law-case: *a civil suit*
3 **suitable** *adj.*
3 **suitcase** *n.*
4 **sum**
  4 *n.* total
  4 *n.* amount of money: *a large sum*
  5 *v.* put together: *sum up*
  5 *n.* problem in arithmetic
1 **summer** *n.*
1 **sun** *n.*
1 **Sunday** *n.*
4 **sunlight** *n.*
2 **sunrise** *n.*
2 **sunset** *n.*
1 **sunshine** *n.*
2 **sunny**
  2 *adj.* bright with light
  4 *adj.* cheerful: *a sunny smile*
5 **super** *adj.*

4 **superior**
  4 *adj.* better than average: *superior intelligence*
  4 *adj.* greater: *superior in number*
  4 *adj.* better than: *this cloth is superior to that*
  5 *n.* person of higher rank: *you must talk to your superiors*
5 **supermarket** *n.*
5 **supersonic** *adj.*
1 **supper** *n.*
2 **supply**
  2 *v.* give, provide
  4 *n.* stock, amount available: *a steady supply of money*
  6 *v.* meet (a need): *should he supply the need for help*
3 **support**
  3 *v.* hold up: *this wall supports the house*
  4 *v.* strengthen, help: *she supported him in his flight*
  5 *v.* provide for: *he supports a large family*
  5 *n.* someone who supports: *Robert is the chief support of the family*
  5 *n.* supporting, being supported: *this bridge needs more support*
  6 *v.* endure: *I can't support it any more*
3 **suppose**
  3 *v.* guess, think: *I suppose he's French*
  4 *v.* imagine: *let's suppose . . .*
  5 *v.* as suggestion: *suppose we go there*
  6 *v.* imply: *creation supposes a creator*
2 **sure**
  2 *adj.* convinced: *I'm sure he knows*
  3 *adj.* decided: *I'm not sure if I'll go*
  5 *adj.* steady: *a sure hand*
  6 *adj.* proved and tested: *there is no sure remedy*
4 **surface**
  4 *n.* the outside of an object
  4 *n.* the top of a liquid
  5 *n.* outward appearance: *you must go beyond the surface*

6 *v.* give a covering to: *they surfaced the road*
5 **surgery**
  5 *n.* treatment by an operation
  5 *n.* consulting room
3 **surname** *n.*
3 **surprise** *n./v.*
3 **surround**
  3 *v.* go around
  6 *n.* floor between the walls and the carpet
4 **surroundings** *n.(pl.)*
4 **survey**
  4 *v.* take a general view: *he surveyed the countryside/the state of the economy*
  5 *n.* general view: *a survey of the situation*
  6 *v.* measure, map out position
  6 *n.* piece of land-surveying
  7 *v.* examine the condition of a house before purchase
4 **suspect**
  4 *v.* be suspicious
  5 *n.* person who may be guilty
5 **suspicion**
  5 *n.* feeling that something is wrong
  7 *n.* tinge: *a suspicion of sadness*
5 **suspicious** *adj.*
4 **swallow**
  4 *v.* take in down the throat
  5 *n.* act of swallowing
  6 *n.* bird
  6 *v.* exhaust: *expenses swallowed up his savings*
3 **swear**
  3 *v.* use bad language
  6 *v.* take an oath
5 **sweat**
  5 *n.* moisture
  5 *v.* produce moisture through the skin
2 **sweater** *n.*
2 **sweep**
  2 *v.* brush
  4 *v.* cause to move quickly: *he was swept along by the current*
  6 *v.* move in a dignified manner: *she swept out of the room*

6 *v.* pass over: *the searchlights swept the sky*
7 *n.* cleaner of chimneys: *chimney sweep*
1 **sweet**
  1 *adj.* like sugar
  3 *adj.* pleasant: *a sweet face*
  3 *adj.* fragrant: *a sweet smell*
  3 *n.* candy
  4 *n.* dessert
5 **sweeten** *v.*
5 **sweetness** *n.*
5 **swell**
  5 *v.* become larger: *her eyelids were swollen with crying*
  6 *v.* have a curved surface: *the sails swelled in the wind*
  7 *n.* increase in sound: *the swell of the organ*
  7 *n.* rise and fall of the sea: *sea-swell*
5 **swelling**
  5 *n.* swollen place
  6 *n.* increase in size
5 **swift** *adj.*
1 **swim**
  1 *v.* move through water
  2 *n.* act of swimming: *go for a swim*
  4 *v.* be covered with: *eyes swimming with tears*
  5 *v.* have a dizzy feeling: *his head swam*
3 **swing**
  3 *v.* move backwards and forwards in a curve: *his arms swung as he walked*
  3 *n.* seat for swinging on
  4 *n.* swinging movement: *the swing of a pendulum*
  4 *v.* turn swiftly: *he swung round*
3 **switch**
  3 *n.* electrical connector
  4 *v.* engage/disengage current: *switch on/off*
  5 *n.* change: *switch in policy*
  5 *v.* change: *his argument switched direction*
3 **sword** *n.*
5 **symbol** *n.*

4 **sympathise** *v.*
4 **sympathy** *n.*
3 **system**
   3 *n.* group of things working in regular relations: *a railway system*

5 *n.* ordered set of ideas: *a system of philosophy*
5 **systematic** *adj.*

T

1 **table**
   1 *n.* piece of furniture
   6 *v.* put forward a proposal: *to table a Bill*
   7 *n.* food: *he keeps a good table*
   7 *n.* list: *table of contents*
5 **tablecloth** *n.*
5 **tablet**
   5 *n.* pill
   7 *n.* flat surface with words cut into it
3 **tail**
   3 *n.* part of animal's body
   6 *n.* something at the end: *the tail of a kite/procession*
   7 *v.* follow: *she tailed his car for two hours*
4 **tailor**
   4 *n.* maker of garment
   6 *v.* cut out and sew
   7 *v.* adapt: *tailored to the purpose*
1 **take**
   1 *v.* lay hold of: *he took my hand*
   2 *v.* carry: *can you take those letters to the post?*
   3 *v.* steal: *who has taken my pen?*
   3 *v.* record: *I took a photograph of the children bathing*
   4 *v.* allow oneself: *we took a holiday last March*
   4 *v.* accept: *what will you take for this car?*
   4 *v.* require: *that job will take about four hours*
   5 *v.* capture: *they took 50 prisoners*
   5 *v.* subscribe to: *which newspaper do you take?*

   6 *v.* regard: *don't take it so gloomily*
5 **take after** *v.* resemble: *he takes after his father*
3 **take away** *v.* subtract
3 **take back** *v.* restore to previous state/position: *take back goods/employee*
4 **take in**
   4 *v.* include
   4 *v.* absorb
   5 *v.* delude
2 **take off**
   2 *v.* remove
   3 *v.* leave the ground (aircraft)
5 **take on** *v.* undertake
5 **take over** *v.* assume control of
5 **take to**
   5 *v.* adopt as habit
   5 *v.* develop a liking for
4 **take up**
   4 *v.* adopt as pastime/job
   4 *v.* occupy time/space
1 **talk**
   1 *v.* speak
   4 *n.* discussion: *they had a long talk*
   4 *n.* speech: *she gave a talk on cookery*
   5 *v.* discuss: *they talked sport*
1 **tall**
   1 *adj.* not short
   6 *adj.* exorbitant: *a tall order*
3 **tame**
   3 *adj.* not wild
   5 *adj.* spiritless, dull
   5 *v.* convert from a wild state

5 **tan**
  5 *n./adj.* sunburnt colour: *she got a good tan*
  5 *v.* become brown in the sun: *she tans easily*
  7 *v.* treat leather
5 **tank**
  5 *n.* container for petrol etc.
  5 *n.* armoured vehicle
  7 *v.* get tanked up
3 **tap**
  3 *n.* controlled opening for gas or liquids
  4 *v.* knock: *she tapped on the door*
  5 *n.* a light touch: *she heard a tap at the window*
  6 *v.* draw off liquid: *they tapped the trees for rubber*
  6 *n.* plug to open and close a cask
  7 *v.* extract information: *they tapped her telephone*
3 **tape**
  3 *n.* narrow strip of material: *3 feet of tape*
  4 *v.* record on magnetic tape
  5 *v.* fasten, tie together
4 **task**
  4 *n.* piece of hard work to be done
  7 *v.* put a strain on: *mathematics tasks his brain*
2 **taste**
  2 *v.* test the flavour of: *she tasted the soup*
  3 *v.* have the flavour of: *it tastes of coffee*
  3 *v.* be aware of the taste: *can you taste soap?*
  4 *n.* flavour: *a good taste*
  4 *n.* one of the five senses
  5 *n.* liking, preference for: *a taste for fast cars*
  6 *n.* discrimination: *she has good taste*
3 **tax**
  3 *n.* payment to the government
  4 *v.* put a tax on: *wine is heavily taxed*
  6 *v.* strain: *he taxed my patience*
  7 *v.* accuse: *he taxed him with neglect of his work*

1 **taxi**
  1 *n.* car for hire
  4 *v.* (of aircraft) move slowly along the ground
5 **taxpayer** *n.*
1 **tea**
  1 *n.* drink
  2 *n.* occasion in the afternoon when tea is drunk
2 **teach** *v.*
1 **teacher** *n.*
3 **teacup** *n.*
3 **team**
  3 *n.* persons playing together
  6 *n.* two or more oxen, horses before a cart
  6 *v.* join: *team up with*
3 **tear**
  3 *n.* drop from eye
  3 *v.* pull apart, rip
  4 *v.* become torn: *this paper tears easily*
  5 *v.* move at great speed: *they tore down the road*
4 **technical** *adj.*
4 **technique**
  4 *n.* technical or mechanical skill in art or craft
  4 *n.* method of doing something expertly
5 **technology** *n.*
5 **teenager** *n.*
2 **telegram** *n.*
1 **telephone** *n./v.*
5 **telescope**
  5 *n.* instrument
  7 *v.* make shorter by sliding one section into another: *the first two coaches of the train telescoped*
1 **television** *n.*
1 **tell**
  1 *v.* make known: *I told him my name*
  2 *v.* relate: *she told the children a story*
  3 *v.* order: *tell him to wait*
  4 *v.* reveal: *he promised never to tell my secret*
  5 *v.* distinguish: *he can't tell red from green*

4 **temper**
  4 *n.* emotional condition of the mind: *in a good temper*
  6 *n.* degree of hardness of a metal
  6 *v.* bring to the required condition: *she tempered the steel*
  7 *v.* moderate: *temper justice with mercy*

5 **temple**
  5 *n.* building for worship
  6 *n.* flat part at sides of the forehead

4 **temporary** *adj.*

4 **tempt**
  4 *v.* persuade to do something unusual: *nothing could tempt him to take such a step*
  4 *v.* attract: *the weather tempted us to swim*
  6 *v.* test: *tempt providence*

5 **temptation** *n.*

1 **ten** *n./adj.*

5 **tenant**
  5 *n.* person who pays rent for a room
  7 *v.* live in as a tenant: *houses tenanted by farm workers*

4 **tend**
  4 *v.* be inclined to move: *prices are tending to go up*
  6 *v.* watch over: *tend a sick animal*

4 **tendency** *n.*

5 **tender**
  5 *adj.* gentle, delicate
  6 *n.* one who looks after something: *the bar-tender*
  6 *v.* offer: *he tendered his resignation*
  6 *n.* offer: *a contract put out to tender*
  7 *n.* small ship for carrying supplies

4 **tennis** *n.*

4 **tense**
  4 *n.* form of a verb
  4 *adj.* tightly stretched, strained
  5 *v.* strain: *he tensed his muscles*

4 **tension**
  4 *n.* degree of tenseness/strain: *nervous tension*
  5 *n.* state of being stretched: *increase the tension of the string*
  6 *n.* voltage: *high tension wires*

3 **tent** *n.*

2 **tenth** *adj.*

3 **term**
  3 *n.* period into which academic year is divided: *the spring term*
  5 *n.* fixed period: *a term of imprisonment*
  6 *n.* conditions offered or agreed to: *terms of surrender*

5 **terminal**
  5 *n.* arrival/departure point: *West London Air Terminal*
  6 *n.* point of connection of an electric circuit
  6 *adj.* taking place every term: *terminal exams*
  7 *adj.* final: *a terminal illness*

5 **terminus** *n.*

3 **terrible**
  3 *adj.* extremely bad: *terrible work*
  4 *adj.* causing great fear or horror: *a terrible war*
  4 *adj.* extreme: *terrible heat*

5 **terribly** *adv.*

5 **terrific**
  5 *adj.* very great, extreme: *driving at a terrific pace*
  7 *adj.* causing fear

4 **territory**
  4 *n.* land: *how much territory does he cover?*
  5 *n.* land under one ruler: *Iraqi territory*

4 **terror**
  4 *n.* great fear
  6 *n.* troublesome person: *a perfect terror*

5 **terrorist** *n.*

3 **test**
  3 *n.* an examination: *he did well in the test*
  3 *v.* examine

4 **text**
  4 *n.* main body of a book
  5 *n.* original words of an author
  5 *n.* short passage as subject for discussion

2 **than** *conj.*

2 **thank**
  2 *v.* express gratitude

6 *v.* (in requests) insist: *I'll thank you
to be quiet*
5 **thankful** *adj.*
2 **thanks**
2 *int.: thanks a lot*
4 *n.(pl.)* gratitude: *she gives you her
thanks*
5 **Thanksgiving** *n.*
1 **thank you** *int.*
1 **that**
1 *adj./pron.*
2 *conj.: it states that they went*
1 **the**
1 *det.* this: *an old man. . . the old
man*
1 *det.* the only one relevant: *the river;
the street; the sun*
1 *det.* (with superlative): *the best way
to get there*
2 *det.* the only one existing: *the
Atlantic*
3 *det.* of a particular invention: *the
telephone is useful*
4 *det.* members of a class: *the rich*
4 *det.* each: *30 miles to the gallon*
5 **the more. . . the more** *conj.: the more
he eats the more he wants*
3 **theatre**
3 *n.* building
4 *n.* hall or room for lectures,
operations etc.: *operating
theatre*
6 *n.* dramatic literature or art: *a
specialist in Greek theatre*
7 *n.* scene of important events: *the
theatre of war*
1 **their** *det.*
2 **theirs** *pron.*
1 **them** *pron.*
1 **themselves** *pron.*
1 **then**
1 *adv.* at that time: *he was living in
Greece then*
3 *adv.* so: *then it isn't here*
5 *adv.* furthermore: *then there's Mr
Jones*
4 **theory**
4 *n.* general principles: *the theory of
navigation*

5 *n.* reasoned explanations of
events: *Darwin's theory of
evolution*
6 *n.* something conjectured/not
proved: *he has a theory about
women*
1 **there**
1 *adv.* in/at/to that place: *put the box
there*
1 *adv.* pointing out: *there's an
elephant – let's take a ride*
1 *adv.* informing: *there are over 30
students in the class*
4 *adv.* on/at that point/matter: *I don't
agree with you there*
5 *adv.* (+verb of motion + noun):
there goes the bus!
6 *int.* exclaiming: *there – you'll be all
right now*
3 **therefore** *conj.*
5 **thermometer** *n.*
1 **these** *pron./det.*
1 **they** *pron.*
1 **thick**
1 *adj.* not thin
5 *adj.* stupid
6 *adj.* intimate: *they are very thick
together*
7 *n.* most crowded part: *in the thick of
activity*
5 **thicken** *v.*
5 **thickness** *n.*
3 **thief** *n.*
1 **thin**
1 *adj.* not thick
3 *n.* make thin
1 **thing**
1 *n.* material object: *I got this thing in
Indonesia*
2 *n.* articles, belongings: *bring your
swimming things*
3 *n.* subject: *that's a thing I want to
ask you about*
4 *n.* circumstances: *that only makes
things worse*
6 *n.* person, animal: *she's a sweet
thing*
6 *n.* the best: *a skiing holiday would
be the very thing*

7 *n.* the question to be considered: *the thing is, what are we to tell him?*

1 **think**

  1 *v.* believe

  2 *v.* exercise the mind

  2 *v.* consider

3 **think of**

  3 *v.* call to mind

  5 *v.* invent

4 **think out** *v.* plan carefully

4 **think over** *v.* consider further

3 **thinker** *n.*

1 **third** *adj.*

3 **thirst**

  3 *n.* need for a drink

  4 *n.* strong desire: *the thirst for knowledge*

1 **thirsty** *adj.*

1 **thirteen** *n./adj.*

1 **thirty** *n./adj.*

1 **this** *det./pron.*

5 **thorn** *n.*

4 **thorough** *adj.*

4 **thoroughly** *adv.*

1 **those** *det./pron.*

3 **though**

  3 *conj.* notwithstanding: *though it was raining, he didn't take an umbrella*

  5 *adv.* however: *you never know, though*

3 **thought**

  3 *n.* idea: *let me have your thoughts on the matter*

  4 *n.* process of thinking: *he was lost in thought*

  5 *n.* intention: *I had no thought of visiting Spain*

  6 *n.* way of thinking: *modern thought is concerned with . . .*

3 **thoughtful**

  3 *adj.* thinking

  6 *adj.* considerate

2 **thousand** *n./adj.*

3 **thread**

  3 *n.* spun cotton

  4 *v.* put cotton etc. through a needle

  5 *n.* chain or line: *the thread of a story*

6 *n.* something very thin: *a thread of light*

7 *n.* ridge around a bolt

4 **threat**

  4 *n.* intention to hurt

  5 *n.* sign of warning: *a threat of rain*

4 **threaten**

  4 *v.* utter a threat

  5 *v.* give warning of

1 **three** *n./adj.*

4 **throat**

  4 *n.* front part of the neck

  4 *n.* passage in the neck where food passes

1 **through**

  1 *prep.* from one side to the other: *he came in through that door*

  2 *prep.* from end to end: *she won't live through the night*

  2 *adv.* from end to end: *read the book right through*

  3 *adv.* all the way to: *the train goes through to Edinburgh*

  3 *prep.* by means of: *I learnt of it through the papers*

  4 *adv.* to the end: *when will you be through with your work*

  5 *adv.* connected: *you're through to New York*

  5 *adv.* completely: *you're wet through*

  6 *adj.* long-distance: *a through train to Moscow*

4 **throughout** *adv./prep.*

2 **throw**

  2 *v.* make a thing move through the air

  3 *v.* put carelessly: *she threw her clothes on the chair*

  6 *v.* give: *she threw a party*

  6 *v.* cause the rider to fall: *two men were thrown during the race*

4 **throw out**

  4 *v.* discard

  4 *v.* eject

3 **thumb**

  3 *n.* fifth finger

  6 *v.* turn over the pages: *he thumbed through the book*

3 **thunder**
   3 *n.* noise showing atmospheric disturbance: *thunder and lightning*
   5 *n.* loud noise like thunder: *the thunder of the guns*
   5 *v.* make thunder: *it was thundering*
   5 *v.* make a loud noise: *the train thundered through the station*
   6 *v.* speak in a loud voice: *he thundered against gambling*
4 **thunderstorm** *n.*
1 **Thursday** *n.*
4 **thus** *conj.*
2 **ticket**
   2 *n.* travel document
   3 *n.* price label
   4 *n.* printed notice of parking offence
   7 *n.* certificate listing qualifications of a pilot etc.
4 **tide**
   4 *n.* rise and fall of the sea
   6 *n.* flow and tendency: *the tide of public opinion*
3 **tidy**
   3 *adj.* neat
   4 *v.* make neat
   6 *adj.* considerable: *a tidy sum of money*
2 **tie**
   2 *n.* article of clothing
   3 *v.* fasten
   4 *n.* thing used to keep things together: *hair ties; family ties*
   5 *n.* equal score: *the game ended in a tie*
   6 *n.* something that limits one's actions: *young children are a tie*
4 **tiger** *n.*
2 **tight**
   2 *adj.* fastened, held closely together: *the cork is too tight*
   3 *adj.* too small: *a tight dress*
   6 *adj.* (colloq.) drunk
5 **tighten** *v.*
5 **tights** *n.(pl.)* garment
5 **tile**
   5 *n.* plate of baked clay
   6 *v.* cover with such plates

2 **till**
   2 *conj./prep.* until
   5 *n.* cash-register
   6 *v.* cultivate the land: *he tilled the soil*
1 **time**
   1 *n.* point of time: *what time is it?*
   2 *n.* stretch of time: *it took more time than expected*
   2 *n.* occasion: *the last time I was there*
   2 *n.* appropriate point or period: *it's time for supper*
   4 *n.* in multiplication: *four times four are sixteen*
   5 *n.* conditions of life: *times were hard*
   5 *n.* rhythm: *keep time with your foot*
   6 *v.* choose moment: *he timed his entry for maximum effect*
4 **timetable** *n.*
2 **tin**
   2 *n.* can
   4 *n.* metal
   4 *v.* put in cans
   6 *v.* coat with tin
4 **tiny** *adj.*
5 **tip**
   5 *n.* pointed end: *the tips of his fingers*
   5 *n.* payment to waiter
   5 *v.* make such payment to a waiter
   6 *v.* knock over
   7 *n.* piece of advice: *a tip about a race*
   7 *n.* place where rubbish is deposited
4 **tire**
   4 *v.* make/become weary
   5 *n.* tyre
1 **tired** *adj.*
3 **title**
   3 *n.* name of a book etc.
   5 *n.* word to describe someone's status: *what is his title?*
   7 *n.* names of persons involved in a production: *the credit titles*
   7 *n.* claim: *what title does he have to this land?*
1 **to**
   1 *prep.* in the direction of: *to London*

1 *part.* (marking infinitive): *to go*
2 *prep.* (indirect object): *I gave it to Katie*
2 *prep.* before: *a quarter to six*
2 *prep.* until: *from Saturday to Monday*
3 *prep.* ratio, reference: *they won by six goals to three*
3 *part.* (with infinitive) in order to: *they came to help me*
4 *prep.* as far as: *wet to the skin*
4 *part.* (for verb): *we didn't want to go, but we had to*
6 *part.* and: *he awoke to find himself tied up*
5 **toast**
　5 *n.* bread browned under the grill
　5 *v.* make toast
　6 *v.* warm oneself thoroughly
3 **tobacco** *n.*
1 **today**
　1 *adv.* this day
　2 *adv.* the present time
3 **toe**
　3 *n.* one of the 'fingers' of the foot
　5 *n.* part of a sock/shoe covering the toe
2 **together**
　2 *adv.* in company: *they left together*
　3 *adv.* united: *tie the ends together*
2 **toilet**
　2 *n.* lavatory
　6 *n.* process in dressing: *she spent a few minutes on her toilet*
5 **tomato** *n.*
1 **tomorrow** *adv.*
2 **ton**
　2 *n.* measure of weight
　4 *n.* large weight: *it weighed a ton*
　6 *n.* measure of the capacity of a ship
4 **tone**
　4 *n.* sound: *the tone of his voice*
　5 *n.* general character: *the tone of the neighbourhood*
　6 *n.* shade of colour: *the warm tones of the picture*
3 **tongue**
　3 *n.* organ in the mouth

4 *n.* language: *his mother tongue*
6 *n.* animal's tongue as food: *they chose tongue from the menu*
7 *n.* something in the shape of a tongue: *a tongue of land*
1 **tonight** *adv.*
1 **too**
　1 *adv.* also: *I've been to Jakarta too*
　3 *adv.* in a higher degree than allowable: *too heavy to lift; too much rain*
2 **tool**
　2 *n.* instrument: *garden tools*
　6 *n.* person used by another: *he was a mere tool in the director's hands*
1 **tooth/teeth**
　1 *n.* white bony object growing in the mouth
　6 *n.* tooth-like part of rake, saw etc.: *the comb has some teeth missing*
4 **toothbrush** *n.*
4 **toothpaste** *n.*
1 **top**
　1 *n.* highest part: *the top of the page*
　1 *n.* upper surface: *on top of the car*
　2 *n.* highest rank: *at the top of his class*
　3 *n.* utmost degree: *at the top of his voice*
　4 *v.* surpass: *exports have topped the £800 million mark*
　5 *v.* reach the top of: *we topped the hill and. . .*
　6 *v.* cut the tops off: *lift and top the turnips*
　6 *n.* toy: *a spinning top*
4 **torch**
　4 *n.* hand-light
　6 *n.* flaming object made of flax etc.
3 **total**
　3 *n.* sum
　3 *adj.* complete
　4 *v.* amount to: *the bill totalled £20*
3 **touch**
　3 *v.* be/come into contact with
　4 *n.* act of touching
　4 *n.* light stroke: *a touch of the brush*
　4 *n.* slight quantity: *a touch of bitterness*

5 *n.* communication: *in touch with the situation*

5 *v.* affect: *her tragic story touched us all*

6 *v.* match: *no one can touch him for speed*

6 *v.* have to do with: *this touches your interests*

7 *n.* play: *the ball is still in touch*

4 **tough**

  4 *adj.* (of meat) hard to get one's teeth into

  4 *adj.* not easily worn out: *tough shoes*

  5 *adj.* able to endure hardship: *tough soldiers*

  5 *adj.* rough and violent: *a tough man*

  6 *adj.* stubborn, unyielding: *he got tough with me*

3 **tour**

  3 *n.* brief visit: *a tour of London*

  3 *n.* journey where several places are visited: *a tour of Italy*

  4 *n.* round of official visits: *the Director goes on tour tomorrow*

  4 *v.* visit

  6 *n.* period of duty overseas: *a two-year tour in India*

3 **tourist** *n.*

2 **toward/s**

  2 *prep.* in the direction of

  4 *prep.* as regards: *his attitude towards his superiors*

  5 *prep.* for the purpose of: *money towards expenses*

  5 *prep.* near: *towards the end of evening*

3 **towel**

  3 *n.* cloth for drying

  5 *v.* dry oneself

1 **town** *n.*

5 **town hall** *n.*

4 **town-planning** *n.*

2 **toy**

  2 *n.* child's plaything

  5 *n.* small animal kept as pet: *a toy poodle*

4 **trace**

  4 *n.* mark, sign: *no trace of the thief*

6 *n.* very small amount: *traces of arsenic*

6 *v.* copy: *he traced the map*

7 *v.* follow or discover through marks: *they traced her parents*

3 **track**

  3 *n.* path prepared for racing: *a race track*

  4 *n.* marks left by animal etc.: *tracks in the snow*

  4 *n.* set of rails for trains

  5 *v.* follow a trail

  7 *n.* belt used on tanks for propulsion

3 **tractor** *n.*

4 **trade**

  4 *n.* buying and selling of goods

  4 *v.* buy and sell

  5 *n.* occupation: *what's his trade?*

5 **trader** *n.*

5 **tradesman** *n.*

4 **tradition** *n.*

4 **traditional** *adj.*

3 **traffic**

  3 *n.* vehicles in street

  6 *n.* illicit trading: *the traffic in drugs*

4 **traffic light** *n.*

5 **trail**

  5 *n.* series of marks: *a trail of smoke*

  5 *n.* track in hunting: *hot on the trail*

  5 *v.* follow the tracks of: *they trailed the bear*

  6 *n.* path through the country: *Nature Trail*

  7 *v.* flow over or along the ground: *trailing plants*

1 **train**

  1 *n.* locomotive (with wagons/coaches)

  4 *v.* give practice: *she trains teachers*

  6 *v.* cause to grow in the required direction: *he trained the roses against the wall*

  7 *n.* series or chain: *he interrupted my train of thought*

  7 *n.* part of a long dress

5 **tram** *n.*

4 **transfer**

  4 *v.* move: *the office transferred to Sheffield*

5 *n.* switch: *he got a transfer to Liverpool*
5 *v.* change from one bus (etc.) to another
6 *v.* hand over possession: *he transferred his shares to his son*
7 *v.* convey from one surface to another
5 **transistor**
5 *n.* radio
6 *n.* electronic device
3 **translate** *v.*
3 **translation** *n.*
4 **transparent**
4 *adj.* allowing light through: *transparent glass*
6 *adj.* about which there is no doubt: *a transparent lie*
3 **transport**
3 *v.* carry goods
3 *n.* organisation for conveying people: *London Transport*
4 *n.* act of conveying: *the transport of goods*
7 *v.* send criminal to another country: *he was transported to Australia*
4 **trap**
4 *n.* device for catching animals: *a mouse-trap*
5 *n.* plan for deceiving: *I set a trap for him*
6 *v.* deceive, catch: *she trapped him*
2 **travel**
2 *v.* make long journeys
5 *n.* travelling: *he's fond of travel*
6 *v.* pass from point to point: *his eyes travelled over the crowd*
2 **traveller**
2 *n.* one who travels
5 *n.* salesman who covers a large area
4 **tray** *n.*
5 **treasure**
5 *n.* store of gold, etc.
5 *n.* something highly valued
6 *v.* value highly
7 *v.* store for future use
5 **treasurer** *n.*
5 **treat**
5 *v.* act towards: *he treated her badly*

5 *v.* give medical care: *how would you treat this illness?*
6 *v.* consider: *treat it as a joke*
6 *v.* deal with: *this problem has already been treated*
6 *v.* put a substance through a process: *the wood was treated for wood-worm*
7 *n.* something that gives pleasure: *a special treat*
7 *n.* hospitality: *it's my treat*
5 **treatment** *n.*
1 **tree** *n.*
4 **tremble**
4 *v.* shake involuntarily: *he trembled with excitement*
4 *v.* move to and fro: *the ground trembled*
6 *v.* be in a state of agitation: *I tremble to think what has happened*
5 **trial**
5 *n.* legal process
5 *n.* testing: *they gave the typist a trial*
6 *n.* something troublesome: *life is full of trials*
4 **triangle** *n.*
5 **tribe** *n.*
5 **trick**
5 *n.* something done to deceive
5 *v.* deceive
5 *n.* mischievous joke
5 *n.* feat of skill: *a card trick*
6 *n.* strange characteristic: *he has a trick of pulling his right ear*
6 *n.* point in cards: *he won a trick*
2 **trip**
2 *n.* journey
4 *v.* fall, stumble
6 *v.* dance with light steps: *she tripped across the grass*
7 *n.* (colloq.) be under the influence of drugs: *he's on a trip*
5 **tropical** *adj.*
2 **trouble**
2 *n.* problem, worry, nuisance
4 *n.* care, attention: *did the work cause you much trouble?*

5 *n.* political or social unrest: *labour troubles*
5 *v.* bother: *don't trouble about it*
6 *n.* illness: *liver trouble*
6 *v.* put someone to an inconvenience: *may I trouble you for the sugar?*
5 **troublesome** *adj.*
1 **trousers** *n.*
1 **truck**
  1 *n.* lorry
  2 *n.* railway wagon
2 **true**
  2 *adj.* agreeing with fact: *a true statement*
  3 *adj.* loyal: *a true friend*
  6 *adj.* rightful: *the true heir*
5 **trumpet**
  5 *n.* instrument
  6 *n.* something shaped like a trumpet
  7 *v.* sound made by elephant
5 **trunk**
  5 *n.* large container
  5 *n.* main stem of a tree
  6 *n.* nose of elephant
  7 *n.* body, without limbs
3 **trust**
  3 *v.* believe in someone's honesty etc.: *I trust him completely*
  4 *n.* confidence, strong belief: *put your trust in him*
  5 *v.* allow to do, knowing situation to be dangerous: *do you trust her to drive the car?*
  6 *n.* responsibility: *a position of trust*
  6 *v.* earnestly hope: *I trust you're in good health*
  7 *n.* legal property held for someone's benefit: *he set up a trust for his children*
  7 *n.* association of (business) firms: *a charitable trust*
3 **truth**
  3 *n.* that which is true: *tell me the truth*
  4 *n.* verity: *the pursuit of truth*
  5 *n.* element accepted as true: *the truths of religion*
1 **try**
  1 *v.* attempt: *he tried to sleep*

4 *v.* test: *they tried the new soap*
5 *v.* apply a process of law: *they tried the man*
4 **try on** *v.* put on garment to check fit
4 **try out** *v.* test
4 **tube**
  4 *n.* hollow cylinder: *a test tube*
  4 *n.* soft metal container: *a tube of toothpaste*
  4 *n.* underground train: *they came by tube*
  5 *n.* valve in TV/radio: *the tube is going*
  6 *n.* hollow organ in the body: *the bronchial tubes*
1 **Tuesday** *n.*
5 **tune**
  5 *n.* melody: *he sang a tune*
  5 *n.* harmony: *the recorders were not in tune*
  6 *v.* (musical) adjust the strings
  6 *v.* adjust the engine of a motor-vehicle: *he's just had his engine tuned*
5 **tunnel**
  5 *n.* underground passage
  6 *v.* burrow, create underground passage
2 **turn**
  2 *v.* change direction: *she turned round*
  3 *v.* change position: *she turned the page*
  4 *v.* rotate: *he turned the wheel*
  4 *n.* a change in direction: *a turn in the road*
  4 *n.* act of turning: *a few turns of the wheel*
  5 *n.* occasion for doing something: *it's your turn*
  6 *n.* change in condition: *he took a turn for the worst*
3 **turn back** *v.* reverse direction of journey
4 **turn down**
  4 *v.* reduce intensity: *turn down the sound*
  5 *v.* refuse: *turn down an application*
4 **turn into** *v.* become

3 **turn off** v. switch off
3 **turn on** v. switch on
3 **turn out**
   3 v. extinguish
   5 v. transpire
   5 v. produce, make
3 **turn over** v. reverse position: *turn over in bed; turn over a page*
3 **turn up**
   3 v. increase intensity: *turn up the sound*
   5 v. appear: *he turned up unexpectedly*
5 **turning** n.
5 **turnover**
   5 n. amount of money passing through a business

6 n. type of tart: *apple turnover*
2 **twelfth** adj.
1 **twelve** n./adj.
2 **twentieth** adj.
1 **twenty** n./adj.
2 **twice** adv.
1 **two** n./adj.
3 **type**
   3 n. kind
   4 n. letters for printing: *what sort of type was used?*
   4 v. use a typewriter
4 **typewriter** n.
4 **typical** adj.
2 **typist** n.
3 **tyre** n.

U

3 **ugly**
   3 adj. unpleasant to look at
   4 adj. menacing: *an ugly sky*
3 **umbrella** n.
2 **unable** adj.
5 **unarmed** adj.
5 **unbutton** v.
5 **uncertain**
   5 adj. changeable: *uncertain weather*
   5 adj. not certainly knowing or known
5 **uncertainty**
   5 n. state of being uncertain
   5 n. something which is uncertain
3 **uncle** n.
5 **uncomfortable** adj.
4 **uncommon** adj.
4 **unconscious**
   4 adj. not conscious
   5 n. region of the mind of which one is unaware
1 **under**
   1 prep. lower than: *the cat was under the table*

   1 prep. movement below: *we passed under two bridges*
   1 prep. (in and) covered by: *he hid under the bedclothes/bushes*
   3 prep. less than: *this weighs under 3 kilos*
   4 prep. in process of: *road under repair*
4 **under control**
5 **undergraduate** n.
4 **underground**
   4 adj. under the surface of the ground
   4 n. tube train
   6 adj. secret
   6 adv. into hiding: *he went underground when he heard the police were after him*
5 **underline**
   5 v. draw a line under
   6 v. emphasise
4 **underneath** prep./adv.
1 **understand**
   1 v. know the meaning

4 *v.* learn, infer: *I understand you are married*
6 *v.* supply mentally: *the verb is understood*
4 **understanding**
  4 *adj.* having or showing insight
  5 *n.* capacity for sympathising
  6 *n.* agreement: *they came to an understanding*
5 **undertake**
  5 *v.* agree to do: *he undertook the premiership*
  6 *v.* promise: *I can't undertake that you'll make a profit*
2 **undo**
  2 *v.* untie
  7 *v.* destroy the result of: *the accident undid all my good work*
5 **undress**
  5 *v.* take off one's clothes
  5 *v.* remove the clothes of
4 **uneasy** *adj.*
5 **unemployment**
  5 *n.* state of being unemployed
  6 *n.* amount of unused labour
4 **unfair** *adj.*
3 **unfortunately** *adv.*
3 **unhappy**
  3 *adj.* not happy
  7 *adj.* not suitable: *an unhappy comment*
4 **uniform**
  4 *n.* dress of the same style
  6 *adj.* the same, not varying
4 **union**
  4 *n.* association formed by the uniting of groups: *a trade union*
  5 *n.* being united: *the union of the three towns*
  6 *n.* state of being in agreement: *live in perfect union*
  6 *n.* general club/society: *the Oxford Union*
5 **unique** *adj.*
5 **unisex** *adj.*
4 **unit**
  4 *n.* single thing etc.: *an armoured unit*

6 *n.* standard measurement: *a unit of length*
4 **unite**
  4 *v.* make or become one: *unite two countries*
  5 *v.* act together: *let us unite in fighting the aggressor*
3 **United Nations, the** *n.*
2 **United States, the** *n.*
5 **unity**
  4 *n.* state of being united
  5 *n.* harmony
4 **universal** *adj.*
5 **universe**
  5 *n.* everything that exists
  5 *n.* system of suns and stars
3 **university** *n.*
4 **unjust** *adj.*
4 **unkind** *adj.*
4 **unknown** *adj.*
5 **unlawful** *adj.*
2 **unless** *conj.*
4 **unlike** *adj./prep.*
4 **unlikely** *adj.*
5 **unload**
  5 *v.* remove a load from
  7 *v.* get rid of: *he unloaded his shares*
5 **unlock** *v.*
3 **unlucky** *adj.*
3 **unnecessary** *adj.*
5 **unpaid** *adj.*
4 **unpleasant** *adj.*
4 **unsatisfactory** *adj.*
4 **untidy** *adj.*
5 **untie** *v.*
2 **until** *conj./prep.*
3 **unusual** *adj.*
4 **unwilling** *adj.*
1 **up**
  1 *prep.* direction: *up the hill*
  1 *adv.* to/in erect position: *he's already up*
  1 *adv.* to a higher place: *lift your head up*
  3 *adv.* to a place of importance: *he's gone up to London*
  4 *adv.* (completeness, finality): *time's up*
  4 *adv.* (intensity): *speak up*

3 **up to date**
5 **uphill**
    5 *adv.* sloping upward: *they walked uphill*
    7 *adj.* difficult: *an uphill struggle*
5 **uphold**
    5 *v.* support, approve
    7 *v.* confirm a decision: *the judge upheld the verdict*
5 **upkeep** *n.*
5 **upland** *n./adj.*
2 **upon** *prep.*
3 **upper**
    3 *adj.* higher
    6 *n.* part of a shoe over the sole
5 **uppermost** *adj./adv.*
5 **upright**
    5 *adj./adv.* erect: *an upright post*
    7 *adj.* honourable: *an upright man*
4 **upset**
    4 *v.* disturb: *don't upset him*
    5 *v.* knock over: *she upset the bottle*
    6 *n.* disturbance: *a stomach upset*
2 **upstairs** *adj./adv.*
4 **upward/s** *adj./adv.*
4 **urge**
    4 *v.* encourage: *I urged him to try harder*

6 *n.* strong desire: *the urge to steal*
3 **urgent**
    3 *adj.* needing prompt action
    6 *adj.* showing that something is urgent: *an urgent voice*
1 **us** *pron.*
2 **use**
    2 *v.* employ: *she used a knife*
    3 *n.* utilisation: *for the use of teachers*
    3 *n.* value: *is this of any use to you?*
    4 *v.* consume: *how much wood did we use last winter?*
3 **used (to)**
    3 *modal* past practice: *he used to smoke a pipe*
    4 *adj.* accustomed: *she's not used to waiting*
3 **useful**
    3 *adj.* helpful: *a useful tool*
    6 *adj.* capable: *a useful player*
5 **usefulness** *n.*
5 **useless**
    5 *adj.* of no use: *a car is useless without petrol*
    5 *adj.* ineffectual, pointless: *it's useless to argue*
2 **usual** *adj.*

V

5 **vacant**
    5 *adj.* not occupied: *a vacant seat*
    7 *adj.* empty: *a vacant stare*
4 **vacation**
    4 *n.* holiday time
    6 *n.* university/law court holidays
    7 *n.* leaving: *his vacation of those premises was most surprising*
5 **vacuum**
    5 *n.* machine for cleaning
    7 *n.* empty space
3 **vain**
    3 *n.* without result: *in vain*

4 *adj.* conceited: *a vain woman*
6 *adj.* without use/value: *a vain attempt*
7 *n.* without due reverence: *take God's name in vain*
5 **valid**
    5 *adj.* having force in law: *a valid ticket*
    6 *adj.* sound, well based: *a valid argument*
    7 *adj.* effective, done with the correct formalities: *a valid claim*
2 **valley** *n.*

2 **valuable** *adj.*
2 **value**
  2 *n.* worth: *the value of the pound has gone down*
  4 *n.* quality of being useful: *the value of exercise*
  4 *n.* worth of something compared to something else: *the book will be of great value in his study*
5 **valueless** *adj.*
5 **valve**
  5 *n.* device for controlling the flow of air, water
  5 *n.* device used in a radio/TV
4 **van**
  4 *n.* motor-vehicle
  6 *n.* railway carriage: *guard's van*
  7 *n.* head of a movement: *in the van of scientific progress*
4 **vanish** *v.*
5 **variation**
  5 *n.* degree of varying: *a variation in temperature*
  7 *n.* melody repeated in different form
4 **variety**
  4 *n.* number of different things: *a variety of reasons*
  5 *n.* not being always the same: *variety of diet*
  6 *n.* kind of entertainment
  7 *n.* (biol.) subdivision of species
3 **various** *adj.*
4 **vary** *v.*
5 **vase** *n.*
4 **vast** *adj.*
2 **vegetable** *n./adj.*
3 **vehicle**
  3 *n.* conveyance: *motor vehicles*
  7 *n.* means of conveying a thought/idea: *art as a vehicle of propaganda*
5 **veil**
  5 *n.* covering for the face
  6 *v.* put a veil over: *many Moslem women are veiled*
  7 *v.* conceal: *he couldn't veil his disgust*
  7 *n.* something that hides or disguises: *a veil of mist*

5 **veranda** *n.*
4 **verse**
  4 *n.* form of writing: *blank verse*
  5 *n.* group of lines of text forming a unit: *a poem of five verses*
  7 *n.* one of the divisions of a chapter in the Bible
5 **vertical** *adj.*
1 **very**
  1 *adv.* (intensive): *very good*
  5 *adj.* extreme: *at the very end*
  6 *adj.* (for emphasis): *he knows our very thoughts*
4 **vessel**
  4 *n.* ship
  7 *n.* hollow receptacle
5 **vest** *n.* undergarment
5 **vice**
  5 *n.* evil: *gluttony is a vice*
  6 *n.* bad habits: *he has no vices*
  7 *n.* apparatus for holding things tightly
5 **victory** *n.*
3 **view**
  3 *n.* natural scenery: *a beautiful view*
  4 *n.* state of seeing or being seen: *he did it in full view of the public*
  5 *n.* personal opinion: *she has very strong views*
  6 *v.* examine, consider: *how do you view the problem?*
  6 *n.* opportunity to see and inspect: *a private view*
  7 *n.* aim, intention: *she did it with a view to saving trouble*
2 **village** *n.*
5 **violence** *n.*
5 **violent**
  5 *adj.* using great force: *a violent blow*
  5 *adj.* severe: *violent toothache*
  6 *adj.* caused by a strong attack: *a violent death*
5 **violin** *n.*
5 **virtue**
  5 *n.* goodness: *truth is a virtue*
  6 *n.* chastity: *of easy virtue*
  7 *n.* efficacy: *the virtue of herbs to heal sickness*

7 *n.* advantage: *what's the virtue of doing it this way?*

5 **vision**

  5 *n.* ability to see: *she suffers from poor vision*

  6 *n.* power of seeing or imagining: *the vision of a poet*

  7 *n.* something seen in a trance-like state: *a vision of eternity*

1 **visit**

  1 *n.* act of visiting

  2 *v.* go to see

  5 *v.* examine: *the kitchens are visited regularly by health inspectors*

2 **visitor** *n.*

4 **vital**

  4 *adj.* supreme: *vital importance*

  6 *adj.* connected with living: *the vital force*

5 **vitamin** *n.*

4 **vocabulary**

  4 *n.* number of words in a language

  5 *n.* number of words known to a person: *his vocabulary is extensive*

  6 *n.* book containing a list of words

2 **voice**

  2 *n.* power/organ for making sounds in humans

  3 *n.* type of sound produced by humans

  6 *v.* put into words: *he voiced his dissatisfaction*

7 *n.* grammar category: *active and passive voices*

5 **volcano** *n.*

5 **volleyball** *n.*

5 **voltage** *n.*

4 **volume**

  4 *n.* loudness: *the volume control*

  4 *n.* one of a set of books: *volume II*

  5 *n.* amount of space occupied by liquid or gas: *the volume of a cask*

  6 *n.* large amount: *the volume of work*

5 **voluntary**

  5 *adj.* doing things willingly, without compulsion: *voluntary work*

  6 *adj.* carried on by voluntary work: *a voluntary school*

  6 *adj.* (of bodily movements) carried on by the will: *voluntary movements*

3 **vote**

  3 *n.* ballot

  4 *v.* express one's wishes by voting: *he didn't vote*

  6 *n.* total number of votes: *the size of the Labour vote*

5 **voter** *n.*

4 **vowel** *n.*

3 **voyage**

  3 *n.* journey by water

  6 *v.* go on a sea-trip

5 **wag**

  5 *v.* move from side to side: *the dog wagged his tail*

  7 *n.* merry person: *he's a bit of a wag*

3 **wage/s**

  3 *n.* payment for work

  7 *n.* reward (fig.): *the wages of sin*

3 **waggon/wagon**

  3 *n.* four-wheeled vehicle

  4 *n.* open railway truck

5 **waist**

  5 *n.* part of body

  6 *n.* part of garment

1 **wait**

  1 *v.* await

  3 *n.* period of waiting

  4 *v.* serve at table

3 **waiter** *n.*

4 **waitress** *n.*
2 **wake**
  2 *v.* stop sleeping
  7 *n.* watch over corpse (in Ireland, N. England)
4 **waken** *v.*
4 **Wales** *n.*
1 **walk**
  1 *v.* move
  1 *n.* journey on foot
  3 *n.* path for walking: *a favourite walk*
  5 *n.* manner of walking: *I recognised him by his walk*
  6 *v.* cause to walk: *horses should be walked after exercise*
  7 *n.* calling: *walk of life*
1 **wall**
  1 *n.* dividing section
  6 *n.* something resembling a wall: *a wall of fire*
  6 *v.* surround with a wall
4 **wallet** *n.*
3 **wander**
  3 *v.* move from place to place: *he wandered over the countryside*
  4 *v.* leave the right path: *the sheep wandered away*
  6 *v.* be absent-minded: *don't wander from the point*
1 **want**
  1 *v.* wish for: *she wants to go on holiday*
  2 *v.* require: *I want to speak to the secretary*
  5 *n.* lack, need: *want of food*
  6 *v.* need: *his hair wants cutting*
  7 *v.* be in need: *they live in want*
  7 *v.* fall short by: *it wants one inch to be the correct length*
3 **war**
  3 *n.* armed conflict
  5 *n.* any kind of struggle: *the war against poverty*
  6 *v.* make war
5 **wartime** *n.*
1 **warm**
  1 *adj.* not cold
  3 *adj.* sympathetic: *a warm heart*
  4 *v.* make warm

5 *adj.* enthusiastic: *a warm supporter*
6 *n.* act of warming: *come and have a warm*
4 **warmth** *n.*
3 **warn** *v.* give notice of danger: *he was warned about the ice*
1 **wash**
  1 *v.* clean by using water etc.
  3 *n.* act of washing
  4 *n.* clothes to be washed: *the weekly wash*
  5 *v.* capable of being washed without damage: *does this material wash?*
  6 *v.* flow over: *the sea washes the cliffs*
  6 *v.* carry away: *he was washed overboard*
  7 *v.* scoop out: *water washed a channel in the sand*
  7 *v.* flow past: *the waves washed the sides of the boat*
  7 *n.* movement of water: *the wash of the waves*
3 **washing machine** *n.*
2 **waste**
  2 *v.* make no good use of
  3 *adj.* useless, thrown away: *waste paper*
  5 *adj.* barren: *waste land*
  5 *n.* failure to use well: *there is too much waste in society*
  5 *n.* refuse
  7 *v.* lose strength by degrees: *he's wasting away*
5 **wasteful** *adj.*
1 **watch**
  1 *n.* time-piece
  1 *v.* look at
  5 *n.* act of watching: *keep watch on those birds*
  6 *n.* period of duty: *the first watch*
5 **watchdog** *n.*
5 **watchman** *n.*
1 **water**
  1 *n.* liquid
  4 *v.* put water on, give water to
  6 *n.* state of the tide: *high water*
  6 *v.* fill with water: *my eyes watered*
5 **waterfall** *n.*

4 **waterproof**
  4 *adj.* impermeable
  6 *n.* raincoat
4 **watery**
  4 *adj.* covered with water: *watery surface*
  4 *adj.* like water
  6 *adj.* pale: *watery colours*
3 **wave**
  3 *n.* ridge of water on the sea
  3 *n.* gesture: *a wave of the hand*
  3 *v.* move as in a greeting: *he waved his hand*
  4 *v.* move: *flags waving in the breeze*
  5 *n.* series of curves: *waves in her hair*
  6 *n.* rapid increase and spread: *a wave of enthusiasm*
  6 *n.* motion carrying heat/light etc.: *sound waves*
5 **wax** *n.* substance produced by bees
1 **way**
  1 *n.* road, street, path
  1 *n.* route: *can you find your way home?*
  1 *n.* direction: *they went that way*
  2 *n.* time spent on journey: *they're still on the way*
  2 *n.* distance: *Edinburgh is a long way off*
  2 *n.* space for movement: *don't stand in the way*
  3 *n.* method: *that's the way to do it*
  4 *n.* custom: *it's not her way to be mean*
  5 *n.* respect: *in some ways I like that painting*
  6 *n.* condition: *she's in a terrible way, I'm afraid*
  7 *n.* forward movement: *the ship still has way on*
1 **we** *pron.*
2 **weak**
  2 *adj.* lacking in strength
  3 *adj.* below the usual standard: *weak eyesight*
  4 *adj.* watery: *weak tea*
  5 *adj.* not proficient: *weak at Latin*
5 **weaken** *v.*

5 **weakness**
  5 *n.* state of being weak
  6 *n.* fault or defect in character
3 **wealth**
  3 *n.* great amount of property/money
  6 *n.* great number of: *a wealth of pictures*
3 **wealthy** *adj.*
5 **weapon** *n.*
1 **wear**
  1 *v.* have on
  5 *v.* (cause to) deteriorate in condition: *my shoes are quite worn*
5 **wear off** *v.* fade and disappear (sensation)
4 **wear out**
  4 *v.* become unusable
  4 *v.* exhaust
1 **weather**
  1 *n.* atmospheric conditions
  5 *v.* come through successfully: *the firm has weathered the financial storm*
  6 *v.* expose to the elements: *he weathered the wood*
  7 *v.* shape, mould: *rocks weathered by the wind*
5 **weave**
  5 *v.* make into cloth
  6 *v.* put together: *to weave a story*
  6 *v.* twist and turn: *he wove his way through the traffic*
  6 *n.* style of weaving: *loose weave*
5 **weaver** *n.*
4 **wedding** *n.*
5 **wedge**
  5 *n.* piece of wood
  5 *v.* fix tightly: *he wedged open the door*
  6 *v.* something shaped like a wedge: *a wedge of cake*
1 **Wednesday** *n.*
5 **weed**
  5 *n.* wild plant
  5 *v.* take weeds out of the ground
  6 *n.* (colloq.) thin feeble person
  6 *v.* remove weaker units: *weed out*
1 **week** *n.*
4 **weekday** *n./adj.*
3 **weekend** *n./adj.*

3 **weekly**
  3 *adj.* something carried out each
  week: *his weekly exercise*
  5 *n.* periodical published weekly
4 **weep**
2 **weigh**
  2 *v.* measure the weight
  3 *v.* have a certain weight: *he weighs
  70 kilos*
  5 *v.* capable of weighing: *this machine
  weighs up to 80 tons*
3 **weight**
  3 *n.* how heavy something is
  4 *n.* load: *the pillars have a great
  weight to bear*
  6 *n.* importance or influence: *his ideas
  carry great weight*
  6 *n.* piece of metal used on scales
  7 *v.* add to, make heavy: *the
  circumstances are weighted in his
  favour*
3 **welcome**
  3 *n.* greeting: *they gave us a good
  welcome*
  3 *int.: welcome to England!*
  5 *adj.* received with pleasure:
  welcome news
  5 *v.* greet: *he welcomed us to his
  home*
1 **well**
  1 *adv.* in a good manner: *the children
  behaved well*
  1 *adj.* in good health
  2 *adv.* thoroughly: *shake the bottle
  well*
  2 *int.* (relief etc.): *well, here we are at
  last*
  3 *adv.* to a considerable extent: *she's
  well over forty*
  4 *adv.* fortunately: *he's well off out of
  it all*
  4 *adv.* in addition to: *as well as*
  5 *adv.* with good reason: *you may well
  be surprised*
  5 *adj.* advisable: *it would be well to
  start early*
  5 *n.* shaft
  6 *adv.* with approval: *he stands well
  with his director*

3 **well-known** *adj.*
3 **well-made** *adj.*
4 **Welsh** *adj.*
5 **Welshman** *n.*
1 **west**
  1 *n.* point of the compass: *steer due
  west*
  3 *adj.* coming from that direction: *the
  west wind*
2 **West, the** *n.*
3 **western**
  4 *adj.* from the west
  5 *n.* novel/film about the American
  West
5 **westward/s** *adj./adv.*
1 **wet**
  1 *adj.* covered with/drenched in
  water: *wet clothes*
  2 *adj.* rainy
  4 *n.* rain: *come in out of the wet*
  6 *v.* make wet: *he wet the bed*
1 **what**
  1 *pron.: what happened?*
  2 *pron.: what is he?*
  2 *pron.* (purpose +for): *what is this
  used for?*
  2 *adj.* (exclamation): *what a good idea!*
  3 *adj.* which: *what books have you
  read about this?*
  5 *adj.* whatever: *give me what books
  you have on this subject*
3 **whatever**
  3 *adj.* of any sort: *whatever nonsense
  they print*
  4 *pron.* no matter what: *whatever
  others may say*
  4 *pron.* anything or everything that:
  do whatever you like!
  6 *pron.* anything similar: *he could
  learn the piano, the guitar or
  whatever*
3 **wheat** *n.*
3 **wheel**
  3 *n.* circular frame
  4 *v.* push or pull: *he wheeled his
  bicycle up the hill*
  6 *v.* (cause to) turn in a curve or
  circle: *the sails of the windmill were
  wheeling round*

1 when

1 *adv.* at what time: *when can you come?*
2 *conj.* at the time that: *it was raining when we arrived*
3 *adv.* (after prep.) what time: *till when can you stay?*
4 *conj.* on which: *Sunday is the day when I am least busy*
5 *conj.* at or during which time: *the Queen will be here in May, when she will open the new hospital*
6 *conj.* although: *why does he walk when he could drive?*

4 whenever

4 *conj.* no matter when: *I'll discuss it whenever you like*
4 *conj.* on any occasion: *whenever he speaks*

1 where

1 *adv.* (position): *where does he live?*
1 *adv.* (direction): *where did she go?*
4 *adv.* in which: *we live in a country where it never snows*
5 *adv.* in the place in which: *I found my books where I had left them*

4 wherever *conj.*
2 whether *conj.*

1 which

1 *adj.* (interrogative): *which way shall we go?*
2 *pron.* (interrogative): *which is longer, the Nile or the Congo?*
3 *pron.* (relative, defining): *the house which is for sale is over there*
4 *pron.* (relative, non-defining): *those trees, which I planted in 1974, have not yet borne any fruit*
5 *pron.* (after prep.): *the points to which you referred are set out here*
6 *pron.* (relative to clause): *it was raining hard, which kept us indoors*

4 whichever

4 *pron.* the one which: *take whichever you like best*
4 *pron.* no matter which: *whichever of them you choose*

2 while

2 *conj.* during the time that: *he fell asleep while he was studying*
4 *conj.* implying a contrast: *she was dressed in blue while Mary was dressed in pink*
5 *n.* period of time: *once in a while*
6 *conj.* implying a concession: *while I agree, I won't support him*

4 whilst *conj.*

4 whip

4 *n.* a lash
4 *v.* strike with a whip
5 *v.* beat eggs, cream etc.
6 *v.* take off suddenly: *he whipped off his coat*
7 *n.* official in a political party: *the Chief Whip*
7 *n.* preparation of beaten eggs, cream, etc.: *prune whip*

3 whisper

3 *v.* say softly
3 *n.* soft voice: *she spoke in a whisper*
5 *n.* sound made by leaves in a light wind
6 *v.* tell privately or secretly
6 *v.* rumour: *it is whispered abroad*

4 whistle

4 *n.* pipe: *he blew his whistle*
5 *n.* sound produced by whistling
5 *v.* make sounds / melody through pursed lips
5 *v.* make a signal: *he whistled to his dog*

1 white

1 *adj.* colour
2 *n.* white material: *dressed in white*
4 *n.* colourless part of an egg
5 *n.* the white part of the eye

5 whiteness *n.*

1 who / whom

1 *pron.* (interrogative): *who is that man?*
3 *pron.* (relative, subject of clause): *the woman who told me has left*
3 *pron.* (relative, object of clause): *the salesman who / whom you met has called again*

4 *pron.* (relative, non-defining): *my wife, who has been abroad, will soon be back*

5 *pron.* (relative, after pronoun): *the boys about whom we spoke . . .*

4 **whoever** *pron.*

2 **whole**
2 *adj.* entire: *the whole cake*
6 *adj.* not injured/damaged: *fruit with a whole skin*

2 **whose**
2 *pron.* (interrogative): *whose is this book?*
4 *pron.* (relative): *the players whose names are listed here train on Mondays*
6 *pron.* (relative after preposition): *the tribes about whose origins you inquired are all Hamitic*

1 **why**
1 *adv.* for what reason: *why are you standing up?*
3 *conj.* for what reason (noun clause object): *I know why he's left*
4 *conj.* for what reason (noun clause subject): *why the law was passed is not known*
5 *conj.* for what reason (relative clause): *the reason why she came only appeared later*

4 **wicked**
4 *adj.* bad, wrong
5 *adj.* spiteful: *a wicked blow*
6 *adj.* mischievous: *a wicked look*

1 **wide**
1 *adj.* broad: *a wide road*
4 *adj.* of great extent: *a man of wide interests*
4 *adj.* fully open: *his mouth was wide open*
4 *adv.* fully: *wide awake*
5 *adv.* over a large area: *travel far and wide*
6 *adv.* far from the point aimed at: *wide of the mark*

4 **widely**
4 *adv.* at wide intervals: *widely scattered*

4 *adv.* to a large extent: *widely different*

5 **widen** *v.*

5 **widespread** *adj.*

4 **widow** *n.*

3 **width**
3 *n.* quality of being wide: *a road of great width*
4 *n.* measurement from side to side: *a width of 10 metres*
5 *n.* piece of material of a certain width: *2 widths of cloth*

1 **wife** *n.*

2 **wild**
2 *adj.* not domesticated: *a wild animal*
3 *adj.* savage: *wild tribes; wild scenery*
5 *adj.* excited, uncontrolled: *wild laughter*
6 *adj.* reckless: *wild scheme*

1 **will**
1 *modal* (future): *tomorrow will be Tuesday*
4 *modal* (inevitability): *accidents will happen*
4 *modal* (generality): *she'll sit there by the hour saying nothing*
5 *n.* mental power: *he has the will to live*
6 *n.* testament
7 *v.* desire: *come when you will*
7 *v.* force: *can you will yourself to keep awake?*

3 **willing**
3 *adj.* ready to help: *willing workers*
5 *adj.* done without hesitation: *willing obedience*

2 **win**
2 *v.* do best: *win a race/scholarship*
5 *n.* success in a game: *five successive wins*
7 *v.* reach by effort: *they won the shore*

1 **wind**
1 *n.* air blowing
3 *v.* (cause to) move in curving/spiral manner
5 *n.* breath needed for running: *out of wind*

6 *v.* be out of breath: *the long climb winded him*
7 *n.* empty words: *politicians are all wind*
7 *n.* instrument: *the wind section*
1 **window** *n.*
4 **wine**
  4 *n.* drink made from grapes
  5 *n.* drink made from other fruit/vegetables: *cherry wine*
3 **wing**
  3 *n.* part of a bird/aeroplane
  5 *n.* football player
  6 *n.* part of an object projecting from one of its sides: *the wing of a house*
  6 *n.* flank of an army
  6 *n.* section of a political party
  7 *n.* section of the theatre near the stage
1 **winter**
  1 *n.* season
  6 *v.* spend the winter season
4 **wipe**
  4 *v.* clean or dry
  5 *n.* act of wiping: *give these plates a wipe*
4 **wipe off** *v.* remove by rubbing
4 **wipe out**
  4 *v.* clean out
  5 *v.* reduce to nothing
3 **wipe up** *v.* clean wet surface with a cloth
3 **wire**
  3 *n.* thread or rope made of metal
  4 *n.* telegram
  5 *v.* send a telegram
  6 *v.* fasten with wire
  7 *v.* instal electrical circuit
4 **wisdom**
  4 *n.* quality of being wise
  6 *n.* wise thoughts/sayings: *the wisdom of the ancients*
3 **wise** *adj.*
3 **wish**
  3 *v.* desire
  4 *n.* longing
  5 *v.* say what one hopes for someone: *she wished them a good journey*
  6 *v.* express a desire: *let's wish*

1 **with**
  1 *prep.* having: *a cup with a broken handle*
  1 *prep.* means: *filled with straw*
  2 *prep.* accompaniment: *go there with him*
  2 *prep.* concerning: *be patient with them*
5 **withdraw**
  5 *v.* draw out, take away: *withdraw money*
  6 *v.* take back: *he refused to withdraw his remark*
  6 *v.* move back: *the troops withdrew from their position*
5 **within** *prep./adv.*
2 **without**
  2 *prep.* not having
  7 *prep./adv.* outside
4 **witness**
  4 *n.* person present at an event
  5 *v.* be present and see
  6 *n.* evidence: *bear witness*
  6 *n.* person who adds his signature to a document
  6 *v.* be present at the signing of a document
  7 *n.* proof: *his driving licence was witness to his identity*
  7 *v.* give evidence of, show: *her pale face witnessed the onset of her illness*
5 **wolf**
  5 *n.* animal
  7 *v.* eat greedily: *he wolfed down the meal*
1 **woman/women** *n.*
4 **wonder**
  4 *v.* feel surprise: *it's not to be wondered at*
  5 *v.* feel curiosity: *I was wondering what he'll say*
  6 *n.* feeling of admiration: *they were filled with wonder*
  6 *n.* thing that causes such feeling: *one of the wonders of our times*
3 **wonderful** *adj.*
1 **wood**
  1 *n.* hard solid substance

2 *n.* area covered with growing trees
6 *n.* cask or barrel: *wine from the wood*
3 **wooden**
   3 *adj.* made of wood
   6 *adj.* stiff, awkward: *her wooden behaviour embarrassed them*
3 **wool** *n.*
5 **woollen** *adj.*
1 **word**
   1 *n.* sounds forming a unit: *the words in a sentence*
   2 *n.* remark or statement: *he didn't say a word*
   5 *n.* news: *send me word of your arrival*
   6 *n.* promise: *his word is his bond*
   6 *v.* express in words: *you should word that more gently*
1 **work**
   1 *n.* use of power: *fond of hard work*
   1 *n.* employment: *he's out of work again*
   1 *v.* engage in activity: *he's working in the garden*
   3 *n.* something made: *the work of a local carpenter*
   3 *n.(pl.)* creation: *the works of Shakespeare*
   4 *n.(pl.)* factory
   4 *v.* operate: *learn to work a machine*
   6 *v.* shape by hammering etc.: *work clay*
4 **work out**
   4 *v.* draw up: *work out a plan*
   4 *v.* solve: *work out a problem*
4 **work surface** *n.*
5 **work up**
   5 *v.* stimulate: *work up interest*
   5 *v.* train: *they worked up to the final*
2 **worker** *n.*
4 **workman** *n.*
4 **workshop** *n.*
1 **world**
   1 *n.* the globe: *he went around the world*
   4 *n.* society and activities of men: *he's got on in the world*

5 *n.* the whole human race: *the world is against me*
6 *n.* a section of mankind: *the literary world*
4 **world-wide** *adj.*
5 **worm**
   5 *n.* creature
   6 *v.* wriggle into/out of: *she wormed her way into his confidence*
   7 *n.* contemptible person: *he's a worm*
3 **worry**
   3 *v.* be anxious: *she worries*
   3 *v.* cause anxiety: *what's worrying you?*
   4 *n.* condition of being worried: *worry showed in her face*
1 **worse** *adj./adv.*
5 **worship**
   5 *n.* respect paid to God
   6 *n.* admiration: *the worship of success*
   6 *v.* pray: *she worships each Sunday*
   7 *v.* adore: *she worships the ground he walks on*
1 **worst** *adj./adv.*
2 **worth**
   2 *adj.* having value: *what is it worth?*
   4 *adj.* giving satisfactory reward: *the exhibition is worth visiting*
   5 *n.* value: *of great worth*
   6 *adj.* owning property to a certain value: *how much is he worth?*
5 **worthless** *adj.*
4 **worthwhile** *adj.* viable: *a worthwhile scheme*
5 **worthy**
   5 *adj.* deserving: *worthy of praise*
   6 *adj.* having merit: *the worthy poor*
   7 *n.* person of distinction: *an Elizabethan worthy*
   7 *n.* person who appears to be distinguished: *the local worthies met the Queen*
2 **would** *modal*
5 **wound**
   5 *n.* injury
   5 *v.* injure
   6 *v.* (fig.) hurt: *her remarks wounded him*

3 **wrap**
  3 *v*. cover, put around: *she wrapped the parcel*
  6 *n*. outer garment: *don't forget your wrap*
5 **wreck**
  5 *n*. remains of large object: *the wreck of the ship*
  6 *v*. destroy: *vandals wrecked the school*
  7 *n*. (fig.) disaster: *the wreck of his hopes; she looks a wreck*
5 **wrist** *n*.
1 **write**
  1 *v*. put down in words
  2 *v*. make letters: *he learnt to write*
4 **write away** *v*. send an order for

2 **write down** *v*. record on paper
4 **write in** *v*. send postal enquiry
4 **write off**
  4 *v*. send postal enquiry/request
  6 *v*. accept loss of: *the car was written off after the accident*
3 **write out** *v*. express in full in writing
4 **write up** *v*. rewrite (notes) in full
2 **writer** *n*.
1 **wrong**
  1 *adj*. immoral: *it is wrong to steal*
  2 *adj*. incorrect: *six wrong answers*
  3 *adv*. out of order: *there's nothing wrong with his car*
  6 *n*. injustice: *the wrongs of society*
  7 *v*. treat unjustly: *he wronged me*

Y

2 **yard**
  2 *n*. enclosed space: *the school yard*
  3 *n*. unit of length
  7 *n*. cross piece fastened to the mast of a ship
4 **yawn**
  4 *v*. open mouth involuntarily when sleepy
  4 *n*. act of yawning
  6 *v*. be wide open: *a yawning crack*
1 **year** *n*.
3 **yearly** *adj./adv*.
1 **yellow**
  1 *adj*. colour
  6 *adj*. cowardly
1 **yes** *int*.
1 **yesterday** *adv*.
2 **yet**
  2 *adv*. up till now
  5 *conj*. nevertheless
4 **yield**
  4 *v*. produce: *trees that yield fruit*

  5 *v*. give way: *he won't yield to pressure*
  6 *n*. amount produced: *a good yield of wheat*
  7 *v*. surrender: *they yielded the fort*
1 **you** *pron*.
1 **young**
  1 *adj*. not old
  4 *n*. young people: *the young today*
  5 *n*. offspring: *the young of the fox*
1 **your** *pron*.
2 **yours** *pron*.
2 **yourself** *pron*.
3 **youth**
  3 *n*. state of being young: *the innocence of youth*
  4 *n*. young man: *three youths attacked her*
  5 *n*. young men and women: *the youth of today*

Z

2 **zero** *n./adj.*
5 **zip**
   5 *n.* type of fastening
   5 *v.* do up by means of this fastening

5 **Zodiac, the** *n.*
4 **zoo** *n.*

Appendix A: Recurrent occasions

All the items listed below are in the main list.

Weekdays and months
Monday Tuesday Wednesday Thursday Friday Saturday Sunday

January February March April May June July August September October November December

All of these items are graded in the main list. Abbreviated forms of these items are dealt with together with other abbreviations in Appendix V.

Festivals and feast-days
Cultural and political relevance determines the importance of feast-days and festivals for each country. The following items have been judged to be of sufficiently general importance for inclusion in CEL. The gradings are shown on the left as in the main list and reflect relevance variously for West Europeans and North Americans.

3 Bank Holiday   5 Good Friday   5 Boxing Day   5 New Year's Day   1 Christmas   5 Thanksgiving   3 Easter

Many nations will want to add *Independence Day*, and recurrent occasions such as the *Queen's Birthday, Mother's Day* and perhaps occasions such as *Remembrance Day* but these are not included in CEL. It is up to the user of this list to add the names of festivals and feast-days which he considers students at specified levels should know.

Appendix B: History and politics

Cultural and political relevance for any one country again (as in Appendix A) determine the range of names of events, periods and organisations which students at given levels should be able to recognise and refer to in English. Each user must therefore make his own list.

Nevertheless the items listed below probably represent a minimum that all students should know in their English names, and are therefore all in CEL, and graded 5, except where otherwise indicated.

Events: the First World War   the French Revolution   the Second World War
Organisations: the Roman Empire   3 the United Nations

Many countries will want to add items such as *the (British) Commonwealth, the European Economic Community, the Organisation of African Unity* or *the Organisation of Petroleum Exporting Countries,* but the choice must lie with the user.

Appendix C: The universe

The current rise in interest in space, science fiction and astrology has brought the planets and stars back into popular language in some countries and contexts of use.

CEL does not however expect students in general to have knowledge of more than the following terms in astronomy and astrology, for which the gradings are shown:

1 sun   1 moon   2 earth   1 star   5 planet
5 the Pole Star   5 the Zodiac

Users must determine how far, in the context under consideration, students should know the following items:

Mercury Venus Mars Jupiter Saturn Uranus Pluto Neptune

the Plough/the Great Bear   the Milky Way   the Southern Cross

Aries the ram	Libra the balance
Taurus the bull	Scorpio the scorpion
Gemini the twins	Sagittarius the archer
Cancer the crab	Capricorn the goat
Leo the lion	Aquarius the water-carrier
Virgo the virgin	Pisces the fishes

Appendix D: Named features of the earth

Considerations of culture, history, politics and geographical proximity all play a part in determining the relevance of geographical features for students at various levels to recognise or name in English.

CEL includes the following items among international and national geographical features. The gradings given are tentative, and intended for students in West European contexts.

Continents: 2 Africa   1 America   2 Asia   1 Europe
Regions: 4 Antarctic   4 Arctic   5 Caribbean   3 Far East   3 Middle East   2 West
Waters: 2 Atlantic   2 Pacific   2 Mediterranean   3 North Sea   3 Channel
Rivers: 4 Amazon   4 Nile   4 Mississippi   4 Missouri   3 Danube   3 Rhine   3 Thames
Mountain ranges: 3 Alps   5 Himalayas
Deserts: 5 Sahara

Many more might justifiably have been included. The user should consider inter alia the following items for possible inclusion.

Continents: Australasia   Oceania   Antarctica
Regions: Mid West   Far West   Near East
Waters: Indian Ocean   Red Sea   the Gulf
Passages: Suez Canal   Panama Canal   Straits of Gibraltar   Straits of Dover   Dardanelles   Straits of Malacca
Closed waters: Great Lakes   Caspian Sea
Rivers: Congo   Niger   Indus   Ganges   Brahmaputra   Yangtze-Kiang   St Lawrence   Volga   Seine   Rhone
Mountain ranges: Andes   Rocky Mountains   Pyrenees
Island groups: British Isles   Channel Islands   West Indies

Appendix E: Country, nationality, national and language

The names for the above four features may be usefully grouped together in one appendix. Users will once again wish to make a further selection to suit their own contexts. CEL includes only those set out below. The gradings are tentative and relate to West European contexts of use.

Country	Nationality (She's/it's-)	National (He's a-)	Language (They speak-)
5 Brazil	5 Brazilian	5 Brazilian	4 Portuguese
2 China	3 Chinese	3 Chinese	3 Chinese
1 France	1 French	2 Frenchman	1 French
1 Germany	1 German	2 German	1 German
2 India	3 Indian	3 Indian	
2 Japan	3 Japanese	3 Japanese	3 Japanese
4 Portugal	4 Portuguese	4 Portuguese	4 Portuguese
4 Soviet Union	2 Russian	2 Russian	2 Russian (etc.)
1 Spain	2 Spanish	3 Spaniard	2 Spanish
1 Britain	1 British	5 Briton	
1 England	1 English	2 Englishman	1 English
4 Scotland	4 Scottish	5 Scotsman	1 English/4 Scots
4 Wales	4 Welsh	5 Welshman	1 English/4 Welsh
4 Ireland	4 Irish	5 Irishman	1 English/4 Irish
2 United Kingdom			1 English (etc.)
2 United States	1 American	2 American	1 English (etc.)
3 Canada	3 Canadian	3 Canadian	1 English/1 French (etc.)
3 Australia	3 Australian	3 Australian	1 English (etc.)
4 New Zealand		5 New Zealander	1 English (etc.)

Appendix F: Capitals, cities and towns

None of the items below occur in CEL; nevertheless it may
reasonably be assumed that students at level 5 should recognise
most of these cities and towns in English, and some of them much
earlier.

It is important not to assume that city names are the same or
nearly the same in a foreign language as in English. (For
example: London and Edinburgh are Londres and Edimbourg in
French; Paris is Parigi in Italian; Cologne is Köln in German;
Prague is Praha in Czech; and Cairo and Bangkok are entirely
different in Arabic and Thai respectively.)

Europe

London	Oxford	Edinburgh	Belfast
Birmingham	Cambridge	Glasgow	Dublin
Manchester			

Paris	Oslo	Madrid	Cologne
Copenhagen	Athens	Brussels	Lisbon
Berlin	Stockholm	Prague	Amsterdam
Rome	Vienna	Moscow	Belgrade

Asia

Tehran	Delhi	Bangkok	Peking
Baghdad	Bombay	Singapore	Shanghai
Jerusalem	Calcutta	Hong Kong	Tokyo

Australasia

Sydney	Canberra	Melbourne	Wellington

Africa

Cairo	Nairobi	Johannesburg
Khartoum	Lagos	Cape Town

North America			*Canada*
Washington	Chicago	San Francisco	Montreal
New York	Boston	Los Angeles	Toronto

Latin America

Rio de Janeiro	Santiago	Mexico City
São Paulo	Buenos Aires	Caracas

Appendix G: Cultural features

The English terms for cultural features are important at various levels depending on the student's context of use. Only a very modest selection is therefore included in CEL. The grading attempted is for West European contexts of use.

Religions

4 Christian	5 Islam	5 Hindu	4 Bible
5 Christianity	5 Muslim	5 Buddhist	2 God
5 Catholic	5 Jewish		
5 Protestant			

Cultural areas

3 Western	5 Oriental	3 American	4 African
2 European	4 Asian	5 Arab	

Cultural periods or movements
5 Middle Ages

Ideas and philosophies
5 Marxist
(There are also *communist, capitalist, socialist* and *conservative* in CEL, beginning with small letters.)

Possible additions to the above items, not in CEL, might include:

Koran   Hinduism   Buddhism   Confucianism   Zen   Baptist   Methodist   Seventh Day Adventist   Mormon

Micronesian   Polynesian   Amerindian

Classical Era   Dark Ages   Renaissance   Reformation   Romantic Era

Freudian

Appendix H: Common first names

Students of English should be familiar enough with a range of first names in common use in English-speaking countries to be able to recognise them for what they are, when they are met unreferenced and unexplained by context, whether grammatical or semantic. None are included in the main list, and no grading is attempted.

The list below covers contemporary usage in Britain, Australia and New Zealand rather than America and Canada, though very much the same names are used commonly throughout. American first names tend to include surnames used as first names (e.g. Stanton, Howard, Irving, Lyndon), and these should be added where appropriate.

Very common first names (short forms and variants in brackets)
For men

Alan	Henry (Harry)
Alfred (Alf, Alfie)	James (Jim, Jimmy)
Andrew (Andy)	John (Johnny, Jack)
Arthur (Art)	Joseph (Joe, Jo)
Charles (Charlie)	Michael (Mick, Mike)
Christopher (Chris)	Peter (Pete)
David (Dave)	Richard (Dick)
Edward (Ted, Teddie)	Robert (Bob, Bobby)
Francis (Frank)	Ronald (Ron, Ronnie)
Frederick (Fred, Freddie)	Thomas (Tom, Tommy)
George	William (Bill, Billy, Will)

For women

Ann, Anne	Margaret
Catherine, Catharine (Kate)	Mary, Marie
Elizabeth (Liz)	Sally
Jane	Susan (Sue)
Joan	

Fairly common first names
For men

Adam	Derek	Hugh
Albert (Bert)	Donald	Jeremy
Antony (Tony)	Douglas	Jonathan
Bernard	Eric	Julian
Brian	Geoffrey (Geoff)	Keith
Colin	Harold (Harry)	Kenneth (Ken)

Appendix H

Kevin
Malcolm
Mark
Martin
Matthew
Nicholas (Nick)
Nigel

Norman
Patrick
Paul
Philip (Phil)
Raymond (Ray)
Robin

Roger
Sidney
Simon
Stephen (Steve)
Victor
Walter

For women

Alice
Alison
Angela
Annabel
Barbara
Brenda
Bridget
Carol
Caroline
Christine
Clare
Diana
Doreen
Doris
Dorothy

Frances
Gillian (Gill)
Helen
Irene
Jacqueline (Jackie)
Janet
Jennifer (Jenny)
Joanne (Joanna)
Joy
Judith (Judy)
Julia
Linda
Louise
Marion
Marjorie

Nancy
Nicola
Pamela (Pam)
Patricia (Pat)
Rachel
Rosemary
Ruth
Sandra
Sara(h)
Sheila (Shelagh)
Teresa (Terry)
Valerie
Vera
Wendy
Yvonne

Appendix K: Irregular forms of nouns, adjectives and adverbs

CEL lists very few irregular plural forms of nouns, but most of the irregular comparative and superlative forms of adjectives and adverbs. For reference purposes the forms are indicated below; those that appear in the main list are asterisked:

Irregular plurals of nouns

1 men*	1 teeth*	5 geese*	3 mice*	1 children*
3 pence*	1 women*	1 feet*		

3 halves	2 leaves	3 loaves	3 shelves	2 wives
2 knives	3 lives	2 selves	3 thieves	5 wolves

Irregular comparatives of adjectives and adverbs

1 better*	1 worse*	2 more*	2 less*
1 best*	1 worst*	2 most*	2 least*

5 farther*	3 further*	5 latter	5 elder	3 former*
5 farthest*	5 furthest*	1 last*	5 eldest	

Appendix L: Plural-form nouns

The nouns listed below are all found in the main CEL list. They are drawn together here for ease of reference, since they form a special group. Their gradings will be found in the main list. What they have in common is their ending in an -*s* that appears to signal plurality. They have a diversity of characteristics, however, including:

i) Most take the plural form of the verb, but a few take the singular *(maths, measles)*.

ii) Some have no singular form *(knickers, outskirts)*.

iii) Some have a singular form with a very different meaning *(customs, means)*.

iv) Some have a singular form with a somewhat divergent meaning or usage *(scales, brains)*.

v) Some have a singular form with the same meaning, but much less frequent use than the plural form *(stairs, regards)*.

arms (weapons)	lodgings	ruins
brains	looks	savings
chips (potatoes)	manners	scales
clothes	maths (mathematics)	scissors
contents	means	shorts
cross-roads	measles	slacks
customs	mumps	spirits
earnings	news	sports
funds	outskirts	stairs
glasses	pains	surroundings
goods	pants	thanks
grounds	physics	tights
hours (office)	pyjamas	trousers
jeans	regards	wages
knickers		

Appendix M: Auxiliaries and modals

All forms of the auxiliaries and modals in English are to be regarded as within CEL, whether entered or not in the main list.

The full list of forms is given below; only the asterisked items are in the main list. The items *need* and *dare* are bracketed because their use as modals is restricted by usage to certain contexts (interrogation, emphasis).

For grading of derived syntactic forms in column 1, refer to *English Grammatical Structure* (EGS) (Longman 1975).

Negative and abbreviated forms in columns 2 to 5 will broadly follow the grading for the positive forms, except where contra-indications are to be found in EGS.

1 *Positive*	2 *Abbreviated*	3 *Negative full*	4 *Negative abbrev'd*	5 *Negative using n't*
1 do*		do not		don't
does		does not		doesn't
did		did not		didn't
1 have*	've	have not	've not	haven't
has	's	has not	's not	hasn't
had	'd	had not	'd not	hadn't
having		not having		
had (past part.)				
1 be*				
am	'm	am not	'm not	
1 is*	's	is not	's not	isn't
are	're	are not	're not	aren't
was		was not		wasn't
were		were not		weren't
being		not being		
1 can*		1 cannot*		can't
2 could*		could not		couldn't
2 may*		may not		mayn't
2 might*		might not		mightn't
1 shall*	'll	shall not	'll not	shan't
2 should*	'd	should not		shouldn't
1 will*	'll	will not	'll not	won't
2 would*	'd	would not	'd not	wouldn't
1 must*		must not		mustn't

183

Appendix M

1 *Positive*	3 *Negative full*	5 *Negative using n't*
2 ought to*	ought not to	oughtn't to
3 used to*	used not to	usedn't to
1 (need)*	need not	needn't
3 (dare)*	dare not	daren't

Appendix N: Compound nouns

The items below *exemplify* the types of compound noun
appropriate to various levels in CEL. In most cases the meaning
of the item can be construed from the meaning, or one meaning, of
the parts; all the items below are in the main list. Compounds
based on phrasal verbs listed in this appendix may be freely
derived from them for use in CEL, provided that the meaning is
also directly transferred.

5 airman	2 haircut	2 postman
4 baby-sitter	3 hairdrier	5 rainfall
3 birth control	3 handout	4 record-player
4 bookshelf	4 handshake	4 seaman
5 breakdown	4 handwriting	5 setback
2 bus stop	4 headache	4 sightseeing
4 bypass	3 housekeeping	5 steering wheel
3 car park	4 income	3 story telling
5 chairman	5 intake	5 taxpayer
2 coffee-pot	5 lay-by	4 teacup
4 dishwasher	2 living room	5 town hall
3 doorstep	5 look-out	5 town-planning
4 dressmaking	5 loudspeaker	4 traffic light
5 dropout	5 milkman	5 upkeep
4 ear-ring	4 nightfall	3 washing machine
5 earthquake	4 output	4 working surface

Appendix O: Compound prepositions and connectors

CEL contains a number of compound prepositions and connectors. These are brought together here for ease of reference.

5 according to *prep.*
4 on account of *prep.*
4 in addition to *prep.*
3 ahead of *prep.*
3 apart from *prep.*
5 as for *prep.*
4 as if *conj.*
2 away from *prep.*
2 because of *prep.*
5 on behalf of *prep.*
3 in case *conj.*
5 due to *prep.*
5 except for *prep.*
2 as far as *conj.*
1 in front of *prep.*
4 if only *conj.*
3 instead of *prep.*

4 as long as *conj.*
4 by means of *prep.*
5 the more . . . the more *conj.*
2 not only . . . but also *conj.*
5 in order that *conj.*
4 in order to *conj.*
1 out of *prep.*
5 owing to *prep.*
5 as regards *prep.*
5 seeing that *conj.*
4 so as to *conj.*
3 as soon as *conj.*
4 so that *conj.*
5 such . . .that *conj.*

In the main list these items are entered alphabetically by the first word. Items containing a major second word listed in its own right (such as *in order that*) are listed both under *in* and under *order*.

186

Appendix P: Compound adjectives

The items below *exemplify* the types of compound adjective allowable in CEL. Similar formulations are to be considered as falling within CEL, provided that the meaning of the whole is derivable from the parts, or corresponds with the meaning of the parent phrasal verb. The grading for a compound adjective will be at least that of its higher level part.

5 drive-in (cinema)   3 first-class (carriage)
5 pick-up (van)   4 part-time (work)
4 stand-up (lunch)   4 second-hand (car)
5 oil-producing (country)

3 well-made   4 kind-hearted
3 well-known   4 left-handed
3 home-made   4 middle-aged

Appendix Q: Phrasal verbs

All the phrasal verbs given below are listed and graded in CEL. This appendix draws together the values which may be used at the levels indicated. Semantic values close to those shown may in general also be used, depending on the context.

ask after	5	enquire about (health)
for	2	request
back out of	5	withdraw from (an agreement)
up	5	support someone (in a contest)
bear up	5	remain firm
break down	5	collapse (in tears)
	3	fail to go on working
in	5	interrupt (a conversation)
	4	enter (a building by force)
off	4	end suddenly
out	4	escape
	5	burst into speech
through	5	overcome (an obstacle)
up	3	separate (partners in a marriage)
	4	smash into many pieces
bring about	4	cause to happen
back	2	return (something to someone)
in	4	introduce (an element)
off	5	succeed against expectations
out	5	make clear
round	5	help back to consciousness
up	3	raise (children, animals)
burst in	4	enter suddenly (a room, conversation)
out	5	explode from a confined space into freedom
call away	3	summon to carry out another activity
by	4	stop at socially while on a journey
for	3	collect someone
	5	require
in	3	visit
	5	ask to visit
off	4	abandon, cancel
on	5	visit
up	5	mobilise (troops for an army)

Appendix Q

care about	3	be concerned
for	4	like
	5	look after
carry off	4	seize and take away
on	3	continue
out	3	complete (a task)
catch on	5	become popular
	5	understand
up with	4	draw level with (someone, the times)
check in	3	register (at a hotel)
out	3	give up (your room at a hotel on leaving)
over	4	see if all is in order
up	4	verify, see if something is correct
clear off	5	disappear quickly (a person)
out	4	empty (a room, a drawer)
up	3	tidy up (the garden, a mess)
	4	stop raining, turn sunny (the weather)
come across	4	find/meet accidentally
	5	be understood
by	5	pass
down	3	be reduced (price)
forward	4	present (itself etc.)
off	5	succeed in happening
on	4	appear (TV, theatre)
out	3	bloom
	5	solve itself
round	5	regain consciousness
	3	visit
	4	recur on regular basis
up against	5	be faced with (a problem)
count in	4	include
on	5	rely on
up	3	find the total
cross out	3	remove (from list, record)
cut across	4	take shorter way (to destination)
back	5	reduce (expenses, manpower)
down	5	reduce (expenses, consumption)
in	5	push suddenly into stream (of speech, traffic)
off	4	stop flow (of supplies, communications)
out	5	delete (from a set)
	5	give up (a habit)
up	3	divide into small pieces

Appendix Q

do away with	5	get rid of
out of	5	stop someone from having
without	3	manage in the absence of
draw in	5	become shorter (daytime)
	4	slow down and stop (train, taxi)
out	5	become longer (daytime)
	3	take money out of bank account
	3	set out on journey (train, ship)
up	4	come to a stop (vehicle)
	5	prepare a written statement (report, document)
drop back	3	fall behind (in performance)
by	4	visit casually
in on	4	visit someone casually
off	4	allow someone to alight
	5	doze off
out	5	withdraw from (a group, society)
face up to	5	accept a challenge
fall back on	5	rely on for support
behind	4	be overtaken (in performance)
for	4	be strongly attracted to
in with	5	meet by chance
	5	agree to (a proposal)
out	5	stop being friends
through	5	fail to materialise
feel like	2	be in the mood for
up to	4	judge oneself to be capable of
fill in	2	complete (a form)
get across	4	communicate
along with	3	manage to live/work together with
(a)round	4	overcome, circumvent (a problem)
	4	become known (within group, community)
at	3	reach, gain access to
	5	suggest
away	3	leave
away with	4	escape with stolen goods
	5	go unpunished
back	2	return
	3	recover possession of
by	3	manage to pass
	4	survive
down	2	descend
	3	write quickly
	3	leave the table (of children)
	5	demoralise

Appendix Q

in	2 enter (vehicle)
	4 collect
off	2 alight from
	4 (cause to) leave
	3 remove (clothing)
	5 (cause to) escape injury/punishment
on	2 put on (clothing)
	3 progress
on with	3 make progress with
	4 manage to work/live with
out	4 leave (bounded space)
out of	4 leave (place, situation)
	4 derive
	5 avoid
over	4 recover from (illness)
	5 make clear
round to	5 have time for
through	4 pass (a test)
	5 consume, master
	4 make contact (by phone)
together	3 meet, assemble
up	2 rise (from bed)
	3 climb
up to	3 reach

give away	5 betray, reveal
back	2 return
in	4 yield
	2 hand in (homework)
out	2 distribute
up	5 surrender (a possession, in a context)
	4 stop doing (smoking, skiing)

go after	2 pursue
by	2 pass
down with	5 become ill with
for	3 go to fetch
in for	5 practise
	5 enter (a competition)
off	3 leave, start
	2 stop working (power supplies)
	4 go bad (milk, meat)
	3 explode (gun, fireworks)
on	2 continue
	2 happen
	5 be spent on
	2 be lit
out	2 stop burning (fire)
	5 ebb
over	4 examine

191

Appendix Q

through	5	endure
	5	examine
under	3	sink
with	3	be part of
	4	match, suit
without	5	not have, yet manage
hand in	3	submit
on	4	pass to next (person, group, generation)
out	2	distribute
over	4	surrender (something, someone)
hang about	4	wait idly
back	5	hesitate
on	3	wait
	4	grip firmly
on to	4	retain
up	3	end telephone conversation
have back	3	have something returned
in	3	have people (visitors, builders) in one's home
on	2	be dressed in
round	4	have (visitors) to one's home
hold back	4	restrain, withhold
in	5	restrain
on	3	wait, keep in position
on to	3	keep, keep hold of
out	4	last, remain
up	4	delay
join in	3	participate
up	4	unite
keep at	5	(cause to) persist at
back	4	(cause to) stay at a distance
	5	withhold (information)
down	5	repress, not raise, control
in	3	detain indoors, restrain
off	4	(cause to) stay away from
	5	(cause to) not to eat or drink something
on	3	continue
	5	retain in employment
up	4	maintain (standards, knowledge)
up with	5	progress at same rate as
knock down	2	cause to fall
out	5	eliminate (in competition)
	5	make unconscious
lay by	5	save
out	3	arrange neatly

192

Appendix Q

leave in	3	allow to remain
on	3	allow to stay in use
out	4	omit
let down	3	lower
	5	disappoint
in	3	allow to enter
off	5	release (from duty, punishment)
	4	allow to explode
out	3	release (from confinement)
through	3	allow to pass
live on	3	survive
	3	support oneself by means of
through	3	undergo period of strain
up to	5	reach expected standard
look after	3	care for
at	2	examine, consider
for	2	try to find
in	5	visit
into	5	investigate
on	3	be a spectator
out	3	take care
over	4	inspect, survey
through	4	scan
up	3	try to find (information)
up to	5	respect
make for	3	move towards (place)
out	5	manage to see
	4	write out (a bill, report)
out of	5	interpret (statement, situation)
up	4	compose, complete
	4	invent
	5	restore (looks, friendship)
up for	5	compensate for
miss out	5	fail to take part
open out	3	broaden, unfold
up	4	unfasten
pass away	5	die
off	4	recede (pain)
	5	take place (ceremony, occasion)
out	3	distribute
	5	lose consciousness

193

Appendix Q

pay back	5	punish (in retribution)
in	3	put money into (a bank account, savings)
off	4	settle (debts)
	5	give final wages to
out	5	disburse
up	5	hand over the full amount due
pick out	4	select
up	5	improve
	2	lift
	4	gather (scattered items)
play away	5	have match away from home
back	2	replay a tape (on recorder)
pull down	4	demolish
in	4	draw to a halt (train, car)
off	4	remove
	5	succeed against odds
on	4	put on clothing
out	4	extract
	4	begin to move (train, ship, car into traffic)
up	4	slow down and stop (bus, car, bike)
put aside	4	reserve
away	3	return to proper place for keeping
back	5	defer
	4	change time on clock
down	3	write down
in for	5	apply for
off	4	postpone
	5	discourage
	5	distract
on	2	get dressed in
	2	switch on (light)
	3	increase (in weight)
out	2	extinguish
	4	issue (information)
through	2	connect (by telephone)
up	3	raise (price)
	5	provide lodging
up with	5	tolerate
ring back	2	telephone again
off	2	end telephone conversation
up	2	telephone
rub out	3	erase
run away with	4	take and remove, contrary to law or custom
down	3	knock down (on road)
	5	lose power

into	5	collide with, meet by chance
off	5	duplicate
out of	4	exhaust stocks
over	4	drive across
	5	scan, summarise
see about	5	organise, remedy
off	5	say goodbye to (at station, airport, etc.)
through	3	discern truth behind falsehood
to	5	ensure action
send for	3	order to come (by post, messenger)
in	4	submit
off	4	dispatch
on	5	forward (letters)
out	5	emit
	3	make person leave room
set back	5	hinder progress
down	5	record on paper
in	5	begin an extended period (weather, season)
off	3	begin a journey
	4	effect (reaction, explosion)
out	3	begin a journey
	3	begin work towards an objective
	3	arrange (items or points)
up	4	establish, organise
show in	3	guide someone in
off	5	display to impress
up	4	be noticeable
	5	arrive
sit for	5	take (examination)
up	5	not go to bed
stand back	3	remain at a distance from
by	5	observe passively
	5	support
for	5	represent
	5	tolerate
in for	5	deputise for
out	5	be noticeable
up for	5	support when under attack
up to	5	resist, endure
stick out	3	(cause to) project
	5	endure
to	5	not abandon (person, task)

Appendix Q

stop behind	3	remain (while group goes on)
in	3	stay indoors (school, house)
off	4	break journey briefly
over	4	break journey for one or two nights
take after	5	resemble
away	3	subtract
back	3	restore to previous state of affairs (goods, employee)
in	4	include
	4	absorb (idea)
	5	delude
off	2	remove
	3	leave ground (aircraft)
on	5	undertake
over	5	assume control of
to	5	adopt as habit
	5	develop a liking for (a person)
up	4	adopt as pastime, job
	4	occupy (space, time)
think of	3	call to mind, consider
	5	invent
out	4	plan carefully
over	4	consider further
throw out	4	discard
	4	eject
try on	4	put on garment to check fit
out	4	test
turn back	3	reverse direction of journey
down	4	reduce intensity (light, sound)
	5	refuse (application)
into	4	(cause to) become
off	3	switch off
on	3	switch on
out	3	extinguish (light, gas)
	5	transpire (events)
	5	produce, make
over	3	reverse position (object, page, body in bed)
up	3	increase intensity (light, sound)
	5	appear (expectedly, unexpectedly)
wear off	5	disappear gradually (coating, impression)
out	4	become unusable (articles)
	4	exhaust (energies)

Appendix Q

wipe off	4	remove by rubbing
out	4	clean the inside
	5	reduce to nothing
up	3	clean wet surface with cloth
work out	4	draw up (plan)
	4	solve (problem)
up	5	stimulate (interest)
	5	train
write away	4	send an order for (by post)
down	2	record on paper
in	4	send postal enquiry for
off	4	send postal enquiry, request for
out	3	express in full in writing
up	4	rewrite (notes) in full

Appendix R: Prepositional phrases

Below are listed types of prepositional phrases proper to CEL. The items given indicate the range that may be used at these levels. All are included in the main list, under the first letter of the initial preposition. Considerations of context will guide judgement as to how far one may go in including phrases of these kinds without explanation or glossing.

1 at breakfast	2 at last	1 at school
2 at church	3 at least	2 at sea
5 at all costs	5 at a loss	2 at a time
5 at all events	2 at once	3 at the same time
1 at first	3 at peace	4 at times
5 at first sight	3 at present	3 at war
5 at hand	5 at a profit	1 at work
1 at home	4 at any rate	
4 by accident	4 by heart	2 by post
1 by air	1 by land	1 by sea
1 by bus	4 by all means	2 by ship
1 by car	3 by mistake	3 by sight
4 by chance	3 by name	4 by surprise
3 by day	3 by night	4 by train
5 by far	2 by oneself	2 by yourself
5 by hand	1 by plane	
4 in all	3 in a hurry	3 in reach
1 in bed	2 in ink	4 in secret
3 in any case	2 in love	3 in sight
4 in common	3 in order	3 in stock
4 in debt	3 in particular	4 in tears
4 in difficulties	2 in pencil	2 in time
2 in danger	2 in pieces	3 in town
1 in the end	3 in place	3 in turn
2 in fact	4 in prison	3 in two
4 in general	3 in private	4 in a way
3 in half	3 in public	5 in other words
2 on business	4 on the one hand	5 on purpose
2 on duty	4 on the other hand	3 on sale
2 on fire	1 on holiday	3 on time
1 on foot	1 on a journey	4 on the whole

Appendix R

5 out of breath
5 out of control
4 out of danger
3 out of date
3 out of doors

4 out of order
3 out of place
5 out of practice
5 out of the question
4 out of reach

4 out of sight
3 out of stock
4 out of turn
3 out of work

3 off duty

4 under control

3 up to date

Appendix S: Strong verbs

The strong verbs listed in CEL may be used in all forms in which they occur as lexical items. The forms are given below for reference purposes. The gradings are given in the main list and apply to all the forms listed, subject to limitations expressed in EGS.

arise / arose / arisen
be / was/were / been
bear / bore / borne
beat / beat / beaten
become / became / become
begin / began / begun
bend / bent / bent
bind / bound / bound
bite / bit / bitten
bleed / bled / bled
blow / blew / blown
break / broke / broken
bring / brought / brought
build / built / built
burn / burnt / burnt
burst / burst / burst
buy / bought / bought
catch / caught / caught
choose / chose / chosen
come / came / come
cost / cost / cost
creep / crept / crept
cut / cut / cut
deal / dealt / dealt
dig / dug / dug
do / did / done
draw / drew / drawn
dream / dreamt / dreamt
drink / drank / drunk
drive / drove / driven
eat / ate / eaten
fall / fell / fallen
feed / fed / fed
feel / felt / felt
fight / fought / fought

find / found / found
fly / flew / flown
forbid / forbade / forbidden
forget / forgot / forgotten
forgive / forgave / forgiven
freeze / froze / frozen
get / got / got
give / gave / given
go / went / gone
grind / ground / ground
grow / grew / grown
hang / hung / hung
have / had / had
hear / heard / heard
hide / hid / hidden
hit / hit / hit
hold / held / held
hurt / hurt / hurt
keep / kept / kept
kneel / knelt / knelt
know / knew / known
lay / laid / laid
lead / led / led
lean / leant / leant
learn / learnt / learnt
leave / left / left
lend / lent / lent
let / let / let
lie / lay / lain
light / lit / lit
lose / lost / lost
make / made / made
mean / meant / meant
meet / met / met
pay / paid / paid

Appendix S

put / put / put
read / read / read
ride / rode / ridden
ring / rang / rung
rise / rose / risen
run / ran / run
say / said / said
see / saw / seen
sell / sold / sold
send / sent / sent
set / set / set
shake / shook / shaken
shine / shone / shone
shoot / shot / shot
show / showed / shown
shrink / shrank / shrunk
shut / shut / shut
sing / sang / sung
sink / sank / sunk
sit / sat / sat
sleep / slept / slept
slide / slid / slid
smell / smelt / smelt
sow / sowed / sown
speak / spoke / spoken
speed / sped / sped
spell / spelt / spelt
spend / spent / spent
spill / spilt / spilt

spin / spun/span / spun
spit / spat / spat
split / split / split
spoil / spoilt / spoilt
spread / spread / spread
spring / sprang / sprung
stand / stood / stood
steal / stole / stolen
stick / stuck / stuck
sting / stung / stung
strike / struck / struck
swear / swore / sworn
sweep / swept / swept
swim / swam / swum
swing / swung / swung
take / took / taken
teach / taught / taught
tear / tore / torn
tell / told / told
think / thought / thought
throw / threw / thrown
wake / woke / woken
wear / wore / worn
weave / wove / woven
weep / wept / wept
win / won / won
wind / wound / wound
write / wrote / written

Appendix T: Numbers

1 Lexical items expressing number in CEL fall into two groups: those explicitly listed, and those implicitly included.

2 The lexical items explicitly listed are summarised here for ease of reference:

one   two   three ... twenty—all at level 1
thirty   forty ... hundred—all at level 1
thousand   million   billion—all at level 2
1 half   1 quarter
2 pair   4 couple   4 dozen
1 none   1 once   2 twice

3 Implicitly included in CEL are all regularly formed items expressing cardinal and ordinal numbers making use of the words in paragraph 2.

4 Ordinals are at level 2, except for *first, second* and *third,* which are at level 1.

5 Certain other words expressing or relating to figures or measurement are also listed in CEL. Examples are:

3 per cent   4 solution   5 amount
3 add   3 subtract   3 multiply   3 divide
2 cost   2 price   3 profit
1 square   2 circle   5 angle
3 wage   3 tax · 3 earn   5 earnings   3 salary
2 pound   3 penny   3 pence   2 dollar   2 cent

Appendix U: Symbols, punctuation marks, typographical and grammatical terms

1   It is assumed that the following non-alphabetical mathematical symbols are understood in their iconic forms by learners at the levels indicated, and that the oral equivalents are in most cases known.

1 £ pound	1 + plus	2 % per cent
1 p penny, pence	1 − minus	5 √ square root
1 $ dollar	2 × times, by	5 a² squared
1 ¢ cent	2 ÷ divided by	2 · point (also .)
4 ° degree	1 = equals	2 , marking thousands

2   It is also assumed that learners at the levels indicated know the following punctuation marks and symbols and their names.

1 . (full) stop	2 's apostrophe	1 ? question mark
1 , comma	3 ( ) brackets	2 ! exclamation mark
2 ; semi-colon	4 — dash	4 ... pause
3 : colon	3 - hyphen	2 ' " inverted commas
	2 good underlining	5 " ditto

3   In addition learners at the levels indicated are assumed to know the significance of typographical terms (and their main usages) below.

1 capital letter	3 indent	2 heading
3 italics	1 margin	1 paragraph
5 phonetics	1 title	2 column

4   At the levels indicated, learners are assumed to understand the meanings of the following grammatical and linguistic terms, and to recognise their abbreviations.

5 *abbr.*	abbreviation	5 *int.*	interjection
5 *adj.*	adjective	3 lang.	language
5 *adv.*	adverb	3 *n.*	noun
5 *aux.*	auxiliary	3 nat.	national
5 colloq.	colloquial	2 opp.	opposite
4 *conj.*	conjunction	4 *pl.*	plural
5 *det.*	determiner	4 *prep.*	preposition
5 *fig.*	figurative	4 *pron.*	pronoun
4 gen.	generally	3 *v.*	verb

Appendix V: Abbreviations

None of the following items are in the main list, but the gradings given classify them within the stock for each specified level.

2	AD	in the year of the Lord
1	am	before noon
4	approx.	approximately
1	Apr.	April
1	Aug.	August
1	Ave.	Avenue
4	b	born
4	b & b	bed and breakfast
3	BA	3 (GB) Bachelor of Arts 2 British Airways
3	BBC	British Broadcasting Corporation
2	BC	2 Before Christ
4	bk	book
5	bn	billion
5	Bro.	Brother (religious order)
5	Bros.	Brothers (commercial company)
3	BSc	(GB) Bachelor of Science
2	C	Centigrade
2	c	2 cent(s) 4 century 3 about 5 cubic
3	Capt.	Captain
5	cc	cubic centimetre(s)
4	ch.	chapter
5	CIA	(US) Central Intelligence Agency
2	cm	centimetre(s)
3	Co.	Company (commercial)
3	c/o	care of
5	Cons.	(GB) Conservative (political party)
3	cont'd	continued
5	Co-op	Co-operative (Society)
1	Dec.	December
4	dep.	departs
5	Dept	Department
3	Dip.	Diploma
1	Dr	Doctor
1	E	east

Appendix V

4 Ed	4 edited by
	4 editor
3 EEC	European Economic Community (the Common Market)
3 e.g.	for example, for instance
4 Eng.	England
2 etc.; &c	and the rest
5 F	Fahrenheit
2 f	female
1 Feb.	February
5 Fed.	5 Federal
	5 Federated
	5 Federation
5 fem.	5 female
	5 feminine (grammar)
5 Fr	5 Father
	5 franc
1 Fri.	Friday
2 ft	2 foot
	2 feet
1 GB	Great Britain
5 GCE	(GB) General Certificate of Education
3 Gen.	General
2 gm	gram(s)
5 GMT	Greenwich Mean Time
4 govt	government
4 h & c	hot and cold (water)
4 H-bomb	hydrogen bomb
5 HMS	His/Her Majesty's Ship
5 HMSO	Her/His Majesty's Stationery Office
5 Hon.	5 Honorary
	5 Honourable
5 HP	5 hire purchase
	5 horse power
4 HQ	Headquarters
2 hr(s)	hour(s)
3 I	roman one
3 i.e.	which is to say, in other words
2 in(s)	inch(es)
4 incl.	4 including
	4 inclusive
4 info.	information
4 intro.	introduction
5 IOU	I owe you
5 IRA	Irish Republican Army
4 Is.	Island(s)
1 Jan.	January
5 Jr	Junior
1 Jul.	July

Appendix V

1 Jun.	June
2 kg(s)	kilogram(s)
2 km(s)	kilometre(s)
4 L	lake
1 l	left
5 Lab.	(GB) Labour (political party)
4 lang.	language
4 lat.	latitude
2 lb	pound (weight)
5 Lib.	5 (GB) Liberal (political party)
	5 Liberation
5 lit.	5 literature
	5 literary
4 long.	longitude
3 LP	long-playing (record)
4 LSD	lysergic acid diethylamide (drug inducing hallucinations)
3 Lt	Lieutenant
3 Ltd	Limited
2 m	2 male
	2 metre(s)
	3 million
3 MA	Master of Arts
1 Mar.	March
5 masc.	masculine (grammar)
4 math.	(US) mathematics
4 maths	(GB) mathematics
3 max.	maximum
3 min.	minimum
4 misc.	miscellaneous
2 mm(s)	millimetre(s)
1 Mon.	Monday
5 MP	Member of Parliament (House of Commons)
4 mpg	miles per gallon
3 mph	miles per hour
1 Mr	mister
1 Mrs	missis
1 Ms	Mrs or Miss
4 Mt	Mount
1 N	north
2 NB	*nota bene* take special note of
2 NE	northeast
5 no.(s)	number(s)
1 Nov.	November
2 nr	near
2 NW	northwest
4 NZ	New Zealand
1 Oct.	October
5 OHMS	(GB) On Her/His Majesty's Service

Appendix V

4	O level	(GB) Ordinary level (examination)
3	opp.	opposite
3	oz	ounce(s)
2	P	Parking
3	p	penny
		pence
4	para.(s)	paragraph(s)
3	PhD	Doctor of Philosophy
5	PM	Prime Minister
1	pm	after noon
3	PO	Post Office
3	poss.	3 possible
		3 possibly
4	pp	pages
4	pr	pair
3	Pres.	President
5	pro.	professional
3	Prof.	Professor
2	PS	Postscript
2	PTO	please turn over
4	R	River
1	r	right
5	RAF	Royal Air Force
4	RC	Roman Catholic
1	Rd	Road
4	ref.	reference
4	ret.(d)	retired
5	Rev.(d)	Reverend
5	RN	Royal Navy
3	RSVP	please reply
1	S	south
4	SA	South Africa
4	sae	stamped addressed envelope
1	Sat.	Saturday
4	sch.	School
2	SE	southeast
2	sec.(s)	second(s)
1	Sept.	September
4	sgd	signed
5	Soc.	Society
2	Sq.	Square
5	Sr	5 Senior
		5 Sister
1	St	1 Street
		3 Saint
3	STD	subscriber trunk dialling (telephone)
1	Sun.	Sunday
2	SW	southwest
5	TB	tuberculosis

Appendix V

2 tel.	telephone
2 temp.	2 temperature
	3 temporary
1 Thurs.	Thursday
5 trans.	translated
5 TUC	(GB) Trades Union Congress
1 Tues.	Tuesday
1 TV	television
1 UK	United Kingdom
2 UN	United Nations
5 UNESCO	United Nations Educational, Scientific and Cultural Organisation
3·Univ.	University
3 UNO	United Nations Organisation
1 US	United States
1 USA	United States of America
2 USSR	Union of Soviet Socialist Republics
4 V	Volt
2 v	2 very
	5 see, refer to
3 VAT	Value Added Tax
4 VIP	very important person
4 vocab.	vocabulary
4 vol.	volume
5 VSO	(GB) Voluntary Service Overseas
1 w	west
2 WC	water closet
2 wk	week
2 Xmas	Christmas
2 yr	year

Appendix W: Prefixes

Where CEL lexical items occur with the prefixes below in the meanings listed, the item so formed may in general be regarded as accessible to the student at the level indicated against the prefix, or against basic item, whichever is the higher.

Prefix	Meaning(s)	Examples
5 co/con/cor/col	with/joint	co-operate; context
5 dis	opposite/not	dislike; discover
4 in/im/il/ir	opposite/not	incorrect; improbable
5 inter	between/among	international; intercourse
4 mid	middle	mid-air; mid-sentence
3 mini	little	mini-skirt; minicab
4 mis	wrongly/astray	mislead; mistake
3 non	not	non-smoker; non-iron
5 post	after	postgraduate; postscript
4 pre	before	prefix; prepaid
5 out	do better/faster etc.	outlive; outgrow
4 over	too much	overdo; overtime
3 re	again/back	rebuild; reclaim
3 self	to/for oneself	self-help; self-interest
5 sub	under/lower	subway; sublet
5 sub	less than	subnormal
4 super	above/more than	supermarket
4 trans	across	transform; transaction
4 un	reverse action	undo; unpack
3 un	opposite/not	unfair; unexpected
5 under	too little	underdone

Appendix X: Suffixes

Where CEL lexical items occur with the suffixes below in the meanings listed, the item so formed may in general be regarded as accessible to the sudent at the level indicated against the prefix, or against the basic item, whichever is the higher.

Suffix	Meaning(s)	Examples
2 able	able to be X-ed	acceptable; drinkable
5 ation	state/action	exploration; qualification
5 ation	institution	organisation
4 ed	having X	pointed; blue-eyed
4 ee	(passive suffix)	trainee; employee
2 en	make/become more	widen; quicken
1 er	doing/living in X	rider; Londoner
5 ery	collectivity	machinery
2 ese	nationality/language	Chinese; Portuguese
3 ess	female	waitress; actress
3 ette	compact	cigarette; laundrette
3 ful	amount contained	mouthful; spoonful
2 ful	full of/having/giving	useful; hopeful
4 hood	status	boyhood; brotherhood
1 ing	activity/state	bathing; betting
3 ing	result of activity	painting; earnings
3 ish	somewhat	reddish; tallish
2 ist	member of group/etc.	capitalist; artist
5 ity	state/quality	popularity; possibility
4 ise/ize	(causative)	modernise
3 less	without/not giving	childless; restless
4 like	having qualities of X	childlike
3 ly	having qualities of X	womanly; lovely
2 ly	in a manner	happily; strangely
5 ment	state/action	arrangement; judgement
4 ness	state/quality	dullness; kindness
4 ship	status	friendship; membership
4 ward	direction of movement	onward(s); homeward(s)
5 wise	in the manner of	clockwise; crosswise
2 y	like/full of	sandy; hairy
3 y/ie	(familiarity)	daddy; Charlie